WORKING
THE WHEEL

WORKING THE WHEEL

Martin Brundle

with

Maurice Hamilton

EBURY
PRESS

First published in Great Britain 2004

This edition published 2005

1 3 5 7 9 10 8 6 4 2

Ebury Press, an imprint of Ebury Publishing.
Random House, 20 Vauxhall Bridge Road, London SW1V 2SA

Random House Australia (Pty) Limited
20 Alfred Street, Milsons Point, Sydney, New South Wales 2061, Australia

Random House New Zealand Limited
18 Poland Road, Glenfield, Auckland 10, New Zealand

Random House South Africa (Pty) Limited
Isle of Houghton, Corner Boundary Road & Carse O'Gowrie, Houghton, 2198, South Africa

The Random House Group Limited Reg. No. 954009

www.randomhouse.co.uk

A CIP catalogue record for this book is available from the British Library.

Cover design by Two Associates
Text design and typesetting by Textype
Circuit design by Michael Agar

ISBN 0 091 90081 6

Papers used by Ebury Press are natural, recyclable products made from wood grown in sustainable forests.

Printed and bound in the UK by Bookmarque Ltd, Croydon

Acknowledgements

To my wife Liz, daughter Charlie and son Alex. Sorry for the absent weeks and months during my travels: thank you for your love and understanding.

Also to my sister Helen and my brother Robin. Thank you for your constant, generous and enthusiastic support to this day.

For making this, my first book, such a pleasure to create I thank Maurice Hamilton, David Luxton, Hannah MacDonald and all at Ebury Press, Margaret Cole and Michael Agar.

Finally, thanks to Bernie Ecclestone for making Formula One what it is today and, in no particular order, all of my team principals, fellow team members, sponsors, fans, F1 ITV crew, competitors, organisers, officials, marshals and medical crew for helping to either create or save me from the many experiences recounted in this book.

Contents

Introduction

When I went to a Formula 1 race for the first time in 1966, I never imagined that I would become a Grand Prix driver. I feel so privileged to have spent twelve years behind the wheel of some of the best racing cars in the world, and a further eight years as a television commentator. I have learned even more in the latter period than I did as a driver because there has been time to stand back and watch others at work instead of being focused, almost blinkered, on my own career. My role as a commentator has confirmed my love of motor racing, and Formula 1 in particular.

When Maurice Hamilton approached me about writing a book on the racetracks of the world, the idea instantly appealed to me. Here was the chance to write about not only the circuits but also the cars themselves and the colourful people who drive and run them. Therefore each chapter focuses on a different track, through the slot of a full-face crash helmet, and pauses to recall my experiences and those of other drivers in this exciting business. The aim has been to include the fear and the elation, the mishaps and the glory, the brilliant moments and, occasionally, the tragedy. The racetracks may be the central theme but I have endeavoured to paint a picture of what it is really like to work on and around them as a professional driver.

It is often far less glamorous than many people may think. One combination of airport, hotel and paddock can look exactly the same as the next. F1 racing is not as the old movies would have you believe where the winner gets the best-looking girl and returns to the deserted track on the Monday morning to stand moodily amongst the littered, empty grandstands to relive his glorious victory. As soon as the chequered flag falls, drivers are on their way to the next test session, meeting, sponsor function or whatever has been crammed into the limited time between each Grand Prix.

But that does not remove the unique experiences etched on to the mind of a driver; the incredible highs but, more often, the gut-wrenching lows. International sports competitors have more bad days than good days and motor racing is no exception. You are not going to win every time and you learn to soak up the thrilling moments because they are going to help you through the difficult times, many of which are covered in this book.

Adrenalin is the drivers' energy source. It is how they find the reserves to keep pushing on, pushing the throttle, pushing their luck. When they stop racing, drivers handle this enormous vacuum in different ways. Some disappear completely; others, like myself, are hooked on the drug and can't let go. I enjoy it as much now as I did on that day in 1983 when I had my first test in a Grand Prix car.

In the years that followed, I raced against some of the greatest drivers in the world and drove for some of the very best teams. The success of any racing organisation is dependent on the quality of the people within it, multiplied by the amount of money it has to spend. F1 is about the characters involved – the people you work with and those you fight against. This book simply tells it the way it is.

I have also touched on the fundamental technical aspects of racing cars and what happens when a driver takes them to the limit. My hope is that, as a result, television viewers and trackside fans on a Sunday afternoon will have a deeper understanding of the action being played out before them and the challenge presented by the track in question.

The circuits in this book were not chosen purely because they had or have the best sequence of corners or the most difficult bends. They are included because, together, they paint the full picture of a racing driver's world. That is also the reason why Le Mans is on the list; this evocative, superb and, at times, terrifying race is worth a book on its own.

I read a quote recently by an author who claimed that writing a book is the nearest thing to the pain of childbirth that a man can experience. These words caught my attention because we were in the middle of writing this book at the time. I completely disagreed then and continue to do so now because we have had so much fun putting these chapters together.

Maurice has reported on my F1 career from the moment I was unveiled to the British press by Ken Tyrrell in 1984 to when I stopped F1 racing at the end of 1996. He is, of course, a highly respected journalist and motor sport correspondent for the *Observer,* as well as the author of many books, but he is also a friendly rival in his role as F1 commentator for BBC Radio 5 Live. Certainly, our long, amusing and enjoyable conversations have brought back the stories and memories as the miles of these great racetracks have unfolded in my mind's eye. We have had great fun putting this book together and it is not intended to be an autobiography. The aim is to let you, the reader, experience life through the eyes of a racing driver, working the wheel of the fastest and most dramatic cars in the world.

Martin Brundle
King's Lynn
July 2004

Length: 5.303 km

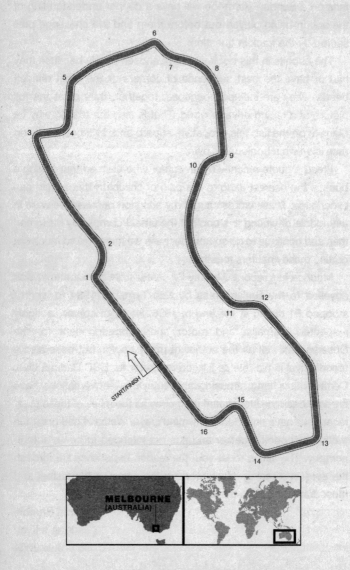

Melbourne

If you took a straw poll among Formula 1 people, I wouldn't mind betting that Melbourne would top the list of favourite races. It's not just that the season opens in a lively, cosmopolitan city – and usually in fine weather at a time when Europe remains in the grip of winter. The fact is that the Albert Park circuit sets the world standard for racetracks in temporary surroundings. I'd even go so far as to say it's better than many of the permanent facilities we visit during the course of the season. But, initially, we didn't think that possible because Melbourne had a very tough act to follow.

The truth was that no one wanted to leave Adelaide, the previous home of the Australian Grand Prix. Melbourne – or wherever you cared to mention – couldn't possibly be better. The final race in South Australia had taken place in November 1995 and it had been a very emotional affair with lots of sad goodbyes. We faced the prospect not only of switching cities, but also appearing first rather than last in the racing calendar. There is, for obvious reasons, a major difference between the opening race of the season and the one that closes it. The first is tense and full of anticipation, the other more laid-back and relaxed. So in Adelaide in 1995 we were contemplating the fact that, in less than four months, we would be back in Australia, but in a completely different venue. We all felt that Melbourne would have to go some to match Adelaide, never mind beat it.

That mood was not helped by arriving in Melbourne in March 1996 to find it was a much bigger city and the Grand Prix was viewed as just another event threatening to clog the streets. In fact, the track was nothing like Adelaide or any other street circuit. Laid out within Albert Park in the city's suburbs, the track had none of the sharp angles around buildings and the street furniture of everyday life. It was a parkland circuit, with long straights and many similar corners. A further contradiction was that, even though these roads were used all year round, they were not subjected to the heavy traffic, and resulting oil and diesel that you would normally associate with a street circuit.

We soon discovered that the circuit was challenging. Because the long, fast corners were so similar, finding a lap time was difficult. If the car was poor in one corner, it was slow everywhere. But there were also lots of idiosyncrasies. A couple of the corners were unsighted and under a canopy of trees. There was not much grip and the corners had difficult turn-ins and quite high-speed exits. But, because grip was low, drivers would regularly slide off the road. It really was quite tricky and, of course, in that first year, we did not have the benefit of testing there beforehand. All in all, it was quite an adventure and we soon forgot about comparisons with Adelaide. In any case, my first association with Melbourne was to be pretty dramatic from beginning to end.

I had joined Jordan for 1996 and got off on the wrong foot when my Peugeot engine blew up on the first day, followed by another engine failure the day after. That meant a loss of vital track time and I then had to play catch-up all weekend. The level of grip was changing all the time, which made setting up the car problematic. Whenever something strange or different happens to the handling, whatever the circuit, you need to know whether it is because of the set-up changes you've made to the car or simply because the track is changing as more tyre rubber is laid down.

There was also a slight element of panic. I was with a new team and I wanted to go well. Rubens Barrichello in the other Jordan-Peugeot was hooked up and there is always pressure when your team-mate is producing the lap times and you are not. It was a sign of clutching at straws when I took the set-up that Rubens had chosen for his car and copied it onto mine. It didn't help; I qualified nineteenth of twenty-two starters. Just to rub it in, Rubens was eighth.

But things seemed to be on the up – they couldn't get much worse – on race morning. The car felt good during the thirty-minute warm-up. I was really charged and determined to make a lot of places in a hurry. I had a tremendous start and passed many cars going towards Turn 3. There was a nice big gap opening up, as the drivers further ahead were following each other towards the right-hander. There is no doubt that I was fired up and ready to brake very late and deep into the corner.

This may have been a parkland track but the cars were reaching 190 mph on the approach to Turn 3 and I was partially unsighted while following another car. It's just like driving in fog. You are familiar with the road ahead but it never seems to arrive quite the way you remember it. Your sense of judgement becomes impaired. It's like that in an F1 car. Your mind is momentarily on something else, you can't fully see and you've travelled quite a distance when the track suddenly narrows on the approach to a corner and you realise you are carrying too much speed. It's the start of the race, your brakes and tyres are not up to temperature and you've got a lot of fuel on board. It is going to be tricky.

Nonetheless, I was doing nicely when, all of a sudden, David Coulthard and Johnny Herbert ran into each other and their cars twisted across the track at point-blank range to fill the space I needed to slow down my car. Doing the wrong side of 170 mph, I hit the back of David's McLaren and that launched me into the sky.

I can picture it now, frame by frame. Seeing everything in slow motion is an ability you have as a racing driver when something happens in front of you. You will see a car spin and, even though you are travelling at warp speed, you work out that he is going to spin to the left, so you calmly decide to go to the right. The whole thing slows down. I don't know how that happens. I've heard other sportsmen say the same about this ability to go into slow motion. I had it happen on the road fairly recently. A driver in front of me suddenly stopped for a pheasant on a country road and came to a complete halt without any warning. It was my racing experience that slowed the whole thing down in my mind and prevented me from going into the back of that car. But I didn't have time for any of that in Melbourne on 10 March 1996.

Normally, you would ride up the back of the car in front and then crash back onto the track. But the Jordan kept climbing. My first thought was: 'This is going to be a big accident.' The second thought was: 'Please don't let me go into the trees.' I remember the car rolling over and, at the time, it seemed to be happening very slowly. My next thought was: 'Don't let me land upside down in the gravel run-off area. If I do that, the roll-over bar behind my helmet will dig in, my head will take the impact – and I'm dead.'

Still upside down, I passed Jean Alesi – who was sixth or

seventh; that's how far I had travelled – as he came into the corner. As luck would have it, I landed on the final piece of Tarmac before the start of the gravel. So that was OK – until the car started to barrel roll.

Photographs taken at the time show that I was still trying to steer the car. That was an instinctive reaction because, in quite a few big accidents, you can still do something with the car to the bitter end, a tactic which had already saved my life in an accident two years earlier. You work the steering or the brake pedal in order to help minimise the impact. The pictures show that I was applying steering lock even though there was only one wheel left on the car and the nose was about to be buried in the wall. I was hanging on!

The car landed upside down and there was not a single mark on me – which is more than can be said for what was left of the Jordan-Peugeot. Then I felt fluid begin to run all over me. I thought it was fuel and I started to panic. I had a big fear of burning to death in a racing car: it must be the most terrible way to go. I realised later that it was actually water from my drink bottle, but I could smell fuel because, although I didn't know it, the car was broken in half. Regardless, I wasn't going to hang around and work out the exact nature of this fluid. My priority was to get out – and fast. There was a gap no bigger than a briefcase between the top of the rollover bar behind my head and the front of the cockpit. Still upside down, I undid my seat belts and more or less fell through the hole.

Because of the violence of the accident, most people thought I was dead. But I did not have a single bruise on my body. Like jumping off a tall building, it's not the fall that kills you, it's the sudden stop. The same applies in a racing car when it crashes. All the violence and bits flying off are actually dissipating energy. The trouble comes for the driver when the car comes to a sudden stop against something solid.

I got out of the car and thought: 'Would you believe it? They've stopped the race. That's a bit of luck! I'll run back and get in the spare car.' It didn't occur to me that they had stopped the race because of my accident. I honestly thought there had been a major incident elsewhere on the circuit. It simply did not register just how big a crash I'd had. Or, at least, not until I thought to look at what was left of my car.

I took a walk around the wreck and I remember thinking: 'What have I done? My first racing lap for Jordan in F1 – and the car's a write-off.' It was broken like an egg. I was more embarrassed than anything else. When you have smashed a car badly, you just want to get away from it, pretend this didn't happen, that it wasn't you. I focused on getting back to the pits for the spare car.

The marshals were panicking. So often in this situation, drivers shrug off well-meaning officials. You are out of the car, you are hot, bothered, fed-up and hyper. People start getting hold of your overalls and your first reaction is to push them away and say you're fine. Of course, they are only trying to do their job and they need to make sure you're not concussed. All I thought about was getting a lift back to the pits and the spare car because it was too far to walk and I knew there would be a restart thanks to the race being only one lap old. In this situation the marshals were really good and quickly understood that I was OK. They produced a minibus, I jumped in and the driver went for it. It was a heavy old vehicle with medical kit rolling round in the rear, he was on the wrong line into every corner and I really thought we were going to crash.

We managed to reach the Jordan garage, which was buzzing. There were all sorts of emotions running wild, not least because at one point they had thought I must be dead. Not only was I alive, I was standing there asking for the spare car. I reassured everyone that I was fine and it seemed to me, perhaps wrongly, that I was the calmest person in the garage – followed by my wife, Liz. I had given her a wink when I walked in and she knew straight away that everything was OK.

The mechanics had already started to prepare the spare car for me; not the work of a moment because it was set up for Rubens. Then a message came through, saying I could not start until I had been checked out by Professor Sid Watkins, the F1 medical chief. I immediately went to the end of the pit lane, by the exit where the official cars are usually parked. I knew Sid would be sitting in the medical car that follows the field on the first lap, but there was no sign of either the car or Sid. And no one seemed to know where he was.

Charlie Whiting, the official starter, was nearby, standing on his rostrum. This had been the first time the start of a race had been controlled completely by electronics. Charlie had simply pushed a button when everyone was ready and the automatic countdown of lights took care of itself. Five red lights came on one by one and then, after a predetermined gap, they all went out and the race was on. (The FIA officials had recognised that drivers don't wait for the green light to appear but, instead, watch for the first sign of the red lights going out.) Having to abandon the race and start again thanks to me was probably the last thing Charlie needed. When I climbed onto his rostrum to ask where I would find 'The Prof', he politely pointed out he was busy.

Someone said Sid was at the other end of the pit lane. It was a sign of how keen I was when I started running. Because I can't run. Ever since the accident that wrecked my left ankle in 1984, I have had great difficulty in running, particularly on a flat surface in

11

flat-soled driving boots. Nevertheless, I eventually found Sid. He gave me the once-over and said he could see I was OK because he had just watched me run all the way down the pit lane. When he asked me the date, I was able to reply without hesitation because 10 March was my dad's birthday. Sid said I was fine and could carry on. In fact, he said later that my pulse was lower than his!

As I ran back down the pit lane, a marshal asked me what Sid had said. I told him that everything was fine and I stuck up my thumb. As I did so, the crowd suddenly erupted. That really threw me because I had no idea I was being watched. When I put my thumb up for the marshal, the crowd thought I was doing it for them. I looked up at the Diamond Vision screen, and there I was. I had been so focused on getting back into the race that I hadn't appreciated there was a considerable audience following my every move.

The spare car was ready by the time I returned to the garage. I climbed on board and drove to the end of the pits, from where I would take the restart once the field had passed the pit lane exit. I remember feeling completely calm. On the second lap, I caught the Ligier of Pedro Diniz and he braked about 50 metres before I thought he would. I gently touched the back of him at the very same corner where I crashed not long before. I only just tagged the Ligier but I spun and stalled the engine. The same crowd, which had watched me barrel roll the first time round, then saw me collide with another car. I radioed the pits and said: 'I think I've had enough for one day.'

The race was won by Damon Hill, but only after Jacques Villeneuve, son of Gilles, in the other Williams-Renault had a problem on what was his F1 debut. One way or another, it was a busy race and everyone in F1, despite initial reservations, warmed to Melbourne. In other places the reverse is also true; there is a flurry of interest at first from the local people, which quickly fades. But the enthusiasm and support in Melbourne simply gets stronger each year.

It may be a temporary track but the work they do is very impressive. Some of the permanent circuits in Europe really struggle to match the standards established at this venue, which has to be built and dismantled every year. Of course, you can't hold a motor race inside the boundary of a major city without prompting some sort of protest and, before our first visit to Melbourne, it began to look as if we might not get a race at all. The word was that demonstrators, angry over the conversion of Albert Park, were going to block all the entrances. In the end, it came to nothing. In fact, according to one newspaper, the loudest dissenting voice came from the Prostitutes' Collective of Victoria. Their spokeswoman complained that business had been disappointing for a male-orientated sport (motor racing, that is).

Of course, the newspapers on the morning of Monday, 11 March 1996 were full of pictures showing a gold Jordan-Peugeot doing cartwheels at Turn 3. Over the years, there have been a number of equally spectacular accidents mainly because, when you leave the road in Melbourne, you usually do so in a major way. There are five areas in Albert Park where you are pretty much V-max, which gives it a Silverstone feel. It is very unusual for a street or a park circuit to have such high speeds.

Melbourne is characterised by very small false kerbs positioned in a sea of Tarmac to define an artificial corner. Turns 11 and 12 on the back straight are super-fast corners, and if you get it wrong on the exit of either, you will spin off across the grass and into the wall. You are sweeping between two walls at 190 mph and then looking for an almost insignificant piece of temporary kerbing in the middle of what appears to be no-man's land and at the apex of a very quick corner. You are literally pointing the nose of your car at a lump of plastic, followed by a second one if it's a chicane. And that is it. You spend the entire weekend focused on what would otherwise be insignificant pieces of material that, ordinarily, you would feel ought to be picked up and tossed in the bin. But they are determining exactly where you should place the car at 150 mph. It's challenging, to say the least.

If the set-up of the car isn't right, this is one circuit where you cannot just hustle through the corners. You can stand up in the seat – metaphorically, of course – at somewhere like Monaco and drive round problems, teeter on the edge and get away with it. At Melbourne, the car can feel great and yet it is so easy to be 1 to 1.5 seconds off the pace whereas 0.25 to 0.5 seconds is the worst you would normally expect.

It is a case of being unable to find the correct line. Certain circuits have a groove – sometimes it is impossible to detect; sometimes it is obvious – and you need to get into this groove in order to be hooked up and build momentum. It's easy to go fast when you do that. If there was a groove at Melbourne, I never found it. It seemed to me that if you pushed too hard, you then out-braked yourself or missed the turning-in point and that would put you off-line for the exit of the corner.

There are one or two tracks where the set-up of the car is everything. That is where you find what I call the Noah's Ark grid because, with one or two exceptions, cars from the same team end up side by side all the way down the grid. They've done more or less the same lap time and, if that happens, then it's safe to say that this is not a circuit that favours the driver over the car. But Melbourne is different again. You don't necessarily get the Noah's Ark grid but you've got to get the car absolutely right. Technically, it's a challenging racetrack. Being the first race of the year, you see a lot of drivers – particularly those new to F1 – in all sorts of muddles and struggling to produce anything like a decent lap time.

That spectacular show in 1996 was to be my only appearance at Melbourne as a racing driver. The following year, Melbourne marked my first race as a full-time broadcaster as I joined Murray Walker in the ITV commentary box. It was rather painful watching the start instead of being a part of it but, at the same time, I found it more fun than I expected. I made a smart decision from the outset by choosing to stand and talk to Murray (who, unlike most commentators, preferred not to sit) and that set the tone of our partnership, as we stood side-by-side talking about our favourite sport.

I recall that in our first link together, which was in a shopping centre about a mile away from the circuit, Murray stood next to a statue of Marilyn Monroe with a floor-mounted fan blowing her dress in a copy of that famous scene in *The Seven Year Itch*. Don't ask me how we fitted that into a Grand Prix link because I just can't remember. Probably because I don't want to!

Naturally, you get a completely different impression of a circuit from the television screen and commentary box compared to the view you get with your backside an inch from the ground in a racing car. There is a lake in the middle of the Albert Park that is often shown in the television pictures as the cars blast by. But, in the car, you would never know there is a park alongside, let alone a lake. You are simply staring up at concrete walls with debris fencing on top and a canopy of trees plus the occasional building beyond. If there are a few correctly positioned Diamond Vision screens, you might catch a glimpse of the lake and, particularly when driving at slower speeds behind the safety car, the drivers do tend to glance at the screens because the pictures give additional information to that supplied by radio and signalling board from the pits.

There is usually a lot to talk about in the Australian Grand Prix, if only because the first race always produces a high attrition rate. Reliability is not yet built in and there are a lot of cars in brake trouble because of the combination of high speeds and slow corners. Teams have not got on top of the cooling problems that come with the high ambient temperatures and severe braking. Added to that, the new boys have to deal with the pressure of one-lap qualifying and the excitement of the first Grand Prix. Melbourne is a huge baptism of fire.

It is also like the first day back at school. On the racetrack, drivers are spinning off all over the place as they get their eye in, and in the paddock, everyone is catching up after the winter. It is a great feeling to be back in the swing of things and yet the first race brings a reminder of how the years roll by. As you check in to your usual hotel, it is impossible not to remark that it can't possibly be a year since you did the very same thing. You feel that at every hotel you go to but, in Melbourne, there is the additional thought that this is the start of another season. You've stepped off the plane at five in the morning, your room is not ready and you suddenly remember the same thing happened the year before, just as you were preparing for the off. There are as many as eighteen races ahead and, at that moment, you are aware that it's a very long haul. And it all starts in Melbourne.

The drivers have to get their heads around the fact that the points on offer in Melbourne mean just as much as those available when the season moves into a showdown in the later stages. They have to remember that all the points count and anything earned in Melbourne could have a profound effect when the totting up is done seven months later.

Moving away from the cockpit also allowed me to sample all the press conferences for the first time. The pattern at this first race is amusing. Everyone is ready to go and full of enthusiasm for a car they say is the best because it has incorporated lessons learned from last year's car, which, they now admit, maybe wasn't so good. And, of course, most of the teams will say the same thing, in the same place, twelve months later. 'But,' they say, 'this car is going to be so fast it's going to run into the back of itself. That's because it's got X more downforce and Y more horse-power, which,' they add, 'we should have realised before building last year's car' (which cost £20m). Every team starts off with the genuine belief that this is going to be their year.

Everyone has targets and yet they have to be careful not to raise expectations too high. You will have a team that is spending 'only' $150m and aiming at fifth in the world championship. Hearing that, an outsider would be forgiven for saying: 'What! Only fifth? Go home. What's the point in going halfway round the world if your target is fifth?' But there is no point in saying you're going to win the world championship when, in reality, it is out of the question.

It's an interesting point because, at this race, there is a lot of positioning. It is the start of a new year and it is Bullshit Central as everyone lays out their store in a positive way, but covering their backsides at the same time. F1 is a very small world. Everyone, from those in key positions to mechanics and journalists, moves from team to team – but within the same insular environment. Arrive in Melbourne and suddenly everyone is back in the crucible again; the same 300 metres of pit lane which is the centre of this particular universe.

Everyone has an opinion on what's going to happen, what the new regulations mean, and how effective the various cars are going to be. Somehow, the drivers have to skim over all this, which is why they look pretty bored in some of the press conferences because they know that the only serious piece of talking is done on the track. They don't want to say they're going to do this or win that because they know that every single word they say in Melbourne will be taken down and used in evidence against them later in the year.

The lovely thing about Melbourne itself is that, like Adelaide, it is a short drive to the beach. There is no doubt that if it is a fun city, it is a fun Grand Prix. And a better Grand Prix because everyone goes there with a spring in their step. You definitely head off to Melbourne with a different feeling to that engendered by some of the tracks we come across mid-season in Europe.

The only problem for me is that everybody I have ever met in Victoria seems to have been standing at Turn 3 on that Sunday afternoon in 1996. I have signed hundreds of photos of the accident and bits of bodywork from the crash. Several years later, I still get pictures sent to me, at least twice a week from all over the world, with a request to sign them. When you consider what could have happened, I was incredibly lucky. Despite, or perhaps because of, surviving that momentary horror, I have really good feelings about the Grand Prix in Melbourne.

Rio de Janeiro

If asked to choose a location for your first Grand Prix as a driver, you couldn't do much better than pick Rio de Janeiro. Of course, choice didn't come into it when I made my F1 debut; the Brazilian Grand Prix was then first on the schedule and that is where I found myself in March 1984, entering this amazing new world. It was exciting enough stepping up to the top level of motor sport but being in Brazil – and Rio in particular – added even more colour and exhilaration to a significant new phase of my life.

Mention the Brazilian Grand Prix and you instantly think of highly emotional events in a Third World setting. It doesn't matter whether the race is in either of the venues in Rio or São Paulo, the entire weekend has a samba beat and a level of excitement I have not experienced in many other countries. But, of the two, Rio remains one of the most thrilling and intimidating cities I have ever been to.

I actually went there for the first time in January 1984 to carry out a test in order to win the drive with the Tyrrell team. I can see it as clear as day now: getting off the plane with the Tyrrell boys, a keen young lad feeling as if his wife had packed his bag and

Length: 4.932 km

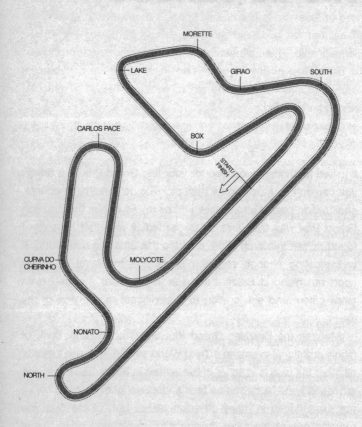

RIO DE JANEIRO
(BRAZIL)

sent him off with a chocolate bar to South America. This really was a new world in every sense. I had been having fun as a more or less amateur driver in Formula 3, where I met Ayrton Senna and we had enjoyed a ding-dong battle for the 1983 championship. Then, almost overnight, I found myself arriving in Rio de Janeiro on the verge of becoming an F1 driver. Today, twenty-four is considered too old to start in F1. But, in 1984, I seemed barely a lad.

We explored Copacabana and Ipanema and it soon struck me that you had to be really careful in Brazil. I was wearing a relatively cheap and cheerful watch, but even that was getting a lot of attention. We were walking along the beach and a young guy, with a few mates in close attendance, came up and asked for the time. He spoke very poor English and made a bad attempt at portraying himself as an American tourist. Never having experienced this sort of thing before and being as green as they come, I could hardly believe that these guys were actually valuing my watch. Fortunately, they must have figured it was not worth stealing.

During this first visit, I spent a lot of time with Danny Sullivan, the American driver whose place I was taking at Tyrrell. When we were out one evening, a group of pretty young girls came up to Danny and put their arms around him. When he started pushing them off, I wondered what on earth was wrong with him. But Danny knew the form only too well: while one girl is smiling at you and another is kissing you, a third is removing the wallet from your back pocket.

The constant element of risk continued on the roads around Rio. We usually drove ramshackle hire cars known as Gols. These were Brazilian versions of the VW Scirocco, and ran on alcohol fuel. Not only was your hearing assaulted by the popping and banging engine but the sugar-based fuel produced a powerfully sweet and pungent aroma.

A party piece for the Tyrrell boys – practical jokers almost to a man – was to wire up a switch in the minibus we used to travel to and from the racetrack. The switch turned the engine on and off, and would be flicked in one of the many tunnels on our route. The alcohol fuel would build up, ignite and attempt to blow the exhaust clean off, the enormous bang amplified by the walls of the tunnel. It was a mystery to the driver and team manager, Brian Lisles, who initially knew nothing of the secret switch.

The state of the roads in 1984 had to be seen to be believed. The potholes were so big that you could park a car in some of them and we were often stopping to change punctured tyres. There were times when driving on the road would be more thrilling than the race.

A top priority on the initial drive to the track was to stop at a supermarket and buy a load of disinfectant. Then, without further ado and before a spanner had been lifted, the sinks and toilets in the circuit's garage would receive serious bleach punishment. It was clear that nothing happened on this track for 355 days of the year. Then, as the race drew nearer, the entire place would be transformed. Scores of people would turn up in minibuses and trucks and start painting everything in sight. Arriving at the Jacarepagua Autodrome on the actual weekend gave an indication of what must be commonplace for the Queen on her travels; the smell of fresh paint is everywhere. It is the same in São Paulo, scene of the Brazilian Grand Prix since 1990, but it seemed exaggerated in Rio, particularly as we would go testing there beforehand and watch the preparations unfold from scratch.

In this respect, Formula 1 is definitely not as much fun as it used to be. Because of cost-cutting, pre-season testing is limited to tracks in Europe. Twenty years ago, we would have a ten-day Rio test, followed by a ten-day break in the middle and then the Grand Prix. It meant we had a three-week trip to Rio, which was absolutely the business. Today's F1 teams would trade anything for the schedules we used to have.

Filling in the time was not a problem, thanks to sunshine and high temperatures. Money would be changed on a daily basis because it was the best way to cope with rampant inflation, which could see the rate move by as much as 10 per cent in twenty-four hours. This meant a regular ritual of trying to find the best black market rate, which usually involved negotiations in a toilet cubicle or outside the front door of the hotel – where you were taking your life in your hands in any case. But it was the only way to operate because the rate for your pound at the beginning of the trip might be double at the end. It was as dramatic as that.

Such raging inflation had the effect of adding zeros to the currency at an alarming rate. Then, one year, you would arrive and find the Brazilians had knocked all the noughts off the end, changed the name of the currency and started again. There was no point whatsoever in returning home with Brazilian cruzados because the notes would only be good for lighting the fire by the time you wished to return.

Brazil gave me my first experience of the *churrascaria*, an extraordinary style of restaurant where, in simple terms, they keep bringing all sorts of meat to the table until you can eat no more. There is no menu and the routine is very simple. You arrive, help yourself to salad, sit down and wait for the beginning of a process that, if unfamiliar, can be startling. A huge spear of freshly cooked meat will appear over your left shoulder while, from the right, comes a sharp knife to cut a delicious slice of whatever it is. Each person has a little disc – red on one side, green on the other – by their place and you turn it to red if you want a breather. Switch back to green and a huge joint of something else soon comes winging past your left ear. You know the meat is fresh because you can see it being cooked over charcoal fires. This adds to the atmosphere of a large family restaurant that is really buzzing. Fancying myself as a bit of an entrepreneur, I thought of starting something like this in the UK. It seems so straightforward but *churrascarias* are not so exciting or lucrative in Europe.

There were times when a driver felt he really needed all the nourishment he could get because the Rio circuit was one of the toughest in the world. Not only was it then the first race of the year, it was also run anti-clockwise. That may not seem a major issue but, believe me, it is a problem for drivers, particularly after they have spent the winter and most of the previous season using tracks run in a clockwise direction. Your neck becomes accustomed to predominantly right-hand corners. In the heat of Rio there is not only a succession of left-handers but many of them are long and fast.

I'll never forget watching the 1982 Brazilian Grand Prix on television and seeing Nelson Piquet win the race with his head literally hanging out of the side of the cockpit like some demented bull; he was flopping all over the place. Drivers did not have the headrests and protective collars you see now.

I did twelve laps in the Tyrrell on that first test day – and I was history for an hour or two afterwards. This was a completely different ball game and I was not ready for it. I had just come out of F3, was young and fit. But the left-hand corners and the heat just killed me. In addition I had previously been testing at

Silverstone when there was no one else on the track. The circuit was busy in Rio and I went into the wrong pits, which was a great laugh for the F1 mechanics. But when I finally stopped at the right garage, I had to get out and be sick; it was just so incredibly hot. Rio was physically demanding for an experienced driver, never mind a new boy.

There were the series of left-handers leading on to a long back straight, but the corner that finished you off was a very fast 180-degree left curve at the end of it. That was where your neck would cry 'enough'. It is the most pathetic feeling in the world when your neck gives up and you're trying to drive a racing car. Your balance goes out of kilter and, as hard as you might try, you can't do anything about it. Then you begin to suffer as your head starts to jolt back and forward when braking and accelerating. But the corners provide the biggest problem and you find you are looking through the extreme end of the slot in your crash helmet while desperately trying to steer the car through the corner. Inevitably, you end up slowing down because, as soon as your neck goes, your shoulders follow.

It is similar to being too cold and your hands won't function properly. You want to undo your coat or something like that and you can't. When your neck muscles give up, it's that same feeling of utter hopelessness. And as soon as the car starts to get away from you, a crash is inevitable because you are behind the car. You've got to back off a little, which, of course, goes against the grain.

When driving a car – any car – you don't think about how you position your head when cornering. You do it automatically as a means of maintaining a sense of balance. It is like asking a motor-cyclist to go round a corner and not lean, but to keep the bike upright. The rider will instinctively lean into a corner and you will notice that passengers in a fast-moving road car will do the same thing.

It is, in effect, lowering the centre of gravity of your head, which is about 10 per cent of your bodyweight. When you start doing the sums and add the weight of a crash helmet and then multiply the total by three or maybe four – depending on the amount of G-force being created by the corner – then you begin to get an impression of what happens as that weight is pushed sideways. Neck muscles are simply not designed to cope. When the muscles begin to go into spasm, that's the hopeless moment. You can't recover them. Or, at least, not while driving.

The frustrating thing is that they seem to recover quickly once out of the car – it's something to do with the high amount of blood in the neck area – but then they fade very quickly again. There are machines available now that exercise these muscles but no one has found anything that replicates the exact angle of your head and neck when driving a racing car. You are lying down with your chin close to your chest while dealing with a force that is part accelerative G and part lateral G. The enormous acceleration of an F1 car – mind-blowing in the turbo days – produces a force from the front, followed by sideways force in a corner, and all of this with your chin on your chest and the neck muscles attempting to cope with the weight of your head and crash helmet. The only way I found to train those muscles properly was by driving a racing car.

Drivers still struggle today. You will see it at Interlagos, which is also anticlockwise with more left-handers than right-handers to get back to the beginning. But that does not tell the whole story. It is a question of how quickly the left-handers follow each other and how fast they are. String three or four of these together and your neck muscles are history.

So, at Rio, you would start bracing yourself for the long left-hander when charging down the back straight. That was an extraordinary section of the track, a strange combination of being in the outback and yet being watched by this massive, colourful mob in a grandstand that stretched the length of the straight. Even travelling at close to 200 mph, you would be aware of the blur of colour on your right and, if you missed that, there was always a reminder in the shape of litter and plastic bags swirling onto the track – very similar to the back straight at Interlagos.

It was the kind of place where, if you stopped, everything seemed hot and bothered and dried out. And just to add to that feeling, the car would invariably set fire to the grass alongside the track. All of this would be the focus of a packed, uncovered grandstand. The locals would sit in the scorching heat all day and I'll never forget the image on race morning of a fire engine hosing them down. Some of the fans had a little bit of covering over their heads but they were delighted to be soaked. That's Brazilian dedication for you.

The Rio track was usually bathed in a curious sort of light. I don't know why that was – perhaps because of its proximity to the sea or the effect of smog from the city – but photographers loved working there. Certainly, it made their journey worthwhile because, believe me, getting to and from the track in those days was more dangerous than the race itself. Some of the most amazing experiences I had in a car in Brazil were on the public roads. You took your life into your hands because everyone was ducking and diving, and there appeared to be no rules whatsoever. There were accidents and punctures galore.

Quite often, the hardest part of the Grand Prix weekend would be the journey to the airport on the evening of the race. You would have to cope with spectator traffic, which met traffic travelling home from the coast. The ensuing mass of motors and mayhem then had to filter through tunnels before reaching Rio. The bad news for us was that the airport was on the far side of the city.

I can remember being stuck in a huge jam with Liz and my dad. We were going to miss the plane. Getting desperate, we decided to turn off the main road – I use the term advisedly – and take minor routes, followed by back gardens which took us through fences and onto rough ground, our general direction being maintained by glimpses of the sea on the right. We ended up racing my team-mate, Stefan Bellof, like some bizarre car-chase from a cheap movie. I've never had a journey like it in my life. And none of the locals seemed to mind.

This was par for the course. Whatever form of transport you used, moving around Rio was an adventure. It was possible to sit in a taxi and see the road – through the floor. But all of this merely added to the sense of excitement that would have been building from the moment of arrival for the first race of the season. And, in my case in 1984, my very first Grand Prix.

I qualified nineteenth, the fastest of the four non-turbo cars present. Given that the Tyrrell did not have the benefit of a turbocharged engine, this was where I expected to be because it was always going to be a struggle using a normally aspirated V8 against the likes of Ferrari, Renault and Williams-Honda.

On top of that, Ken Tyrrell had no sponsors. There was nothing on the side of the blue car except 'Tyrrell' in big white letters. It was a case of doing what we could. If the car was comparatively slow, then at least it would be reliable, always a useful asset as others ran into trouble with their new machinery at the start of the season. We may have been nowhere during qualifying, when engine performance was everything, but at least I knew that the Tyrrell was actually quite nimble when compared to some of the cumbersome turbo cars in race trim. Because of the savage amounts of power available, these cars would chew up their tyres. At least the Tyrrell-Ford could never be accused by Goodyear of creating that problem.

Our trump card would actually turn out to be fuel consumption. A new rule for 1984 limited each car to 220 litres of fuel. This crippled the turbo teams, particularly now that refuelling had been banned during the races. The Brazilian Grand Prix may have become an economy run for the leaders but I was too busy doing my own thing to worry about that.

The original objective may have been simply to finish my first Grand Prix but I found myself in the thick of the action from the start. I completed the first lap in fifteenth place and gradually moved forward, mainly because those ahead ran into trouble rather than through demon overtaking moves on my part.

But I was still running and, on this particular day, that's what mattered, as Ayrton Senna (also making his F1 debut) retired his Toleman, Bellof stopped with a broken throttle cable on his Tyrrell, Michele Alboreto's Ferrari succumbed to brake trouble and handed the lead to Niki Lauda, who then went out with an electrical problem on his McLaren-TAG. Derek Warwick then looked certain to score his first win but a thirty-second lead vanished when the front suspension failed on his Renault. There were ten laps to go by that stage and Derek's departure moved me into sixth place. I was going to score a championship point!

It gave me a lift because that race was incredibly hard work. Only towards the end did I think I might not make it but adrenalin gets you a long way. It is the most marvellous stuff; who needs heroin and cocaine when you can have adrenalin? All racing drivers and top sports people are adrenalin junkies. It lifts you and gets you there in the end. Whether you've wrung every tenth of a second out of that car for the whole race is another matter. You only feel really tired at the end, providing, of course, you haven't got cramp or your neck muscles give up.

I got through the race with no major scares or frights and received a final bonus with two laps to go when Patrick Tambay's Renault ran out of fuel and handed me fifth place. Two championship points, no less. You can imagine what I was thinking: 'I can't believe this. I'm a Grand Prix driver. I'm twenty-four; I'm fit; I feel fantastic. Of course I've finished fifth! I won nine races in Formula 3 last year. What's all the fuss about finishing fifth?'

Even so, I was on a high when I climbed from that car after the toughest hour and three-quarters I had ever experienced in motor racing. Not surprising, really, because my previous single-seater races had lasted no more than half an hour. Despite this, I had conflicting emotions brought on by the feeling that fifth place might not be such a big deal. In fact, as I was to discover, scoring points would be rare and something to savour. That's the curious thing about F1. You are there because you have won consistently throughout your career and then, all of a sudden, winning becomes much more difficult and fifth place is perceived as a major achievement. Even so, I remember that Ken Tyrrell seemed quite calm about it. Underneath, he must have been delighted. I do recall him laughing; a loud chortle that would become very familiar. But his muted reaction added to the uncertainty I felt on my return to the garage after leaving my car in *parc ferme*.

A guy came up to me and asked: 'What were all those ball bearings scattered all around the ground after your pit stop?'

I said: 'What ball bearings? What are you talking about?'

'Well,' said the guy, 'after you'd made your pit stop, I walked across some spilt water – and I nearly fell over.'

It turned out that the Tyrrell team had a device known as the Duck Gun or the Torpedo, a homemade mechanism with tubes and air cylinders. It was used for replenishing the water injection tanks during the race – but there was some lead in there as well to act as ballast. Ken had worked out that a car could be weighed after a race, but not during it. Whether it was legal or not is another matter. Naive as I was, I had no idea what was going on. Later in the season it would give me and the team a lot of pain, and we were ultimately thrown out of the championship.

Nevertheless, when I got back home there was a great deal of fuss in the local newspapers in East Anglia, but it began to dawn on me when I read reports in the specialist press that I was one of the very few drivers in F1 history to score points in his first Grand Prix. The financial rewards were absolutely clear. The points would bring travel concessions and bonuses for a team that was really struggling. I was on £30,000 for my first year – minus all my expenses. Whenever I went to a race or a test or needed to find the money for my insurance, I had to pay. You can imagine how eye-watering the premiums are for a Grand Prix driver's death and injury cover and, in the end, with all the other costs taken into consideration, there was not a lot of change from £30,000. But I was on a share of the prize money too, so that fifth place finish was a big deal for me as well. I probably earned about £2,000 from that race.

The circuit will always have good memories even though, when you look closely at the place and conditions, you wonder why. It was very hard work driving a Grand Prix car there and the whole circuit and its surroundings had a grubby feel. In those days there was a nearby rubbish tip or a sewage farm – I'm not sure which but, either way, the pong could be pretty dreadful if the wind was blowing the wrong way. And yet it was a fun place to be. The race in 1989 is a good example.

I was driving for Brabham and, before we could even think about doing anything serious, we had to go through the ritual of pre-qualifying first thing on the Friday morning just to have the right to go out and practise. The entry was so large that there were too many cars for the pits available. It was so cramped, we didn't even have the privilege of a pit in which to use the disinfectant. We were shoved into a temporary lean-to canvas affair at the back of the pits.

We made it through pre-qualifying. That was the good news. The bad news was that we then had an hour in which to move the cars and all our equipment into a proper garage, one that was being vacated by a team that had failed to pre-qualify. Sweat was pouring off the mechanics as they humped all the toolboxes and air cylinders and other heavy pieces into the garage and tried to get the cars ready for the start of official practice. They had just about completed the job when my team-mate, Stefano Modena, walked in and looked as though he had seen a ghost.

'No! No!' he said. 'I don't want my car on the left. I'll only have it on the right.' Stefano was a lovely guy. But he was very, very superstitious. He simply would not get into his car if it was on the left side of the garage. There was nothing for it but to move cars and equipment around. You can imagine the effect this had on the mechanics who had just got everything together in record time.

I, on the other hand, am not superstitious but I certainly did not have much good luck in Rio. I finished fifth again for Tyrrell in 1986 but retired with mechanical trouble in the other three races. The first Grand Prix was obviously the highlight and I look back on that with great satisfaction. It was a terrific result under any circumstances with a cash-strapped team, never mind it being my debut.

I do remember that Derek Warwick had very kindly showed me round the circuit before the race, pointing out the potential pitfalls. He didn't show me any more racetracks after that.

Length: 4.309 km

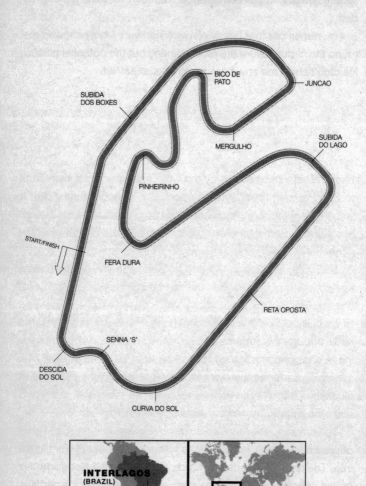

SUBIDA
DOS BOXES

BICO DE
PATO

JUNCAO

MERGULHO

SUBIDA
DO LAGO

PINHEIRINHO

START/FINISH

FERA DURA

RETA OPOSTA

SENNA 'S'

DESCIDA
DO SOL

CURVA DO SOL

INTERLAGOS
(BRAZIL)

Interlagos

I have always been struck by the way Brazilian drivers rush back to São Paulo at the slightest opportunity. Ayrton Senna did it. It was the same for Mauricio Gugelmin. And, these days, you won't see Rubens Barrichello for dust if he has free time between his commitments for Ferrari.

São Paulo and Rio de Janeiro both provide the slightly bizarre mix of a wonderful racetrack in run-down surroundings. In Rio, the view from my five-star hotel room took in the *favelas* clinging to the hillsides and it is the same when you drive to Interlagos, the route through the suburbs of São Paulo passing communities living in shacks piled one on top of the other. It is a massive city, stretching as far as the eye can see when you come into land at Guarulhos airport. The minute you step off the plane, even at 5 a.m., the air is sultry and carries a pungent, soggy smell.

The drive into Rio has awe-inspiring scenery. In reply, São Paulo offers a river, which, judging by its colour, you wouldn't want to fall into. The ringroad heading towards Interlagos runs alongside this brown ribbon of water and the journey can take an hour – perhaps three if you hit the chaotic traffic at the wrong time. The risk factor on the roads may not be as high as in Rio but, nevertheless, you need to keep your wits about you while waiting for the unexpected move from fellow motorists in decrepit vehicles, which look dangerous to sit in, never mind drive. That said, São Paulo is more sophisticated than Rio in many ways. There are posh suburbs downtown and plenty of good places to go, once you know where they are. There is a buzz about the place, but it lacks the colour and vibrancy of Rio.

Where the two cities differ yet again is at the racetracks themselves. Jacarepagua, for all its character and challenge, did not possess the appeal and sense of tradition that is evident from the moment you drive through the gates of Interlagos. For a start, one is in flat countryside some distance from the city whereas Interlagos is on high ground, but on the edge of a busy suburb. Built in the 1940s, Interlagos is reminiscent of an English football ground surrounded by terraced streets. The impression of entering a motor racing institution is similar to the unmistakable aura that greets you at Monza, Indianapolis and other historic venues: you know you have arrived at one of sport's great theatres.

Interlagos has a gladiatorial feel, thanks to being situated in a natural amphitheatre. The pits are on a plateau and the track immediately plunges downhill, swoops around the bottom of the bowl and then begins the return climb to the pit straight. The present layout was first used when the Grand Prix returned to Interlagos in 1990 and the sense of presence is heightened by visible traces of the older, longer circuit that was abandoned for safety and economic reasons ten years before.

The original 4.9-mile track swept past the pits and into a very long banked curve that still stands today. Images from the past instantly return as you recall reports and television pictures of heroes such as Ronnie Peterson, flat out and drifting sideways in his Lotus. Then you take a closer look at the tiny crash barriers and the absence of run-off area and it is pretty obvious why the original circuit could no longer sustain Grand Prix racing.

The old track has, in many places, been used as a base for grandstands, all of which are packed on race day. You see people queuing for two miles down the side of the road as they wait to get in and be a part of the lovely South American chaos that always ensues. There are always about fifty people trying to check your pass at the gate: two would actually get the job done and the other forty-eight so-called officials are usually in the way. There is the inescapable feeling that nobody is quite in charge and yet it functions somehow. That said, Interlagos remains one of the most difficult tracks from an access point of view – something I was to be reminded of when, in 2003, I accidentally found myself outside the track minutes before the start. But more of that later.

As in Rio, the fans arrive early and make a lot of cheerful noise. The atmosphere is enhanced greatly by a seemingly endless run of grandstands that line the outside of the track from the top of the final climb, all the way along the pit straight and beyond the braking area for the first corner. There is a tunnel effect created by the stands high on your right and a very tall pit wall on the left. It is like going into a concrete cutting.

The starting grid is in the middle of all this and I cringe when I see a car stuck in that pit straight area. Because of the high walls either side, it is difficult to remove a stranded car quickly. When the race is running, other drivers are climbing the hill and approaching the blind brow leading onto the straight at 200 mph. The marshals are doing their best, but it's heart-in-the-mouth stuff at the sight of those cars sweeping over the crest.

There was a huge shunt at this point during the race in 2003 when Mark Webber, trying to cool his wet weather tyres on a dry-ing track, went off-line looking for a wet piece of road – and found one. His Jaguar suddenly lost grip and went straight into the wall. Fernando Alonso, despite yellow warning flags and radio messages from the team telling him to slow down, steamed into the pile of debris and came close to wiping himself out. All because that curve is blind and there is no room for error.

The difficulty is that the pit straight, or at least the start of it, is not actually a straight. Usually that is not a problem; there are plenty of racetracks in the world where a curve is easy to negotiate and is effectively a straight line. But, at Interlagos, this section is curved just enough to make the accompanying bumps and little blind crests a massive challenge – particularly when it rains. In fact, it is terrifying in the wet because you know you have to go flat out and yet, all of a sudden, you can just be a few centimetres off-line one way or the other. Catch a bump or a patch of Tarmac at a slightly different angle than before, and the whole thing is out of control almost before you know it. The back end of the car can get away from you very easily.

Conversely, Interlagos – renamed, but rarely referred to as, Autodromo Jose Carlos Pace in honour of the F1 driver killed in a light plane crash in March 1977 – provides one of the most atmospheric starting grids in the world. The samba drums have been going full pelt from an early hour and the steeply raked grandstand seems to tower over the track. The stadium effect is amplified even further by a dip in the track halfway down the grid. It is the most dramatic pre-race grid walk that I do for ITV, a brilliant place for connecting the racetrack with the crowd. The only other location I can think of which produces a similar effect is Casino Square at Monaco.

In 2003, I left it quite late before leaving the grid and making my way to the commentary box. It was lashing down at the time. While that was adding to the uncertainty and tension of the moment, it was not helping my preparation for a commentary that would last for close to two hours. I thought I knew a shortcut which would take me through a gap in the fence and round the back of the public enclosures, the commentary boxes being above the grandstand before the first corner. Not only did I get lost, I somehow managed to end up outside the track, more or less on the street. This presented an obvious problem. I had my accreditation round my neck but the aforementioned collection of so-called officials at this particular gate had either not seen a media pass before or they were understandably suspicious of a guy who seemed to be trying to blag his way in by pretending to be a television reporter.

With time ticking away and water trickling down my neck, the sound of the cars preparing to go off on the final parade lap must have prompted a certain amount of desperation on my part as I persuaded them to let me in. The race was about to start and my fellow commentator James Allen did not know where I was. Neither, for a couple of terrible moments, did I.

I was approaching the back of the commentary boxes from an unfamiliar angle and the route involved walking along a platform at the back of the grandstand, directly beneath the edge of the tented roof. This being a temporary affair, rainwater was gathering in dips in the canvas and, every now and then, the whole thing would move and empty itself without warning in a mini-deluge. All over the walkway. I could not have been any wetter by the time I reached the ITV box. At least the promise of a dramatic start quickly banished any thought of self-pity.

The grid at Interlagos is also unique because the front half runs uphill while the back half is on a downhill slope. Sensors in the racetrack check that cars don't move until the moment the race starts. For the drivers, it is a matter of trying to hold the right revs and stop the car moving forwards or backwards, depending which part of the grid you are on. As starts go, this one is really tricky and it is no surprise to see cars become stranded.

Those that do get going then rush into the braking area for the first corner, which is just beyond another crest. Instead of charging flat out into that banked first corner, which the Petersons and Fittipaldis used to tackle with such flair thirty years ago, the track now turns sharp left, and dives downhill. The braking area for this first turn is wide with plenty of grip on offer, which means you can approach the left-hander on either side of the track, a benefit that has resulted in some great overtaking manoeuvres.

Juan Pablo Montoya and David Coulthard both got the better of Michael Schumacher here in 2001. There were others that didn't succeed, such as Michael Andretti bouncing along the outside wall eight years earlier and almost three-wheeling his way as far as the spectator enclosure. As if it wasn't tricky enough at this point on the circuit, drivers had the additional hazard of an advertising hoarding, which was suspended over the braking area, coming loose and crashing onto the road in 2000. Nobody was hurt but, in many ways, that startling incident summed up motor racing in Brazil.

Television cannot capture the simmering chaos of Interlagos. The helicopter cameras make the place look fantastic, positioned as it is between two lakes (hence the name). The grubby city in the background and the tumbledown buildings in the surrounding area are kept out of shot. Millions of viewers see lakes and a gorgeous green area, all of which looks very impressive. But it is a different matter when you are on the ground. The car parks quickly become a mud bath on a wet day and the toilet facilities are only to be used in an absolute emergency. Even then, you think twice.

Drainage is a particular problem at Interlagos. I recall a strange incident just before the start of the race in 1996. This was a particularly difficult period for me because I had just survived the massive accident in Melbourne two weeks before and then my dad died. I had qualified sixth at Interlagos but even that seemed to be of little use when the rain really came down on race morning. As it happened, I was the first to leave the pit lane when it opened to allow cars onto the grid. I reached the end of the pits and the standing water was so deep that the Jordan, even at 5 mph, created a bow wave that then came off the front wing, filled the cockpit and drenched me.

I crept round the lap and, even though I had wet tyres on, I couldn't prevent the car from aquaplaning. I returned to the pits, got out of the car and told everyone that there was no way they could start the race. It never occurred to me or anyone else in the team that the clock was still running. Drivers have fifteen minutes to leave the pits and make their way to the grid. Fail to do that, and you start the race from the pit lane.

It had stopped raining and, all of a sudden, we realised the pit lane was about to close. There was immediate panic because I had convinced everyone, including my team-mate Rubens Barrichello, that the race was not going to run on time. We got out with seconds to spare.

The track was drying by then although there was a huge black cloud on the horizon. I was on wet-weather tyres, but some instinct told me I should change them. The guys in the pits wanted me to stay out. In their view, this was the clever thing to do because that big black cloud would be here any minute. The rain never came. I was lapped. Then I spun into Turn 1, which was pathetic driving. I was angry about the tyre choice because I had been running really well all weekend.

WORKING THE WHEEL

Experience says that you have to be on the right tyres. A pit stop and changing to the right tyres is better than several laps on the wrong tyres. There is no point in staying out in a vain attempt to make the wrong decision come right. The track that day was too dry for wets. It was a bad couple of weeks.

It has to be said, however, that rain in Brazil does not come in half measures. The problem with inadequate drainage came to a dramatic head during the extremely wet race in 2003. The worst spot was at Turns 2 and 3, the right and left at the bottom of the hill, a part of the track that acted – or tried to – like a plug hole for surrounding slopes disgorging loads of water. The track was drying everywhere else but, at this particular point, a river was flowing across the road. Drivers lost control and, in some cases, hit cars that had already come to a halt against the tyre barrier. There could have been some very serious moments, particularly when Michael Schumacher almost slid into a massive rescue vehicle that was trying to remove an abandoned car. Motor racing is dangerous enough without having officials add to the hazards.

However, the drivers are their own worst enemies, not respecting double-waved yellow flags that indicate a very dangerous situation: in effect, 'people on the track, slow down, be prepared to stop'.

Accidents are generally caused either by driver error or mechanical failure. During the 1994 Brazilian Grand Prix, I was involved in a serious crash that was brought about by a mixture of both. It was the nearest I had ever come to dying.

It was my first race for McLaren and I would quickly come to learn that the Peugeot engine had a habit of shedding its flywheel with dramatic results. The loss of the flywheel would have been nothing more than a frustrating failure had it simply dropped off the back of the engine. But it didn't stop at that. With the flywheel revolving at around 14,000 revolutions per minute – or 230 per second – the forces involved would take it through the bottom of the transmission casing and onto the racetrack, where it would instantly bounce back and cause all sorts of mayhem beneath the car. Its favourite trick was to go through the gearbox and set fire to the oil.

I had already endured a difficult qualifying at Interlagos that year thanks to a sticking throttle that had me running off the road and visiting just about every part of the track. Having qualified eighteenth, the race itself was turning out to be much better as I moved through the field and found myself in seventh place on lap thirty-seven. The problem with the sticking throttle had been cured. Not so, the flying flywheel.

It came off just as I accelerated out of Turn 3 and onto the back straight. There were no pyrotechnics this time and I radioed the pits to say something had gone wrong. The team stressed that I had to return the car to the pits somehow. I was working out how to do that while preparing to keep out of everyone's way.

The next thing I knew, I was in the gravel trap at the next corner, regaining consciousness and trying to work out how I had travelled half the length of the straight and left the road without knowing anything about it. I climbed from the car and turned round to find there was complete mayhem behind me. I could see that Jos Verstappen, Eddie Irvine and Eric Bernard were also vacating damaged cars.

I was later able to piece together that all three had been closing on me, but at differing speeds. Bernard, the first and the slowest, had been caught by surprise when I suddenly ran into trouble. Irvine was about to lap the Frenchman but Eddie had Verstappen in his slipstream and the Benetton was about to attempt a pass by trapping Irvine's Jordan behind Bernard's Ligier. Irvine, faced with either slamming into the back of the slowing Ligier or taking avoiding action, swung left. Verstappen, unaware of my problem and now beginning to draw alongside Irvine, moved left as well, didn't lift his foot from the throttle, put a rear wheel on the grass and was immediately pitched sideways. At about 180 mph.

Verstappen hit the left-rear wheel of my car and became airborne, barrel-rolling across the top of me. A rear wheel hit my head. I've since seen a picture where my head is not visible, as if it has been knocked off. In fact, I was leaning forward, my head almost in my lap. The roll hoop behind my head carried a huge scar in the outline of a Benetton wheel, a mark that also appeared on my crash helmet. The car had taken most of the impact but if that wheel had been a few centimetres further forward, I would not be here to tell the tale.

The accident may have been due to an unfortunate set of circumstances but there have been many incidents going into that corner that are due more to misjudgement than anything else. It is one of those corners that tend to suck you in and you are in trouble before you realise it. The reason is that the approach is slightly downhill and bumpy. You've had a good run down the back straight and everything seems quite easy. But it is necessary to brake a touch earlier than you imagine because, when you get into the corner, it is off-camber and that compounds the error of carrying too much speed. Often the accident has happened on the way in. If someone's car is working well under braking then they will be considerably later on the brakes than someone who is not. That's also when trouble can arise.

Even if you negotiate the corner correctly, there is another trap waiting, almost immediately, for the unwary. This kink to the left looks harmless but it is just enough to get the car out of shape if you're not careful. The trouble is, you are under full acceleration –

even in the wet – when coming out of the corner at the end of the straight. If you catch it wrong, the car is out of control in an instant and straight into the barrier. Olivier Panis had a big crash there, as did Irvine when he destroyed his Ferrari during practice in 1996. Eddie's look of complete bewilderment afterwards said everything about the nasty nature of that innocent-looking little kink.

The beauty of Interlagos – or not, if you are getting tired towards the end of the race – is that there is very little time to relax. Power out of that kink and you are heading towards Fera Dura, a really tricky right-hander that has a blind apex, just over a crest. The corner actually has a double apex and, just as you think you've got it all together, the bend tightens on the exit – while starting to go downhill again. It's a tremendous corner because all of this happens at about 140 mph. There used to be acres of bumpy gravel traps that would rip off front wings if you so much as thought about running wide. It is Tarmac now, so drivers can make mistakes and get away with it. Whether that is good or bad is another question.

From this point on, you are into a really busy section of the circuit. Interlagos is an extremely challenging track of two parts: there are the sweepy high-speed sections and then the middle sector that follows Fera Dura. The track continues to fall, twist left and then rise towards Bico de Pato, a very slow right that turns back on itself. This corner presents a combination that is difficult because an F1 car is designed more with high speed in mind and wants to understeer (go straight on) in tight corners. It is hard to find a rhythm in the middle sector and you can often lose more time there than you can gain on the rest of the track. It means Interlagos is a tough circuit on which to find the best set-up and, even when you do, it is just as difficult to produce a really good lap.

WORKING THE WHEEL

Having negotiated Bico de Pato, you are straight into Mergulho, a fast left-hander. I suffered the indignity of crashing there on the first lap of the Grand Prix in 1993. Mergulho has since been resurfaced but, at the time, it was very uneven and I lost it on a bump – as you often do on a first lap.

In the early stages of a Grand Prix, especially if you are carrying a lot of fuel, your suspension can simply run out of travel at a place like Mergulho where a fast downhill corner feeds into a compression before rising quite steeply uphill. When the car either bottoms out on the track surface or it runs out of suspension travel, then the tyres have to do the work of the suspension. They compress but, unlike suspension, which has springs and shock absorbers to control the deflection, the tyres simply spread momentarily and then pop back up again, making the car skip. Of course, with the track also turning left at this point, you are then thrown off to the right and heading for a big accident.

That's what happened to me in the dip. I went straight into the tyre wall, which made a hell of a mess of the car. There have been many accidents at that corner and, to compound the driver's agony, he then has to walk up the hill to the pits – looking out for snakes or whatever else might be in the grass – and tell a very unhappy team boss that his race car has just been destroyed.

Interlagos has caused problems for just about every driver at some point or other. Even the local hero, Ayrton Senna, actually spun here while leading in 1994. He had started from pole but the Williams, which was difficult that year, got away from him at Juncao, the left-hander that starts the climb towards the pits. The locals so wanted him to win and he was doing his best to deliver and stay ahead of Michael Schumacher, very much the heir apparent at the time. It was to be the beginning of a troubled time for Ayrton that ended with his death a few weeks later at Imola.

No one ever doubted Senna's determination to do the business at home, particularly after winning in 1991, when they had to lift him from his McLaren at the finish. It's strange how these things happen but, despite wins everywhere else in the world at the time, Senna had never won at home, something he wanted more than anything. Finally, it seemed to be a done deal in 1991 as he held a thirty-second lead. Then the gearbox started to play up as he lost fourth, then third, then fifth. And, just to add to the agony, a light drizzle started. Senna was slithering along on slick tyres. With just one lap to go, Riccardo Patrese's Williams had reduced the gap to three seconds. Senna, now struggling with a box of neutrals, found sixth gear and kept it there for fear he might lose that, too. He was convinced Patrese was going to steal the victory in the last couple of miles. In fact, the Williams had gearbox trouble as well and Senna reached the flag, exhausted both mentally and physically by the battle with the gear lever. When Ayrton finally reached the podium, he could barely raise the trophy.

Somehow, that scene was in keeping with a venue that has an intriguing quality and yet is frayed round the edges. Some of the facilities have to be seen to be believed. The garage space has to double as offices and dining facilities. You might be standing at the back of Ferrari, a team spending hundreds of millions of dollars, with the smell of hot engines and food blending into one bizarre mix. Dinner is being cooked while engines are being revved to check for leaks. Meanwhile, on the other side of a temporary partition, personnel are attempting to have a meeting. Wonderful facilities at places such as Sepang in Malaysia are becoming the standard and yet everyone puts up with a great deal in Brazil simply because F1 needs to be in South America if it is to justify its claim as a true world championship.

There is no doubt that the Brazilian Grand Prix at Interlagos is

Imola

Imola will be for ever associated with the death of Ayrton Senna. This colourful track in north-west Italy has many attributes, but the events on the afternoon of 1 May 1994 will come to mind before anything else. It could hardly be otherwise. Senna's crash at Tamburello looked harmless enough – perhaps the fourth-worst accident I have seen at that corner – but the fact that the triple World Champion died of a freak injury did nothing to reduce the horror and sadness which came with the loss of a sporting icon. Because Imola was the scene of the tragedy, the circuit would be forever tainted.

I say 'circuit' rather than 'San Marino Grand Prix' because this is the one of those strange anomalies associated with F1 racing. I am not alone among the F1 community in saying I have never set foot in San Marino. I don't even know where it is. I am told the tiny principality is 50 miles away with a population of less than 30,000 but, in truth, that is largely irrelevant.

The title was invented as a clever means of giving Italy two rounds of the World Championship. With Monza having claimed the Italian Grand Prix from Day 1, Imola never had a look-in. Or, at least, not until this rolling track in the Emilia Romagna region

Length: 4.933 km

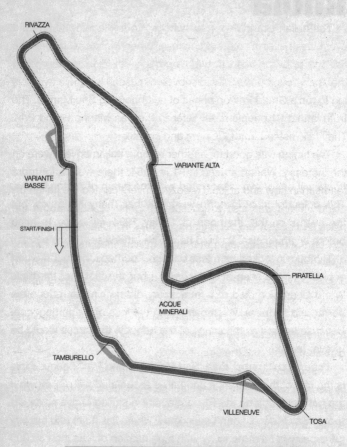

RIVAZZA

VARIANTE ALTA

VARIANTE
BASSE

START/FINISH

PIRATELLA

ACQUE
MINERALI

TAMBURELLO

VILLENEUVE

TOSA

IMOLA
(SAN MARINO)

received a face-lift and, co-incidentally, Monza ran into political difficulties.

The Italian Grand Prix was switched to Imola in 1980 and the event was hailed as a great success. When Monza reclaimed the title the following year, the Imola organisers, keen to cash in on their new-found popularity, discovered a useful loophole by offering to run a Grand Prix on behalf of neighbouring San Marino. The truth is that F1 people rarely refer to the San Marino Grand Prix. They talk instead of Imola: pure and simple.

The timing was good for another reason. Italian drivers were on the increase. When I arrived in F1 in 1984, there were a lot more teams than now and at least a dozen drivers carried the Italian tricolour. There was also a tidy sum of money floating about the place and deals were done along the lines of: 'I'll give you five million on the understanding that three million finds its way into my Swiss bank account.' By sponsoring F1 and swerving the taxman at the same time, these local businessmen were offering young Italian drivers a huge opportunity to find their way into the seat of a Grand Prix car. All of this added to the feeling of passion and tradition for motor sport in Italy. Imola would provide a perfect canvas. Or, at least, the circuit would.

The local area is notable for dreadful hotels, and the curious landscape can present a beautiful Italian house next to a factory, with more houses on the other side and then perhaps a car dealership and a couple of grain silos. It is a strange mix of residential and industrial united by a slightly tatty look.

Even the racetrack, built in the early 1950s, has become frayed around the edges and the first surprise is to find it located alongside a river, within the boundary of the town. When you head for the circuit to start practice on Friday, you join a queue of workers on their way to local factories and offices. But once inside the paddock, there is a definite feeling of being at a track buzzing with atmosphere.

The corners on this elongated circuit carry many evocative names – Tamburello, Tosa, Piratella, Acque Minerali, Rivazza – but the drivers simply use numbers these days. While talking to Jenson Button during practice in 2004, I said his BAR-Honda seemed to be struggling a little through Piratella. 'Which one is that?' he asked. When I explained it was the left-hander at the top of the hill, he said: 'Ah, you mean Turn 8!' It is just the way drivers and engineers work these days.

Before Senna's accident, Imola was dominated by the main straight, which ran all the way from the pits, through the long, fast left at Tamburello and curved to the right on its way to Tosa at the far end of the track. Tamburello was full throttle in the dry. It actually meant that the driver was a reluctant passenger because there was no skill involved in sitting with his right foot hard on the throttle while waiting for the work of the tyre manufacturer, car designer, engineers and engine-builder to show itself. It was also difficult for the engine people standing in the pits because they had to suffer untold agonies while listening to their pride and joy screaming for about seventeen seconds as the car disappeared out of sight and rushed towards Tosa.

Tosa hairpin used to be the scene of some incredible moments on the first lap. Just imagine the scenario: the usual sound and fury as drivers accelerate off the grid, go flat out all the way through Tamburello and into the right-hand kink before jumping on the brakes for Tosa. But the front tyres have very little temperature; the rear tyres are only marginally warmer because they have been transmitting the power. Even worse, the brakes are stone cold because they have not been used since the parade lap between thirty seconds and a minute before, depending where you were on the grid. Add in the weight from a full tank of fuel and you get the picture as the field charges along a high-speed straight and arrives at a tight left-hander with no grip and ineffective brakes but a determination to overtake while still running in such close company. Pandemonium barely begins to describe the scene as more than twenty cars fight for position.

Saying that, one of my worst experiences at Tosa happened in a practice session in 1984. We ran the Tyrrell with a full tank of fuel; a necessary check because mid-race refuelling was not allowed, as I've said, and the extra weight had a massive effect on the handling of the car. Putting 200 litres of fuel into a 500 kg car meant the addition of between 25 and 30 per cent extra weight. It meant altering the set-up because the car was an entirely different beast compared to the one used for qualifying.

As I passed the pits to begin a run, the Tyrrell lost one of the pins holding my rear brake pads in place. As I went through Tamburello and headed towards Tosa, the brake pads jangled out and fell onto the track. I knew nothing of this until I got on the brakes – and quickly discovered there was something terribly wrong. I hit the pedal for all it was worth, but this was merely pushing the brake pistons towards the disc. Before they got that far, they popped out of their seals, which meant the fluid escaped and I had no rear brakes at all. I was doing 180 mph with a full tank of fuel. There were two independent braking systems on the car, so the front brakes locked just before I left the track.

There was very little run-off area at Tosa but, fortunately for me, they had a double row of tyres linked together in a crescent shape. That's where I went in. The impact was such that my crash helmet bent the steering wheel. As I was thrown back into the seat – the tightly strapped seat harness having stretched due to the enormous forces involved – the fuel behind my shoulders surged forward. The petrol was carried in a rubber cell located behind a metal bulkhead separating it from the cockpit. As I rebounded off the steering wheel, 200 litres were still coming my way. The enormous bulk of fuel hit me from behind.

Meanwhile, the tyre barrier had done its job and brought everything to a halt. Two hours later, I was back on the track in the same car. I may have suffered for two years after that with a bad shoulder and neck before it finally sorted itself out, but the truth was that I had been really very lucky.

Once practice was finished at the end of the day, Ken Tyrrell and some of the engineers and mechanics spread across the track and began walking, looking for the missing brake pads. When they reached Tamburello, an Italian fan climbed over the fence. 'You want this?' he asked, holding a brake pad in his hand. He had seen the pad come out of my car, bounce down the track and come to rest against the fence. Later, he picked it up and thought he had a souvenir until he saw the Tyrrell crew clearly looking for something.

Since Tamburello did not require use of the brakes, I had got through the left-hander without incident – which is more than could be said for several drivers over the years. There have been some major collisions with the wall lining the outside of the corner.

During practice in 1987, Nelson Piquet's Williams had a tyre failure and slammed sideways into the concrete, where it left very clear impressions of the right-hand wheels and tyres. Michele Alboreto was knocked about badly when the front wing failed on his Arrows on the way into the same corner. And, during the race in 1989, Gerhard Berger's Ferrari slid into the wall, broke up and caught fire. In each case, the driver escaped with minor injury.

Senna, on the other hand, was so unlucky. The actual chassis of his Williams was completely intact, so much so that there was hardly a bruise, never mind a broken bone. But he died because a piece of suspension, attached to the right front wheel and torn off by the impact, hit him on the head. It was a big accident, but others have been far more horrifying. That added to the feeling of utter disbelief on a weekend none of us will ever forget.

A seemingly endless string of nasty events began during practice on Friday when Rubens Barrichello touched a kerb and his Jordan took off and ran along the top of a tyre barrier. Luckily, instead of going through a spectator fence, the car stayed trackside. Rubens was concussed but otherwise OK. The incident was seen as a typical motor racing accident with no serious consequences. After all, F1 was very safe; there had not been a fatality at a race for twelve years. That rather blasé view was about to be shattered.

The following day, Roland Ratzenberger smashed his Simtek into a wall. The front wings, which had been dislodged on a high kerb, had suddenly come off the car on the very quick approach to Tosa. Ratzenberger, attempting to qualify for what would have been his second Grand Prix, was killed instantly.

The only memory I have of him is a really nice one. I was sitting in a restaurant in the Transamerica Hotel in São Paulo when this bright-eyed, smiling face appeared in front of me. 'Hi! I'm Roland,' he said. 'Nice to meet you.' This was the first race of the year and here was a driver, new to F1, introducing himself to other drivers. That sort of thing is unheard of and it was such a refreshing change. Even from such a brief acquaintance, it was easy to see that Roland was a genuinely nice guy.

There was nothing he could have done about the accident. It was a product of one of the hazards of racing at Imola where it is necessary to bounce over the kerbs. If you are too aggressive, there is always the chance that a front wing might be fractured.

In Ratzenberger's case, he then encountered the worst-case scenario where the long straight leading to Tosa put the aerodynamics under very high loads that seek out that fracture and break the wing. At which point it goes under a front wheel, the downforce is gone and the car skids like a toboggan. The driver is a passenger from then on.

It really hits hard when an accident like that comes out of the blue. You ask why it happened to a nice guy like that. Why today? Why there? You just feel so helpless and sad.

The feeling of being 'on edge' accelerated on race day when a start-line collision left debris all over the track and brought out the safety car. Having started thirteenth on the grid in my McLaren – the car that Senna had vacated when he moved to Williams – I was in a queue led by Senna and Michael Schumacher's Benetton. It took four laps for the wreckage to be cleared. Then it was straight back to racing when the green flag was shown.

At the start of the second lap, more drama, this time at Tamburello. We were so busy dodging bits and pieces on the track that it was difficult to tell who had gone off. I had registered the fact that it was a Williams and thought it must be Damon Hill. The car looked to be in one piece and I didn't think much more about it.

When we returned to the start/finish area and came to a stop, I discovered it was Senna's car and concern began to creep in when, in the midst of an eerie hush, the television monitors were switched off. Ron Dennis of McLaren stood with my team-mate, Mika Hakkinen, while Martin Whitmarsh, the managing director, came to talk to me. As professionals they instinctively felt the need to manage the situation. Another bad sign.

Then the word went round that Ayrton was all right because he had moved his head after the accident. That was true. But, although we didn't know it, the movement had been nothing more than a final, gentle spasm.

Why did his car go straight on at Tamburello rather than continue to negotiate the left-hand curve at 190 mph? I don't know the precise reason. But I do know that a period spent running behind a safety car can turn F1 cars into absolute bitches to drive. The tyre temperatures fall, which means the pressures go down and, in turn, the car's ride height will drop. In this instance, the cars were not just kissing the track, but were running on the ground. The aerodynamic loads, instead of being dealt with by the tyres, were going through the chassis. The result is that you are being steered by the chassis and skid blocks rather than the wheels. You no longer have the compliance created by the suspension and tyres. The car becomes unstable. That said, one of the suggestions put forward was that there was a problem with the steering column.

Added to this, Senna was pushing really hard in order to stay ahead of Schumacher, who had already won the first two races of the season. Ayrton, who was generally suspicious of the world at large, had convinced himself that Schumacher's Benetton had some sort of electronic assistance and, if nothing else, this was adding to Senna's hunger to beat them.

There was little or no news coming through by the time we prepared to restart. All we were told was that Senna was in a serious condition. Writing these lines more than a decade later, it makes me feel sick to think that we then raced past a pool of his blood for fifty-three laps. That may seem hypocritical when you consider that Ratzenberger had died the previous day and we had carried on, business as usual. His car had failed and, in truth, there was little else we could do. But I make no apologies for saying that Sunday was a different matter. This was Ayrton Senna, an icon who we all looked up to, a mighty personality who almost transcended F1 and whom we all felt was invincible. He had so much God-given skill, such exquisite car control, that it seemed nothing could ever happen to him.

We finished the race. The word remained that Senna was badly injured. Everyone went through the motions as a podium procedure was held and the packing-up process began. The expression 'you could cut the atmosphere with a knife' was never more appropriate when applied to the Imola paddock in the late afternoon of 1 May 1994. A couple of hours later, our worst fears were confirmed.

People were crying, others just quietly going about their business, keen to be done with this place. It was as silent as you will ever find the paddock of a busy racetrack. The crowd melted quietly away. No one quite knew how to handle this situation, or how to present themselves, or what to do. It was such an enormous shock.

Like so many others, I questioned my further participation in motor sport, such was the impact of Senna's death. After long hours of thought and discussion, I decided to carry on. This was the only sensible answer, as driving a racing car was my purpose in life at that time.

I had many personal memories of the great man, including our epic battles in the 1983 F3 season, which resulted in significant accidents and confrontation, and culminated with him being extremely magnanimous at the season's end. We tripped into each other several more times in F1 and, ironically, the night before his death, I happened to walk into the hotel lift in which we were the sole occupants. The polite but tense conversation will live with me for ever.

The after-effects of the accident would reverberate around the motor racing world and Imola, of course, would not be immune. When we returned twelve months later, a chicane had been added at Tamburello, and another at Villeneuve, named after Gilles Villeneuve who had crashed spectacularly in his Ferrari at this point on the fast approach to Tosa. In each case, there was little option but to build a chicane thanks to the circuit's tight boundaries. At Tamburello, for instance, there is a public park on the inside of the corner and a river beyond the wall on the outside. There was simply no option but, as chicanes go, these are very acceptable.

The approach to the Tamburello chicane remains very fast, as does the exit. In between, there are hefty kerbs, which now characterise Imola to such an extent that, if your car cannot deal with these kerbs, you will never set a competitive lap time. The Tamburello chicane is a similar layout to Villeneuve. In each case, they have taken away a flat-out, top-gear curve, where the driver was in the lap of the gods, and put in a challenge. I'm very comfortable with that.

The only thing that's missing is the big stop and the overtaking opportunity into Tosa. It is now simply a quick squirt of power from Villeneuve and then into the left-hander. The days are gone when drivers would finish the race and, almost without exception, launch into wide-eyed stories such as: 'You wouldn't believe what he did to me at Tosa!' Or: 'You should have seen the move I pulled going in there.' We have had one or two minor incidents since, but nothing like the high-speed heroics of years gone by.

Now, Tosa is all about making a clean exit and powering up a steep hill. This is the far end of the circuit and it certainly feels like bandit territory if you break down in anything other than a Ferrari. There is a snake pit of fans ready to boo, jeer and verbally abuse any opposition to the team in red.

The hill leads to Piratella, a corner that lost much of its challenge when semi-automatic gearboxes became *de rigueur*. In the days of manual gearboxes, if your coordination wasn't up to scratch when downshifting while cresting the hill, you would get into a mess, enter the left-hander much too fast and run wide. There used to be numerous accidents at Piratella as cars careered into the bank, but not any more thanks to the ease of simply flicking a paddle on the back of the steering wheel and letting the electronics do the rest, coupled with a now beautifully smooth and cambered surface.

Having reached the top of the circuit, you are straight into a bumpy downhill section that provides such good acceleration you would swear the car suddenly has another 100 bhp as gravity comes into play. Waiting in the dip at the bottom is Acque Minerali.

This two-part right-hander has been re-profiled a couple of times. Originally, you went straight into an immensely bumpy braking zone beneath a canopy of trees. Get it wrong and a steel barrier was waiting dead ahead. They then put in a really fast approach to the second part with a huge run-off area; again, I thought they did a very good job.

It remains bumpy through Acque Minerali, which is as it should be rather than trying to provide a super-smooth surface. The bumps mean you can see the drivers and cars working while trying to stay on-line. It is more difficult than you think, as I found to my cost in 1996 when I crashed a Jordan after getting into trouble on the bumps. Any corner where you go steaming in and need to turn a second time at the right moment is always a test. Just for good measure, you are also turning into the foot of a hill. It has a twist and tightens on the exit, all of which adds to the challenge of a great corner.

The next hill is not quite as steep as the rise to Piratella but the driver is already preparing himself for Variante Alta (High Chicane), a fast and tricky chicane, which is unsighted when arriving at 180 mph. There is no room for error here because the high kerbs on the way in will punish any misjudgement by throwing the car off-line, across the grass at the exit – and straight into a wall. Inevitably, the speed and angle of the impact will pluck the right-hand suspension and do a lot of damage to the chassis.

Variante Alta is a terribly expensive place to crash a car, which is tricky because sometimes even the smallest error can suddenly leap out of proportion. The Australian driver, Mark Webber, summed it up perfectly when he said to me in an interview: 'Jeez mate, you need a lucky bounce up there.'

It's true. An F1 car with just 15 mm of ride height is not cut out for leaping through the air at high speed. It is a case of hustling the car on the way into the right-left and driving through it if you get the lucky bounce or, if not, hanging on and hoping to gather it together, just as we saw Michael Schumacher do so brilliantly while vainly attempting to take pole position from Jenson Button during qualifying in 2004.

Variante Alta also sums up Imola in other ways, as the track here appears to dissect the local community as if it were running through back gardens. There are olive groves and small holdings inside the circuit where people carry out their business, lead normal lives and hang over the fence to watch the action when there is racing or testing.

You also notice it on the next section where the track swoops downhill again, curving right under a bridge and lining up for the two Rivazza corners at the bottom. A very high wall running close to the track and allowing a minimum of run-off area forms the boundary at this point. That's because there are roads and houses immediately beyond the wall and locals make the most of a rare free view.

It is a good place to watch because the drivers are very busy when they start braking from 185 mph on the curve leading to the corner. Sometimes, as happens in Italy, the marshals get too close when enjoying the action. Italian marshals love to be right on the edge of the racetrack. A number of times during testing I've gone to the circuit officials and said: 'I don't want to be looking at a marshal when I'm in the braking zone. However fast he thinks his reactions might be, they will not be fast enough if I have brake failure. I'm going to wipe him out and, equally, he might wipe me out if he has a fire extinguisher in his hands.'

Besides, drivers arriving at Rivazza already have their hands full because of the nature of the left-hander. It is easy to lock the left-front brake and it is tempting for a driver following to think there could be an opportunity to overtake. It would be a risky move because the driver in front has to know you are coming. He will be so busy braking, downshifting and looking for the apex of the left-hander that, when caught by surprise, he will have already begun to turn into the corner on the assumption that no one could possibly be leaving their braking late enough to come down the inside.

You have got to make it clear before the previous right-hand curve that you are going to have a go. It is essential to be alongside and announce your presence. The hard part will be braking late and making it stick. The likelihood is that you will lock a brake, skate past the apex and the other driver will tuck back inside and retake the initiative.

There is a very short straight to the second Rivazza, a corner that invites the driver to push hard. It is a case of coming off the throttle briefly before applying power again and hanging on. Sometimes you slide off the kerb, and sometimes you don't:

sometimes you catch the grass on the outside, and sometimes not. Another great corner.

The run towards the pits used to have two chicanes. The first – which has since been removed – was very fast and absolutely terrifying. There was a nasty kerb to dissuade drivers from taking a shortcut on the way in but, frequently, this piece of concrete merely succeeded in acting as a launch pad. It was complete madness but it was also a wonderful feeling to be on top of the car and get this chicane absolutely right because it was difficult to do for every lap of a race thanks to the track surface changing, along with the tyres and handling of the car. Get it wrong just once and you were airborne. Every driver has had a scary moment there and this is where Barrichello was launched onto the tyre barrier at the start of that terrible weekend in 1994.

Now, drivers accelerate hard from Rivazza and into an area of very heavy braking for the final chicane. This used to be much closer to the pit buildings than it is now and it was disconcerting to be heading at high speed towards a gable-end. If you had brake failure there, you were looking at a massive head-on with a tyre barrier.

The chicane has since been pulled back but a hazard remains because the approach is also the start of the pit lane entry. The danger is steaming into the chicane tucked beneath the rear wing of the car in front – and he carries on at speed into the pit lane, leaving you looking foolish as you struggle to swing left at the last second into the chicane. That can be so frustrating, particularly if the rest of the lap has been as perfect as you could ever hope for.

I had a verbal run-in with Jean Alesi at this spot in 1992. We were very evenly matched that year, Jean in a Ferrari while I was enjoying the Benetton. We always seemed to be fighting over the same piece of track and, all too often, running into each other. At

Imola, Jean felt I had screwed up one of his qualifying laps as I was returning to the pits. Coming out of Rivazza, I had pulled over for him. I didn't want to get my tyres too dirty and gave him what I thought was plenty of space. Uncertain about whether or not I had seen him, Alesi didn't commit to the pass and got very upset. When the session finished we ended up, toe-to-toe, at that corner of the pit building. Unfortunately for me, Ferrari was in the first pit garage and Jean's mechanics were right with him. He said to me: 'I will kill you!' He's calmed down since – he's actually a good friend of mine now – but that's what he said at the time.

I didn't respond very well. Opposite this scene was a grand-stand brimming with Ferrari supporters and they quickly caught the drift of what was going on. I was replying in an unprintable way to Jean's threat. This was not the first time there had been words because we had already collided in Brazil. I may have been furious but I had the good sense to look at the mechanics, take a note of the mounting abuse from the crowd and decide it was perhaps wise not to continue this debate and to seek the sanctuary of the Benetton pit.

For one reason or another, Imola has been the scene of many arguments, both on the track and off, which has caused drivers to fall out. In 1982, a war over control of the sport meant there was a reduced entry when nearly all of the British-based independent teams such as Williams, McLaren and Lotus stayed away in protest. Not that the locals cared because Ferrari and major man-ufacturers such as Renault were part of the thin field.

The Ferrari drivers Gilles Villeneuve and Didier Pironi had the final half of the race to themselves that year but Pironi went against a personal agreement and won. Villeneuve was so incensed that he swore never to speak to the Frenchman again. It was a tragic threat. Two weeks later, Villeneuve was killed when out to beat Pironi's time during final qualifying for the Belgian Grand Prix.

Seven years later, Imola was the catalyst for similar intense animosity between Ayrton Senna and Alain Prost when Senna upset his McLaren team-mate by putting his own interpretation on a tactical agreement about not overtaking each other into Tosa on the first lap. Senna respected that initially, but not when the race was restarted following Berger's fiery accident at Tamburello, the Brazilian claiming the arrangement did not apply in that instance. Prost, who lost the race, did not see it that way.

The irony is that after many years of personal hostility between these two, there were clear signs of a rapprochement on the weekend of 1 May 1994. Prost had retired and Senna was actually missing the rivalry provided by one of the few drivers capable of matching his speed – and said as much. The tragedy that week-end meant that they never got to sort out their differences.

I loved driving at Imola. I can honestly say there was never a lap that I didn't enjoy, not even when the layout was changed. It has a unique feel even though there has never been a super-quick cor-ner here in terms of shifting down a gear and powering through. And now, when working as a commentator, I continue to enjoy the atmosphere despite, or arguably because of, its slightly dog-eared look.

In 2004, I took a walk to a statue of Senna placed just inside the track at Tamburello. It is a striking piece of work: Ayrton, sat on his plinth, looking down with an angelic, crestfallen face. It is actually quite spooky. One of the reasons could be that this man and this corner will forever sum up Imola in the minds of millions.

Length: 3.340 km

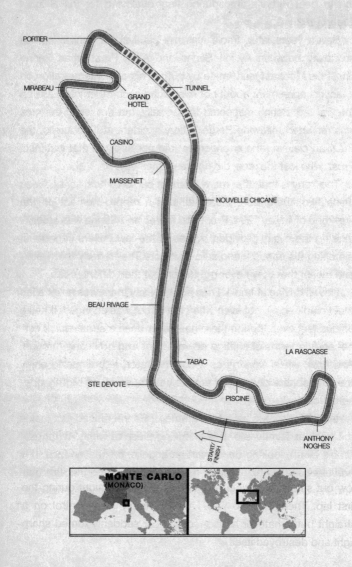

PORTIER

MIRABEAU

GRAND HOTEL

TUNNEL

CASINO

MASSENET

NOUVELLE CHICANE

BEAU RIVAGE

LA RASCASSE

TABAC

STE DEVOTE

PISCINE

ANTHONY NOGHES

START/FINISH

MONTE CARLO
(MONACO)

Monaco

There can be nothing more frustrating for a young driver than going to Monaco for the first time and not being allowed to race. I spent my first weekend there driving a clapped-out van around the streets and I hated every minute of it. It was hardly the image normally associated with the most glamorous motor race in the world.

This was in 1982 when I was racing Formula 3 and the Monaco F3 event was going to be the highlight of my year. Everything about racing at Monaco represents the ultimate challenge. There is a passion, an aura, an expectation. It's the 'Big One'. As a Grand Prix driver you want to win your home race, plus Monaco. And maybe, if pushed, you'd take the Monaco Grand Prix over everything else. When you are in Formula 3, just being there is a pleasure in itself. Or it should be if you have a car to race.

I was driving for David Price Racing at the time. But on the way to Monaco, we took in a race at Dijon, where I had a crash that continues to mystify me to this day. I had qualified on the front row but smashed my car to bits on the back straight during the first lap. There was no way I would simply lose control on a straight but, whatever happened, my car suddenly turned sharp right and destroyed itself.

The good news was that I was unhurt. The bad news was that I had no car to race at Monaco. As a penance, Dave Price made me drive the support vehicle all weekend. It was a sound tactic by Dave; it made my hunger to do well at Monaco fiercely strong, something that still exists to this day. Instead of rushing through the streets in a smart racing car, I was at the wheel of an elderly Volkswagen van and, worse still, I had to get up at six in the morning to drive it. I had to breakfast with the rest of the team as they planned the weekend and, every time I saw the sponsor, it seemed to me that I was the subject of a look of disgust. I then had to watch these guys race, and it broke my heart. Here I was at the Mecca of motor racing, and yet I could not get out there and take it on.

There are occasions when you see a place for the first time and it is disappointing. The reverse is true of Monaco. Quite often complete strangers will say they never really believed me when I described the circuit on television as being very steep, narrow and bumpy but, when they had seen it and climbed the hill to Casino Square, they suddenly understood the point I was trying to make. You wonder how it is possible to hold a motor race in this extraordinary place.

Even though I have taken part in ten Monaco Grands Prix, I often think the same thing when looking around the streets in daily use. This is the one circuit where it is impossible to film my usual pre-race track guide for ITV. Cars are parked on both sides of the road and the only time the track is clear is when it is 'live' and active. The minute the cars stop running, the police are keen to get back to normal as soon as possible by opening the barriers and allowing everyday traffic to flow once more. On race day, it is a very special place, the focus of the world of sport for those few wonderful minutes, and when you're on the podium with Prince Rainier, that red-carpeted platform is the centre of the universe.

Yet, the following morning, ladies walk their poodles and it's a traffic jam again.

I learned this from hard experience when I finally got to race at Monaco in 1983. The paddock for the Formula 3 teams was miles from the pits, tucked away in an area high above the Beach Plaza hotel at the far end of the track. Proof that motor racing takes over on Grand Prix week came when we were allowed to drive our cars through the streets in order to reach the racetrack. That was fine when we went to practice at six in the morning on Friday. It was a completely different proposition when trying to make our way back mid-morning.

As soon as practice was over, officials opened the roads, even though we had not finished packing up our kit in the pits. Suddenly I faced the prospect of getting to the far side of town – in a Formula 3 car. It has to be one of the most bizarre experiences in a racing driver's life to find himself sitting at traffic lights, blipping the engine of a car that barely reaches halfway up the wheel of the bus or truck sitting alongside. At Monaco, the problem is made worse by the instant gridlock that takes over the streets within minutes. By the time I had climbed the hill to Casino Square and sat in queues of traffic, the engine had overheated, and it was well and truly cooked as I eventually struggled into the F3 paddock.

When I began working for television, I did not need to be told that on-track filming would be difficult. You can't get a feel for the circuit by walking, driving or taking a scooter because of traffic coming from both directions. You simply cannot get a perspective. This place only unfolds in front of your eyes when you finally go out in a racing car. That's because, in no way, shape or form can Monaco be considered a conventional racetrack.

It's a pure street circuit although, over the years, it has become more and more of a road course as the surface has been made smoother and more consistent. Manhole covers have been disappearing; barriers replaced by very low kerbs. There is space to breathe and a lot of the unique challenge has gone.

That said, half of it remains a true street circuit in that the road is crowned to deal with rainwater. A racetrack doesn't have a crown; it is cambered one way or the other. That makes a huge difference. At Monaco, you don't always take the obvious racing line around the track because of the crown, gutters, dips, manhole covers, white lines and all the other bits and pieces associated with normal city street furniture. There's the diesel and grit and rubbish that goes down all year round. A racing driver faces a completely different scenario at Monte Carlo.

Because a racing car has very little travel in the suspension and the tyres, it has to be coaxed across the crown. The car will resist initially and then move very quickly down the other side. You approach a corner knowing that, at some point, you've got to cross this smooth hump in the middle of the road. The car is almost certainly going to hit the ground during the process of braking, moving across the crown and into the corner.

That's why you see wheels hanging in the air, particularly at the right-hander at Mirabeau. The car will turn into the corner and, where the road falls away, the right-front wheel will be 10 cm off the ground. That's because there is no give in the car. The chassis is stiff, the suspension travel small and the ride height very low. The road literally falls away from the wheel, which means it's difficult to stop the right front brake from locking.

You have to know the racetrack intimately. There is, for example, another right-hander, just after Mirabeau, on the run down to the sea front. The pavement has a gentle slope, so you aim at that and head towards the barrier knowing that the car will grip before you get there. Occasionally it doesn't. Michael Schumacher hit the barrier there on the first lap in 1996; Teo Fabi did the same thing in a Benetton and the chassis broke like an egg.

You need to treat the entire race weekend as a series of building blocks. Gradually, you are piecing it together, adding experience of the changing surface, learning as you go, increasing pace – but not too much too soon. You have to get to know Monaco more than any other racing circuit because the usual rules don't apply. Normally you approach, say, a left-hander on the right-hand side of the track and take the line of least resistance to minimise the angle of the corner as you go through. That's not how it happens on this circuit.

Two corners illustrate the point: Tabac and another left-hander just before it, the approach to the chicane leading onto the harbour front. You begin to look left into the chicane or into Tabac and, imperceptibly, the car has started moving across the road to the right. It moves less than half a metre but, because you've got to run close to the barrier on the right as you approach the corner and you are getting ready to turn left, the car will shimmy across the road and scuff the barrier before you know it. The fall of the road to the gutter draws you in.

I took the front wing off my Benetton at the chicane in 1992 and had to make a pit stop. At Tabac, three years later in a Ligier, I inadvertently got so close to the barrier on the right that I couldn't get any steering lock to turn left. I ran wide into the corner and spun off backwards into the wall. Then Jean Alesi in the leading Ferrari came round the corner, panicked and hit the wall!

These incidents are typical of how the tiniest slip of concentration can bite you at Monaco. We saw it in 1988. Ayrton Senna had an easy win within his grasp when he just clipped the barrier and it sent his McLaren across the road and into steel rails on the other side. It is so, so easy to fall into that trap. You've done the same thing every lap for the previous sixty laps or so and, all of a sudden, it's a case of: 'Whoa! How did that happen?'

The tolerances are so small and the car is moving around all the time as the track conditions change. You are getting tired or the track has lost a bit of grip or you arrive a fraction too fast and, almost without realising it, you are 2 cm further over from where you need to be. Bang! Game over. And, as I proved during qualifying in 1984, the accident can come from something going wrong with the car when it ought to be in tip-top condition and when the driver is never going to be more alert and on the case. This was one of the weirdest experiences I have ever had in a racing car.

It was my first F1 season and my car, the Tyrrell-Ford, was very quick at Monaco, even though we seemed to struggle for raw pace elsewhere. There were only twenty starters allowed from an entry of twenty-seven. We were struggling for both grip on the track and money in the bank. At best, we were going to squeeze onto the back of the grid. If we could do that, we knew we would be in good shape over the duration of the race. But, when it came to out-and-out performance during a single qualifying lap, we were up against it.

At the time, the chicane leading onto the harbour front was much faster than it is now; a quick flick left and right before screaming towards Tabac. I was right on the limit, making the most of sticky qualifying tyres and a car very light with the minimum of fuel on board. As I rushed into Tabac, my brake pedal went soft. And there is absolutely no run-off at Tabac.

The brake balance bar on the Tyrrell travelled in front of the throttle pedal. As the brake pedal went soft, not only did I have very little braking effect (the brakes had perhaps over-heated), the brake balance adjuster rod also pushed the throttle. The harder I pressed the brake pedal, the more I pushed open the throttle.

I went straight into the barrier. It was a huge, huge impact. People who were on the spot still talk about the violence of the thud. The car was thrown sideways and my helmet hit the barrier before we slid down the road with one side of the car missing and my right hand brushing the track. Jeff Bloxham, the Autosport photographer, took a sequence of shots and close inspection shows my eyes had gone black. I was obviously out for the count. Witnesses were convinced I was dead.

The wreckage, still on its side, came to a halt. I must have regained consciousness very quickly because I was soon out of the car and I can remember hearing the crowd cheering. Because this had happened on a stretch of the track that runs behind the pits – a place where F1 people would regularly come to watch – I knew by instinct roughly where I was and how to get back to the pits on foot.

Practice had been stopped to allow the mess to be cleared. While that was happening, I ran back with the single intention of getting into the spare car and qualifying for the Grand Prix. The back-up Tyrrell was waiting. I was twenty-second fastest at that point; two places short of making the race.

I climbed into the car and I remember saying to Liz: 'I'm so thirsty. I've got to have a drink.' She couldn't find me a drink: there was no water; nothing in the pits. Liz and Norah Tyrrell used to make the sandwiches in the back of the Goodyear motorhome in those days. Nobody seemed to have any water and I was unreasonably thirsty, an obvious sign that my body had experienced a major shock.

Ken Tyrrell plugged his radio headset into my car and told me there were eight minutes remaining.

I said: 'No problem. Which circuit am I at? Which way do I turn when I get out of the pits?' I can clearly remember wondering if I went right or left when I reached the end of the pit lane. At which point, Ken reached into the cockpit and switched off the engine. I was sent back to the hotel. There was no thought in those days of a check-up in the medical centre.

As time passed, I was in more and more pain because I had ricked all my neck muscles. Eventually I found my way to the room of Willi Dungl, the man who had helped Niki Lauda recover from his near-death experience at the old Nürburgring eight years before and was now working with Lauda at McLaren. Dungl proceeded to strap me up with tape and magnets to pull the rubbish from my body. I thought that was a load of rubbish in itself because, at the time, I felt absolutely dreadful – but lucky to be alive.

My best result at Monaco came ten years later when I finished second. But it says everything about the character of the place and the depth of the challenge that I take greater pleasure from finishing sixth in 1989. In fact, I'd say it was one of the best drives of my F1 career.

This was with Brabham, a once-great name that was slowly going into decline. We may have been struggling everywhere we went, thanks to a shortage of money and development, but the one thing in our favour at Monaco was a contract with Pirelli. These tyres may have been fairly average on the more traditional type of track but at Monaco they really worked.

In 1989, I qualified in fourth place. That was an incredible achievement for our little team, particularly when you consider that I had been twenty-second on the grid at the previous Grand Prix, and thirteenth the race before that. During final qualifying on Saturday, I'd thumped the barrier coming out of Casino Square and had a spin at the swimming pool. I went into the pits to calm down, think it all though and get my head straightened. Then I went out and nailed it. To be on the second row was a major result at the end of the very difficult two days spent building up speed.

In the race itself I made the most of my position with a great start. The car was working beautifully. I was into third place and easily keeping pace with the leaders. I knew I was on for a massive result. Because we were in with a real chance, the team had replaced everything on the car before the race. They had even changed the battery. It was brand new. But it was also a dud. Suddenly, I had no power and struggled into the pits at the end of the forty-eighth lap. The battery was under my seat, so I had to get out of the car while they removed the seat and replaced the battery. I lost just over two minutes.

Before that stage of the race, I was never going to take a risk because I couldn't afford to throw away a rare points-scoring opportunity with a silly mistake. All of a sudden I was no longer going to score any points, so I threw caution to the wind and returned to the track to enjoy myself during the remaining twenty-nine laps. Any car I came across, I overtook. Instantly. It was incredible; the car was nimble, had a lot of grip, fresh tyres. Perfect. My team-mate finished third and I had been half a minute ahead of him. Now I was sixth, but I was delighted with my race.

Monaco is hard because there is no pre-race testing and the cars are not really designed for that sort of circuit. You are always compromising the set-up on the car because the track conditions change all the time. The surface is constantly moving, in that dirt and rubbish gather, tyre rubber is going down but the track is always getting better and better. It's coming to you in such a way that you can go through the full extremes of the car's set-up.

You have got to keep pace with the track conditions and be

ready to deliver when the time is right. Start off cautiously, keep building and building, begin to push the car, don't touch the barriers and then push some more and really have it ready for your qualifying lap because the grid position here is everything. With overtaking in the race so difficult, the end result – barring a driver error or mechanical mishap – is determined by where you are on the starting grid.

As my accident in 1984 proved, Monaco differs from other tracks in that there is absolutely no room for error or mechanical mishap. The barrier at the exit of the first corner, Ste Devote, sits on the edge of the track and the crest at the top of the hill that follows is completely blind. If you want to know what that's like and there's not much traffic around, sit on the road – don't stand up because you will have double the driver's vision – and imagine doing 175 mph with your backside a couple of centimetres from the ground. You have the crest before you and, beyond it, the imposing casino. There is a crash barrier in front of it as the track sweeps left past the Hotel de Paris and into Casino Square. As you arrive like a rocket – and that hardly feels like an exaggeration at those speeds – over the top of the hill, you have to make that corner. There are no ifs or buts.

Traps are waiting for the unwary every inch of the way. The barrier on the left suddenly moves out for the front portal of the Hotel de Paris and then goes back in again. Normally, you are actually trying to hit that barrier, knowing that the momentum of the car will pull you away to the right. But if you're on a slow lap out of the pits and automatically following the barrier on the left as it guides you through the corner – as Johnny Dumfries did in his Lotus in 1986 – you'll tear off a front wheel. Just like that.

I spun there in a Jordan during the race in 1996. I had just made a pit stop and the Jordan boys had done a fantastic job changing from wet-weather to slick tyres for a drying track. I was in with a chance of a good result. The sun was shining on the hill, the track was dry and I took a lot of speed into the corner – and caught a damp patch in the shadow of the hotel. That sort of thing is one of the many building blocks or mental notes you make over the years as a driver.

It becomes a long list as you record the idiosyncrasies from Casino Square to Mirabeau and further downhill to the sea front via the hairpin at the Grand Hotel. Then the flat-out blast through the tunnel towards the harbour chicane and Tabac, followed by the swimming pool, Rascasse and the final right-hander leading onto the pit straight.

Of course, actually driving the car is just one part of being in Monte Carlo on race weekend. It's a very difficult place to function, particularly for the mechanics, the team personnel and the media – as I have discovered in recent years. If anything, the driver probably has the least problems! The mechanics used to work in temporary pits and were always carting stuff backwards and forwards. The TV compound and the commentary boxes and the studio are a mile apart. You can't cross or use the track after some unearthly hour in the morning, which means you have to hike halfway round the town to get anywhere.

As a driver, you end up in the paddock and simply walk over the bridge to the pits. The driver is less affected by the logistics and the hassle but, having said that, the pressure is higher because it's Monaco. And that pressure can come in all sorts of ways.

Take what should be the simple business of going for a pee in the pits. Before the modifications in 2004, you had to leave the back of the pits, go down the steps outside the swimming pool and find your way to the public loo. It would take forever and then you would have to stand in a queue. So it would be simpler to pee in a bottle or up the back of a tyre truck when no one was looking! It has been getting better – but not by much.

The pit lane was always a bit scary from a driver's point of view. It was too narrow with too many people and no room for the mechanics to work on too many cars. You had to pick your way through this lot during practice. Even during the race there seemed to be too many punters in the pits. It was always a miracle that we didn't have a few broken limbs every year in the old Monaco pits.

The problem ended in 2004 when the organisers went to great lengths to extend the pit lane and build new garages. But, this being Monaco, everything appeared upside down and inside out. Instead of looking onto the pit straight, as at any other track, the Monaco pit lane overlooks part of the final section of the lap from the exit of the swimming pool to Rascasse.

The garages with offices above are temporary, which is just as well because, in such glamorous surroundings, this building stands out as an ugly facility that would be hard-pressed to win planning permission on a dodgy industrial estate. For once in Monte Carlo, looks don't count; the important point is that life is so much easier for the mechanics now that the cars and equipment can be locked up at night rather than dragged back and forth from the paddock.

Only a few of the teams operated from their pit wall stands – or Prat Perches as they are affectionately known – in the former position. There was little point because the engineers could not see the pit lane: they chose, instead, to work from the upstairs offices.

This removed all the colour from what had been the pit wall opposite the TV and radio commentary boxes. The ITV technicians needed a kilometre of cable to connect the boxes to the TV compound. We wondered if it was worth the trouble because broadcasters could only look at the back of the pit buildings that blocked the view of the pit lane. We could no longer see the pit stops or the mechanics preparing to go to work. It has been a long-standing joke among motor racing journalists that, in Bernie Ecclestone's perfect world, we should be in an underground car park somewhere out of sight and not under his feet. That would never work because we need to hear if a car sounds sick and we also need to be part of the action in order to convey the excitement of the event and the crowd.

We are, however, in the fortunate position of being able to savour the atmosphere by enjoying special access and walking round the track during practice. It is more frightening watching rather than driving the car. In the car you can feel the grip, the car is talking to you and fits like a glove, you are absolutely with it and you know it's going to stick.

But when you watch at the exit of Casino Square or the approach to the swimming pool, it is a different proposition entirely. If you are an F1 fan and want to see the drivers at work, there is nowhere better than Monaco. It brings home the energy and violence of these cars and leaves no doubt about the drivers' commitment. Even though I drove F1 cars for twelve years, the trackside experience at Monaco makes the hairs on the back of my neck stand up. It is truly sensational.

I have always felt that Monaco could be called the Everest of motor sport. But recent changes, particularly the revised section between the swimming pool and Rascasse, have removed high kerbs, smoothed the surface and taken away barriers. This is not Monaco as it should be. It is like climbing Everest to find they have installed a few escalators on the way up. The track has got to be a threat. There must be a penalty for getting it wrong. Make a mistake and it should be instant wall and retirement. If they remove the natural obstacles of a street circuit, then the drivers are no longer doing something that very few people can do. The circuit is no longer the challenge it seems.

You could say the same for some of the legendary places in Monaco racing folklore. We used to visit Rosie's Bar, halfway up the hill to Casino Square. There was memorabilia on the walls but, apart from being a traditional watering hole for drivers in the 1950s and 1960s, it did not have a great deal going for it. Few of the current generation of F1 people mourned its passing to make way for the ever-present building work which seems to pervade the Principality.

Thursday night has a party feel because the Monegasques always ensure Friday falls on a Bank Holiday and cleverly use the time off to extract more money from the visitors. The Tip-Top bar, located halfway down the hill between Casino and Mirabeau, used to be a popular spot. The bar was so small that customers and the merely curious would spill onto the pavement and eventually onto the track.

The trick was to buy a bottle of beer for an outrageous price and then nurse it for the rest of the evening in the hope that a Grand Prix driver might drop by. It was a good thing for a driver to do because he could take the rare chance to buy his mechanics a beer and socialise. The problem was, as the sport became more popular and people became more forward, a driver risked having someone with too many beers boring him to death with a long and rambling story about how he saw the driver race at Hockenheim or some such place six years before.

Even if a driver did not turn up, the Tip-Top was an amazing place to be. It seemed so strange to be leaning against the crash barrier, shooting the breeze and watching people drive back and forth in outrageously exotic road cars, on the actual racetrack that, earlier in the day, F1 cars had used when charging down the hill from Casino. The Tip-Top is not as popular as it was, Stars'n'Bars by the F1 paddock having become the favoured place for the teams and race fans. This is a short walk from the harbour, which is always a popular place on Friday. For drivers, this is a strange day when nothing of major importance happens. You might have a few technical meetings with the team and perhaps attend a function or two with sponsors in the evening. But, after a day spent practising on this extraordinary circuit, it feels as though you have gone into suspended animation on Friday. You are at the racetrack but it doesn't seem like it.

The fans gather on one of the main jetties. You will see mums and dads with kids kitted out in team T-shirts, looking at the most glamorous collection of boats you are ever likely to see in one harbour, hoping to catch sight of a driver or a team boss. Nowhere else in the world can F1 fans soak up the atmosphere in this way. I took my mum to Monaco in 1987 and she still talks about it to this day. It is a truly memorable experience and I think those of us working in F1 often become blasé and forget how significant Monaco is to race fans.

I have never stayed on a boat, mainly because they don't agree with me. My father chose that option one year and I went to visit him. I had to leave after thirty minutes; the sight of other craft moving up and down while moored alongside was more than I could take. In the first year of their F1 involvement, ITV set up a temporary studio on the deck of a boat, a potentially romantic and spectacular setting that was never repeated after one of the presenters became seasick. It could really cut up rough in the harbour but a recently built breaker on the outer edge of the port has calmed things down.

The weather at Monaco can be notoriously fickle. It is common to see a large black cloud hanging over the top of the mountain that rises steeply behind the Principality. Monaco seems to have its own little weather system and it always rained when I least needed it. If you think the streets are treacherous in the dry, then driving in the rain is something else again. Your eyes are on stalks and your senses on full overdrive because it is so difficult to keep control and avoid slithering into the barriers. The car becomes unpredictable and it is easy to catch a camber, a white line or a manhole cover, then snatch a brake and you're straight into the wall.

It is only when you come to a rude halt and climb from the car that you suddenly notice the crowd. When working hard at the wheel, all you see is the barrier towering above you. Your perspective is low and forward. You can see the crowd if you look up after you've done a great lap or you've had a good result and you are on your slowing-down lap. But I would say you are more interested in catching a glimpse of a big screen to get a feel for what's going on in the race. Most of the time, you are totally immersed in your own world and, hopefully, it will come to a wonderful end when you are one of the first three cars allowed to pull up in front of the Royal Box.

I made it after finishing second for McLaren in 1994. To be standing up there alongside Michael Schumacher, for whom I had the utmost respect, was a very special moment. Yet, strange as it may seem, that particular race – the whole weekend, in fact – was not one for which I have warm memories.

Ayrton Senna and Roland Ratzenberger had been killed two weeks before at Imola and then, during the first day's practice at Monaco, Karl Wendlinger had crashed and was rushed unconscious to hospital. The Grand Prix Drivers Association had been reformed and I ended up as chairman. There were all-day meetings and a minute's silence on the grid. I thought it was the wrong thing to do. We were about to start the toughest GP of the year and there we were standing on the grid with the young drivers looking like rabbits caught in headlights. You could see they didn't know what to do or think. It was that kind of weekend.

It had been a difficult season at McLaren but this was always going to be one of my best shots. We hadn't got the power from the Peugeot engine but I knew I was strong around Monaco. I had confidence that I could get the job done.

The problem was the Peugeot engine had a habit of throwing off its flywheel, as I had discovered so dramatically in Brazil. And if it wasn't doing that, the engine would run long enough to get rid of most of its oil and water. Which it did at Monaco. Big time. For the last ten laps, I had a car that had little oil and even less water. How it kept going, I'll never know.

It was a strong drive and I was a contender for most of the afternoon. Although I was never going to beat Michael, I was close enough to keep him honest. He went off on oil at Ste Devote – another example of how this track can bite you when you least expect it – and he managed to rescue it. Unfortunately for me! But at least I made it to the most famous podium of all.

When a car is working at Monaco, as it did for me in 1989, you feel there is nothing you can't achieve. It's almost like you are building into a frenzy. The corners are flowing, the car is always moving and yet you can cope with everything: the bumps; the manhole covers; braking zones; a manual gear shift, blood pouring from your right palm, 2,700 shifts during a Grand Prix, miss just one of them and you can damage the gearbox badly enough to bring trouble later on. You get into a fantastic rhythm and it's like playing a video game on fast-forward. The corners keep coming

Paul Ricard

When you talk about a racetrack then, naturally, the circuit itself becomes the focus. After all, we are discussing the difficulties and the idiosyncrasies of each venue as a place of work for the drivers. Paul Ricard is one of the few exceptions. Even though the track had plenty of challenges to offer when it staged rounds of the world championship between 1971 and 1990, Ricard was all about the ambience, the surroundings and, not least, the drive to and from the circuit.

For me, Ricard represented everything that the French Grand Prix should stand for. This may seem a strange thing to say when you consider that Magny-Cours has been the race's home since 1991 and I spent many hours testing there while driving for Ligier. But the point is, while I have some affection for Magny-Cours, it is through familiarity rather than any feeling of passion and true enjoyment. Paul Ricard had that in spades.

Take the location, high on a plateau above the Mediterranean coast near Toulon: add a date in July and there was an automatic summer holiday feel, massaged by amazing blue skies and a little altitude. F1 people would stay in or around the resort of Bandol. The twisting climb from the seaside to the track became as

Length: 3.812 km

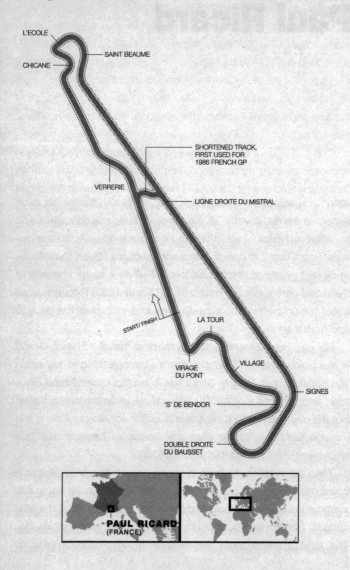

L'ECOLE

SAINT BEAUME

CHICANE

SHORTENED TRACK,
FIRST USED FOR
1986 FRENCH GP

VERRERIE

LIGNE DROITE DU MISTRAL

START/ FINISH

LA TOUR

VIRAGE
DU PONT

VILLAGE

SIGNES

'S' DE BENDOR

DOUBLE DROITE
DU BAUSSET

PAUL RICARD
(FRANCE)

legendary in F1 as many of the racetracks themselves. This route should not be confused with the more northerly run from Ricard, the road on which Frank Williams had his terrible accident while returning to Nice airport in March 1986. The climb from Bandol was more of a commuter run for anyone engaged in the business of motor racing and you can be sure that any racing driver or team boss of that era could provide at least one anecdote about journeys up and down that hill.

It is a series of switch-backs, hairpins and downhill braking sections; an amazing challenge, so much so on the uphill journey that you would almost be out of breath before reaching the circuit for a day's work. At other venues, the route to the track is from a city or a suburban hotel where you mix with commuters at first then join the flow of race traffic. It is a job to be done, one that you hope will not be compromised by hold-ups and queues that could easily start the day on a frustrating note.

The drive to Paul Ricard is completely different. It does seem strange to be talking about a road instead of the track it serves, but everyone in motor racing feels the same about this magnificent piece of tortuous highway. It is scary, dangerous and, I have to admit, some outrageous things have happened on that road over the years. On a race weekend there would be an incredible buzz associated with covering the dozen miles or so to and from the track. Inevitably, there would be a local hotshoe in his Renault 5 who lived or worked in the area and knew the road very well. You would find him taking great pleasure in blowing the doors of any Grand Prix driver foolish enough to take him on. Then, in the middle of all this, particularly on a Sunday morning, the hill would have a sprinkling of wannabe Tour de France cyclists, heads down, pedalling like mad and seemingly oblivious to the potential danger created by getting in the way of the four-wheeled brigade.

It was a potent cocktail on race weekends and, in hindsight, there was some shameful behaviour on that road.

The true and proper pleasure would come during quieter moments when you were taking part in a private test session. The drive would set you up for the day, particularly when you reached the top and took time to enjoy the view of the hills and surrounding countryside. There were certain days, particularly in the spring, when the crystal-clear skies had a slight chill first thing in the morning. It was a unique feeling created by the climate, the clarity of the sky, the slightly barren and rocky landscape surrounding a very fast racetrack.

The circuit was built in the late 1960s by Paul Ricard, maker of the famous pastis. He managed to find one of the few flat pieces of land in his local area, something which ordinarily would go against a location as the basis for an interesting circuit layout. But M. Ricard built a facility that was ahead of its time and unusual in many ways.

The pits, for example, were set back quite some distance from the track and this allowed the introduction of a split arrangement. The first half of the pit lane would exit over a bridge with the entrance to the second half passing beneath. Very strange, but interesting nonetheless. It would never be allowed today because of the need for cars to rush in and out of the pits to refuel. Even in the 1970s and 1980s, the access was very tight and I can remember my car catching fire and causing all sorts of chaos as I sat, stuck at one of the narrow entrances.

Paul Ricard is long and narrow in shape. During the early years, the full circuit was used and although it was flat, it gave the drivers a lot to think about. Because of the elongated shape, long straights dominated, with some very fast sections. Bearing in mind that the track was built in the late 1960s, the run-off areas were very small and there was widespread use of catch-fencing, deemed at the time to be the only way of stopping a wayward car but, in reality, something which usually did more harm than good. The fencing and wires were likely to strangle a driver and, if they failed, then there was a strong possibility of being hit on the head by a pole supporting the fencing.

The lap started with this super-fast section through a left-right chicane some distance down the main straight. Cars would reach 180 mph and it was here that Elio de Angelis suffered a fatal accident during testing in 1986. The chicane was flat out – but not easily so. If your car was reasonably well balanced and not hitting the ground, you could go full throttle through there, albeit with your heart in your mouth. But if anything went wrong, it was going to hurt. It is believed that the rear wing broke on de Angelis's Brabham as he went through the chicane. He lost control at the exit and the speed and forces involved were so great that the car vaulted the crash barrier. He had no chance.

Elio was the archetypal Grand Prix driver. Italian, with debonair looks, he was not only a very quick driver. He was also very polite, an extremely nice person and a major party animal. Elio would either be dancing with the most stunning girl in the room or back in the hotel lounge entertaining everyone on the piano. He was a gifted classical pianist and a sportsman who had everything. He was the sort of guy who would be in a novel about motor racing, someone who was almost too good to be true. His death came as a terrible shock and created a profound sense of loss.

I had been testing at Ricard that day but, because my car had broken down, I had left early for the airport. I remember sitting in the lounge when one of my engineers from Renault came in and asked if I had heard about de Angelis. When he said Elio was dead, I felt physically sick. At that time, Ricardo Paletti had been the last driver to die when he was involved in a collision on the grid at the Canadian Grand Prix, two years before I started in F1 in 1984. My team-mate, Stefan Bellof, had died in 1985 in a sports-car race, the category of racing that, two weeks earlier, had killed another F1 driver, Manfred Winklehock. But, as each year in F1 passed without a fatal accident, Grand Prix racing had somehow seemed above all that.

The feeling of loss is exacerbated when it is not only a house-hold name but also a guy you had been with earlier in the day. It's that suddenness, the absolute finality, which shakes you to the core. A famous racing driver and great guy is dead and gone. That's it. Nothing is going to change that. There's nothing you can do.

Of course, you want to know all the details. You want to know exactly where he left the road and why. Was it driver error? Was it the car? Why didn't the track or medical crew save him? You need the answers to all of those aspects, not in any ghoulish sense but more as reassurance that the same thing could not happen again. To you, or others.

Learning about an accident like that is a reality check. If you put the risks out of your mind and say, 'it will never happen to me', then you will die. I have only ever met a few drivers who were totally fearless – and they're all dead. Every single one. You have to have some fear, but you have to manage that fear. It is neces-sary to have an element of self-preservation while acknowledging the reality associated with the sport.

Whenever you climb into the cockpit of an F1 car, the immedi-ate feeling is that it is so fast, so much quicker than anything else. The top speeds are maybe only 50 mph more than, say, a Formula 3 car. And perhaps they are just 10 mph faster through a slow cor-ner. But the F1 car has wider tyres and carries a lot more weight and mass. When you start adding speed to the mass and factor in the ability of one car to trip over another, then you began to appreciate the potentially explosive forces involved.

You learn very early on – in my case, during a practice session in Dallas, halfway through my first season in 1984 – that this is not a little F3 car. It is a Grand Prix car and, while it may only be a little bit faster everywhere on the circuit, it is in an entirely different league. A different sport almost.

You acknowledge the risks; you come to terms with them. How is it, for example, that you can be doing 180 mph in the rain, you can't see where you are going, and yet you put your foot down even harder? What makes a racing driver do that? There is an element of fear and yet the desire to win drives you on. You know it's dangerous but you hope you won't be killed. You hope you don't get badly injured. You have to acknowledge it may happen but, in your personal estimation, the gains are considerably greater than the risks. I don't mean financial gains necessarily, although that is an aspect of it. I'm talking about the pleasure, the glory and the satisfaction of winning. It can even be as straightforward as the satisfaction associated with simply driving a Grand Prix car, let alone being on the podium, winning the race or, as I know from sportscar racing, becoming World Champion.

That intense sense of fulfilment is worth the risk from a driver's point of view. Other people can't understand why you want to risk your life in a sport, especially when you are going round and round in circles at up to 200 mph. What's the point? They don't understand because they are not passionate about motor sport. It's as simple as that.

You understand the risks and yet, when something happens to another driver, it smacks you in the face. It's really painful. I think most people can relate to it if they have experienced a sudden death in the family, and the sick feeling of shock and disbelief that follows. And yet there is something slightly perverse about a driver's reaction to a fatality in motor sport. A lot of drivers, particularly those without a decent seat, will begin to enquire about who the dead driver's replacement might be. The phone starts ringing. It's business as usual. It sounds a calculating attitude to take but the bald fact is that, at any given time, there are fewer than thirty F1 drivers worldwide and usually fewer than ten cars capable of regularly winning. Drivers tend to face competitive reality rather than coping with the terrible sense of loss.

The alleged mechanical failure on Elio's car notwithstanding, it goes without saying that the first chicane at Paul Ricard had to be treated with great respect. From there on, the run down to the bottom of the circuit had a series of big stops, tight corners and sweeping right-handers; long, fast corners that destroy race tyres.

Then onto the Mistral Straight, so called because the flat-out blast along the back of the circuit would often be assisted by a strong tail wind from the famous Mistral. And, boy, was that straight long and very fast. It was where, I regret to say, I committed one of the silliest acts I have ever been responsible for in an F1 car.

This was during the time when I drove the Tyrrell-Renault, which did not have a lot of downforce, but the works Renault engine ensured that the car was very quick in a straight line. During the French GP in 1985, I caught Eddie Cheever, who was fighting for fourteenth place with Teo Fabi at close to 190 mph. I overtook them both. I had a double slipstream and plenty of straight-line speed – but no room. So I added a bit of track.

The Mistral Straight had what could best be described as a semi-surfaced hard shoulder on either side. There was some Tarmac with loose gravel on top. I made an extra lane, half on the track, half off, while doing over 200 mph. The move itself was OK because there was so much grip available at that speed. But I didn't want to think about the risk of a puncture from the gravel.

Besides, I had already begun to steel myself for Signes, the very fast corner at the end of the straight. It is a right-hander, which, depending on the quality of the car, could be taken without lifting your foot from the throttle. Not a place for the faint-hearted. You would arrive at about 210 mph and go through the corner at 190 mph, losing speed only because of the scrubbing effect and lateral loads on the tyres. Otherwise, you would concentrate on trying to keep your right foot hard against the throttle pedal while ignoring the very marginal run-off area with its menacing catch-fence poles.

In later years, because Signes was so dangerous, they put in temporary chicanes when we were testing sportscars in preparation for Le Mans. We would be simulating a twenty-four-hour race and, understandably, no one was keen on arriving at Signes at over 200 mph in the dark.

Either way, Signes was definitely a challenge to take flat. In F1, if you had a car that was very fast down the Mistral Straight, you had to take a deep breath as the approach to Signes rapidly came into view. And then try to keep your right foot buried. Easier said than done. It is as if there is a little muscle running between your heart and the back of the Achilles tendon and it involuntarily lifts your foot off the throttle. Your head is saying, 'Go on! Take it flat,' and your heart is saying, 'Nooooo chance.' Your heart usually wins when you get there. It's a sixth sense which seems to know that if the car gets out of shape on the way through, you will be in very big trouble. You will run out of road at the exit and there is a horrible big kerb to finish you off. It will put you into a spin – which is not what anyone wants at those speeds. There have been a lot of scary, scary moments at Signes. And the trouble is, you are by no means finished with the lap.

Following on, almost immediately, there is Beausset, a double-right, which has to be one of the most frustrating corners in the world. Not only is the entry super-fast, particularly if you get Signes just right, but there is also a nasty bump on the way in. Beausset gets tighter and tighter and then turns right when you get there. Racing cars never seem to want to go through that corner. They have an inherent desire to understeer and Beausset encourages the wish to go straight on rather than turn right. The car understeers to the point where the driver simply runs out of steering lock. It is a horrible corner made worse by the fact that it contributes towards a good lap time.

Having struggled through Beausset, you are then confronted by the Pif-Paf, one of those little chicanes where you simply kiss the kerbs – 'pif-paf', as the French would say – on the way through. The track is now heading back towards the pits, but not before taking you through a painfully slow and gripless left where the tyres did not seem to want to bite, then into a fast right at Village, which is OK, followed by another long and bumpy left, which requires the driver to turn in early and hope the car takes the corner without a struggle. The final bend is a clumsy, tight right-hander with an unforgiving kerb and, usually by now, the tyres had completely lost interest. All told, a difficult sequence with, in my case, very painful memories.

I crashed the Toyota Le Mans car at Beausset during a test in 1998. It was my first time out in the new car and I discovered that the pedals were too close together. As the car rode over a big bump, I not only hit the brakes but the throttle as well. In any battle between brakes and engine, the engine will always win. The car shot straight on. But what made matters worse was the fact that I was heading for a bare concrete wall. Jacques Villeneuve had gone off at the same spot in his Williams F1 car during a test the previous week and the track officials had not replaced the tyre barrier in front of the wall. And that was exactly where I was heading. I have never experienced as much pain before or since, not even when I smashed my ankles in Dallas in 1984. That didn't really hurt until I tried to walk away from the smash. But this was agony from the word go. I really squealed.

The trouble with the Toyota was that the front was too strong and it didn't give. There was quite a big gravel trap and I had slowed down to about 50 mph as I headed towards the wall. I remember having time to think: 'This is going to be a nuisance. Am I going to hit the wall? I'm not sure. Think I'll be all right. Am I going to hit it? Oh yeah, I am going to hit it. Damn.' So, I did hit the wall. And, boy, did I know all about it.

I went in perfectly straight, but the nose of the Toyota didn't give. The car had not been crash-tested for energy absorption by that stage – something that is only necessary before it can be raced – which meant the car stopped dead. And I didn't. I was thrown forward and, to compound the whole thing, I only had a temporary seat at the time and my belts weren't quite right. They were holding me at the shoulders and hips, which meant I more or less became bent in the middle, breaking the corner of my twelfth vertebra. The pain was indescribable. It was no consolation to struggle from the car and discover, to my complete amazement, that it was hardly damaged.

The circuit was shortened in later years, but those corners remained. The original track was too long and too fast for television, so they effectively cut across the middle and joined the Mistral Straight about halfway along its considerable length. This removed some of the problems associated with tackling Signes –

but not by much. You might have been doing 10 mph less going into a 200 mph corner, so Signes still required your full attention.

This corner, and the sequence that followed, would work the tyres extremely hard and the problem would be made worse by the track surface. It was a very porous, old-fashioned style of Tarmac that looked as if it offered a lot of grip but, in fact, did nothing of the sort. But what it could do with no trouble at all was rip your tyres to pieces. Even though it has recently been resurfaced, that problem remains. Your first lap is always your fastest, after which the drop in tyre performance is huge.

In 1987, following a pit stop during the race, I didn't even get as far as experiencing the benefit of fresh tyres – mainly because one of them was no longer attached to my car. As I came out of the pits, a rear wheel fell off my Zakspeed and bounced off into the distance. This was one of a catalogue of disasters that year. I three-wheeled to a halt, my race over. I was not happy. I removed the steering wheel so that I could climb out, and flung it as far as I could, shouting: 'Find that as well!' I would have been unable to vent my fury in subsequent years thanks to a rule that said the driver had to replace the steering wheel after evacuating the cockpit. But I was so angry on this occasion, I was past caring about such rules.

The great thing about racing at Paul Ricard was that any frustration could be quickly soothed later in the evening. Bandol boasted great restaurants and wonderful local wine. When testing, we would usually go to Au Fin de Maison, which was a favourite of Ken Tyrrell's. He would talk for weeks beforehand about the ratatouille, and with good reason. The ambience in Bandol was brilliant: the food, the scenery, the weather, the locals playing boules on the sea front. Everything was just right although it was difficult to know what to say about call girls standing beside bonfires every mile or so along the road from the circuit.

These days, the circuit is only used for testing. Paul Ricard has undergone a massive face-lift. It is state of the art with no tyre barriers, gravel traps or catch fencing. The run-off areas are all Tarmac and these are purely for the protection of the drivers. There is no need to worry about spectators because the grandstands have been removed. Punters are not welcome and their absence adds to the rather unusual atmosphere. When you test there it is like running with ghosts of the past.

Even stranger is the fact that we no longer stay in Bandol. A luxury hotel outside the main gate takes care of accommodation. And, if you don't want to stop overnight, the upgraded airport alongside allows you to fly in, drive an F1 or Le Mans car for the day, step into your private jet and fly home. That famous climb from the coast has become more or less redundant. Which is perhaps just as well.

Length: 4.361 km

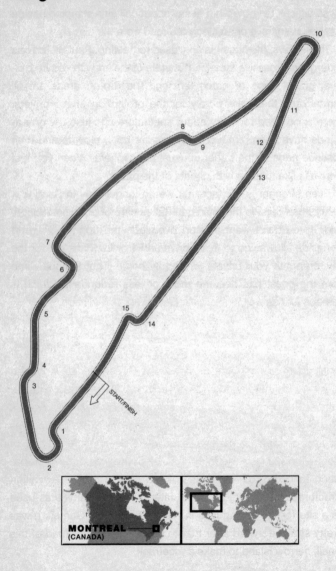

START/FINISH

MONTREAL ◻——
(CANADA)

Montréal

Montréal has to be the only racetrack in the world where you can overtake a ship. It is one of the most bizarre sights in motor sport as F1 cars rush down the back straight while, 400 metres to the left, an ocean-going freighter appears to be riding along the top of a grass bank. If you have forgotten – and it's easily done – that the circuit is actually on a man-made island in the middle of the St Lawrence Seaway, then the sudden appearance of a massive vessel heading towards the Great Lakes can catch you by surprise.

It is part of the charm of the Circuit Gilles Villeneuve, named after the local hero and Ferrari driver who gave the track a dream entry to the F1 world championship when he won the circuit's inaugural Grand Prix in 1978. The island, Île Notre-Dame, was actually created by material excavated during construction of Montréal's excellent Metro system. All of this was done in preparation for Expo '67 and many of the slightly bizarre exhibition structures still remain. Six years later, Île Notre-Dame was used as a site for the rowing lake in the 1976 Olympic Games. It was pretty straightforward after that to use the perimeter road of this small, narrow island to make a racetrack.

Flat it may be, but the circuit's allure in such unusual surroundings is complemented by a track that is actually very challenging and fun to drive. Add to that a knowledgeable and sizeable crowd, many of whom live in the vibrant city on the opposite side of the St Lawrence, and it is no surprise that the Canadian Grand Prix is one of the most popular on the calendar.

Not that the actual setting means a great deal when you are in the car. Rather like the back section of Albert Park in Melbourne, you have no idea that water is close at hand as you rush between concrete walls and steel barriers. I have always gone well at this track, one of the reasons being that it needs a car with a bit of understeer. You have to be good on the brakes, carry a lot of speed into the corners, point the nose in, then get on the throttle with just the merest hint of understeer allowing you to keep the power applied and stop the rear wheels from spinning.

Some drivers don't like understeer. Keke Rosberg, the 1982 World Champion, couldn't drive a car if it wasn't going sideways in a corner (oversteer) and many drivers are of the same view. Others, like myself, Alain Prost and David Coulthard, don't want to fight the machinery. You set up the car to be your friend, not your enemy. If you have a driving style that is particularly suited to understeer, then it works well at Montréal.

The circuit has low grip and it has always been hard on fuel consumption thanks to numerous chicanes. Necessarily, you are always accelerating, braking and then accelerating again, which makes Montréal a rather stop-start racetrack. That said, there are some very tricky corners.

Turn 1 is good. It calls for very hard braking and this has to be done just after a slight but bumpy right-hand curve. This has caught out many drivers as they hit the brakes and spin off –

particularly when it's wet. It is a busy place because Turn 1 is a small left which leads directly into a right at Turn 2. In effect, you use Turn 1 as the braking zone and approach to what is a right-hand hairpin. This combination has been responsible for some enormous first-lap shunts because the cars are still in tight formation after leaving the grid a few seconds before. It just takes one driver to brake late and cars start tripping over each other and flying through the air. Alex Wurz made the most spectacular landing in 1999 when he put his Benetton upside down in the gravel trap.

The correct way to tackle Turn 2 is to hook the car's right-front wheel over the side of the kerb and use it like a railway line to pull you round the corner. Good traction is vital, so you try to make the rear of the car nice and supple in order to get the power onto the road. It's important because the track surface has what could best be described as a washboard effect and, as the tyre rubber goes down, the grip increases noticeably.

Because this track is only used for light traffic between Grands Prix, it needs the passage of F1 cars to clean it up while starting to lay rubber on the racing line. You can really feel the effect of this at Turn 2. Once the grip has been established, the feeling of acceleration is like warp-drive as the triple layers of steel barrier whizz past on either side. It's a mix between Space Mountain at Disney and what it must feel like on an Apollo launch.

There is no time to relax because a difficult right and left are rushing to meet you. The road is slightly downhill and off-camber; tricky enough to have cars smack the barrier. The problem is that the barrier is tight against the back of the kerb at the exit. If you ride the kerb a touch too much, the car is suddenly sucked into the barrier and, before you know it, the right-hand wheels have been ripped off. It has happened many times. A driver picks up a bit of understeer, which doesn't seem to be a problem as he slides onto the kerb, just as he has done before. The difference is that an extra inch further up the concrete is enough to pull the car over the top in an instant. Seconds later, the bemused driver is climbing from a damaged car, not entirely sure why his race is over so suddenly.

Assuming you have kept the car in one piece, it's full throttle into and all the way through a really great corner, a long right-hander between two walls. It's absolutely flat-out – which is why Olivier Panis broke both his legs when his Prost suddenly snapped left and smashed into the barrier during the race in 1997. We've all had some pretty scary moments in that bend but there's no time to think about it because, as soon as you emerge, it's hard on the brakes for a chicane that can be slippery on the way in. This is another place where it is convenient to hook your left-front wheel over the kerb and use it as a tramline to pull the car round the corner and allow a fast exit onto a long and really bumpy straight.

The car darts around quite a bit, particularly in the braking area for the right-hander leading into the next chicane. This was the scene of one of the most unusual and potentially lethal accidents I have ever witnessed.

In 1990, world championship sportscars raced for the first time in Montréal. These cars create a massive amount of downforce, much of it coming from the underside of the chassis, which acts rather like an upside-down wing, sucking the car onto the track. In fact, the force was so great that one of the leading cars actually sucked a manhole cover out of its frame. Two of the following cars hit the bits of metal, which went through the windscreen of a third, the Porsche 956 driven by Jesus Pareja. Worse than that, another piece of the manhole cover ripped open the bottom of the car and went through the fuel tank. The Porsche exploded as if it had been napalmed. The entire effect was exaggerated – if that's possible – because it took place in the murky recesses beneath a vehicle access bridge. It was the most incredible scene and the Spanish driver was fortunate to escape unharmed.

It wasn't as if he hadn't enough to worry about at this point on the circuit. The bumps can cause a wheel to lock when braking and the car will lose about 30 per cent of retardation. For a tyre to grip properly, it has to be turning; a locked tyre is not generating retardation. It's exactly the same theory in other modes of transport. Lock the front wheel on a pushbike and you're straight off, usually over the handlebars. Do that in a racing car, or have the bottom of the car hit the road so that the energy unloads straight into the ground through the chassis rather than through the tyres, and you will miss your braking point and shoot off the road. I'm not alone in having such nasty moments, particularly at that corner on the Circuit Gilles Villeneuve.

Once the braking and turning into the corner have been successfully completed, then the exit is much more straightforward as the rear wheels find grip and hurtle the car onto the back straight. The next potential hazard is quite bizarre, since it has four legs. It is at this point on the track a driver can find he is in a race with a groundhog, which is about the size of a rabbit, scampering along the track. The driver can't swerve out of the way quickly enough and the usual inevitable contact can wreck a front wing, never mind the unfortunate creature.

Assuming there has not been a brush with the local wildlife – which hasn't happened so much in recent years – the very fast trip along this gently curving piece of track brings you to the hairpin at the far end of the circuit. This is one of those places where you brake later and later and later – and seemingly get away with it.

As a result, there have been some great overtaking moves here and plenty of dramatic moments, not least when Jacques Villeneuve left his braking impossibly late and wiped out Ralf Schumacher as the Jordan driver was taking the hairpin in the proper manner.

I can confirm from terrible experience that this is no place to encounter total brake failure. It was in 1985 while driving for Tyrrell, at a time when the brake pads needed bedding in gently before you could use them in the manner intended. The procedure was to blank off the brake ducts in order to generate heat in the pads during the 'cooking' or bedding-in process. Then the tape would be removed and off you would go, safe in the knowledge that the brakes were ready for some harsh if cooler treatment. On this occasion, the problem was that my mechanics forgot to remove the tape from the ducts after I had completed my installation run. I set off to do some serious work and the brake temperatures – for which you have no read-out in the cockpit – just went skywards.

When I approached the hairpin and hit the brakes, the pedal gently made its way to the floor – which was odd for reasons other than having almost no stopping power at 180 mph. Usually, when you lose your brakes, the pedal goes straight to the board. There is no pressure and the brake feels more like a throttle pedal. On this occasion, the brake pedal gave a knife-through-butter feeling. The calliper had become so hot that it opened like a clamshell. It had more or less turned into jelly.

The Tyrrell shot straight into a tyre barrier because, at the time, there was virtually no run-off. That was frightening in itself. The hairpin is surrounded on three sides by grandstands and I remember thinking that this was lunacy as I experienced the consequences of an F1 car with no brakes and virtually nowhere to go. The hairpin has since been brought forward to allow the run-off area to be extended without losing any of the atmosphere generated in this very lively amphitheatre.

The return leg has been changed more than once since F1 first visited Montréal. No sooner have you begun to accelerate from the hairpin than an innocuous-looking left kink beckons. It seems straightforward enough but, in the days when we were being hurled out of the hairpin by turbo power, a bump in the middle of this kink could throw a car clean off the road, almost before the driver had realised what was going on.

In its original form, the track presented the driver with an absolutely terrifying right, left and right. This combination was bumpy and had to be taken flat out. The problem was the swerves were lined by concrete walls and the entry to each change of direction was blind. You went in there with your foot flat to the floor, fighting a car bucking on the uneven surface while praying no one was having an accident just out of sight. If there was a car failure of any kind, there was simply nowhere to go – as I discovered at the scene of someone else's accident in 1985.

The recovery system used by marshals in North America involves sending a breakdown truck, or 'wrecker', as they call it, to the scene of the accident. Philippe Alliot had crashed his RAM (an appropriate name, under the circumstances) and I came through the curves at about 170 mph to find this recovery vehicle positioned halfway across the track pulling Alliot's car out of the wall. All sorts of things flashed through my mind as I took avoiding action, the most prominent being that the last thing you want to do in a low-slung F1 car is lose an argument with a breakdown truck by going beneath it.

After the deaths of Ayrton Senna and Roland Ratzenberger in 1994, the Grand Prix Drivers' Association had decided to take a closer look at the circuits in terms of safety. As the new chairman, I took responsibility for inspecting Silverstone and Montréal and found I was seeing each track in a new light. Previously, when I had walked a circuit with my engineer, the object of the exercise was to spot places where I could go faster and shave fractions of a second from my lap time. Now I was looking at the track and asking: 'Where can I get hurt?' It required a completely different mentality.

In May 1994, the month before the Grand Prix, I walked the Circuit Gilles Villeneuve with Normand Legault, later to become the president of the Grand Prix but, at the time, the general manager of the promoters. I had a map marked with the various speeds – which was just as well because, otherwise, I might not have believed what I was seeing. For instance, as we walked into the braking area for the top hairpin, I consulted the map and said to Normand: 'We're doing 186 mph. Right here.' Then we would look at the escape road, which lay directly ahead. It was tiny.

I had been through this corner hundreds of times but, apart from the brakeless moment in the Tyrrell, I had never thought about the damage that could be done. As a racing driver, you tend not to dwell on things like that. The priority is speed and getting in and out of the corner as quickly as possible. It was the same with the cars of the time; you would simply climb in and drive. Yet, when I come across those cars now, I don't feel safe walking past them, never mind getting in and having a go. Things have progressed so much but, at the time, you don't question anything because it is the state of the art of that particular moment.

When Normand and I reached the very fast right-left-right leading onto the back straight, we decided immediately that something needed to be done. As a temporary measure, we created a chicane with piles of tyres just before the start of the sequences of bends. It was not elegant but we had to do something in the limited amount of time before the 1994 Grand Prix. Not long after that, they got rid of the curves completely and simply made it a quick but open right leading onto the fastest part of the circuit.

As the cars rush down the straight with the rowing lake to the left and perhaps a transatlantic freighter just beyond, the driver's attention is completely focused on the final chicane as he approaches at 210 mph. The right and the left used to be incredibly fast, but the entry was eventually tightened. This reduced speed, particularly at an exit that runs tight against a concrete wall on the right-hand side. Ironically, despite the changes, that wall has claimed some very famous names, so much so that it is unofficially known as 'The World Champions' Wall'. Michael Schumacher, Jacques Villeneuve, Damon Hill and Nigel Mansell have all come to grief there.

It's easily done. It is very difficult to pick out the entrance when charging down the straight with your backside an inch above the ground. If you make a mistake on the way in and just clip a kerb, the speed is such that it is often difficult to sort the car out before hitting the wall. There is little margin for error. From the moment you turn 90 degrees to the right, the car is pointing at the wall. The trick is to get into the left as cleanly as possible and just flirt with the wall by skimming it on the way out. A nice feeling when you get it right; horrible and painful when you get it wrong. And, sometimes, the penalty for a mistake can be carried forward to the next corner.

In 1995, I was really flying while holding fifth place in a Ligier with seven laps to go. I was being chased by Gerhard Berger's Ferrari and I made a slight mistake going through the chicane.

That brief loss of momentum was enough to allow Gerhard to think about taking a run at me on the approach to Turn 1. He was not close enough. Worse than that, he missed his braking point, took to the grass on the left, came down the inside and completely wiped me out as I turned into the left-hander. We ended in a heap but, fortunately, neither of us was hurt.

I walked over to Gerhard, who was sitting on the barrier with his head in his hands, saying: 'I'm really sorry, I'm really sorry.' But I could see he was somewhere else. It turned out that he had some personal issues. As we stood beside the racetrack, he simply said: 'My head is somewhere else today.'

There was no answer to that. What was I supposed to say? 'Oh, that's OK then, Gerhard. I'm out of the race and a points finish. But, never mind. Hope your problem gets sorted soon.' It was the most ridiculous accident. I don't think he knew why he took to the grass or what he was intending to do. Sadly, I had no idea he was coming down the inside. Had I known, I would have let him sail past and have his own accident.

Why didn't I see him coming? Because the mirrors are small, thanks to aerodynamic efficiency being everything on an F1 car. Although the regulations in recent years have called for larger mirrors, they are about as much use as a chocolate fireguard. In effect, you are peering into a small piece of glass mounted very close by. You are looking over your own back tyres and through the rear-wing elements. It is true that officials go to great lengths to make sure the driver can see beyond the rear wing but, even so, the field of vision remains very small. If another car is off to one side, the chances of seeing it are slim and the problem is compounded by the mirrors, which are attached to the bodywork and vibrating like crazy.

In Berger's case, he was coming from an unusual angle – to say the least – and it was one of those situations where I must have looked really stupid in the eyes of TV viewers who could see the whole thing clearly unfolding. In any case, my concentration was focused on the braking point and the corner. You have a sixth sense perception of roughly what's going on, but you can't be sitting there thinking: 'I wonder if Gerhard has gone down the grass this time?'

That retirement was obviously disappointing but the frustration was nothing compared to three years previously when I lost the chance to win the race. I was driving for Benetton in 1992 and felt on top of my game. I was quick throughout practice, seventh on the grid but second fastest in the warm-up on race morning. The car felt really good in race trim.

Senna dropped out after leading for thirty-seven laps. Michael Schumacher, my team-mate, wouldn't let me past even though I was much faster. He held me up for two-thirds of the race and admits, now, that it was a pretty stupid thing to do. I finally got by when I wrong-footed Michael as we lapped a Minardi. He didn't see me for dust after that. I was really in the groove with a car that was perfectly set-up on a circuit that suited my driving style. Things went even better when Riccardo Patrese, running second in his Williams-Renault, dropped out with gearbox trouble.

Berger was leading and I was catching him by 0.75 seconds a lap. There were twenty-five laps to go and Gerhard was having trouble with gear selection. This was looking good. I saw Michael's Benetton disappearing from my mirrors. Gerhard, meanwhile, was coming back to me. I had never had a chance like this before. I remember thinking: 'I can win this race.' I felt this immense surge of power and confidence. It was such a good feeling.

Then, just two laps after taking second place, a gear seemed to disengage as I accelerated out of one of the chicanes on the back stretch. I radioed the pits to say that I had a problem. But then it re-engaged and I radioed back to say that I was all right.

As I drove into the next lap, the final-drive gear disengaged at Turn 5. And stayed that way. That was it. I had no drive. My race was finished and with it went the chance of my first F1 victory.

I coasted to a halt exactly where Senna had stopped. A mix of emotions surged through my head: utter disappointment; sudden loss of elation; confusion. Why did this happen at such a critical moment? What was the cause of the problem, anyway?

It was later discovered that the bolts had been put the wrong way round in the differential. They had come undone and eventually fallen out. The crown wheel and pinion had gradually stopped talking to each other and the feeling of the transmission engaging and disengaging was the final process before the differential actually came apart. It was only a matter of time.

I climbed from the car. Senna was standing by the barrier, watching the race and waiting for a scooter to take him back to the pits. He looked at me and said: 'Tough, isn't it?' I could only mumble in agreement.

Then I noticed that Senna was giving my car a really good inspection and paying particular attention to the state of my tyres. Then he went back to his car, put his helmet on, plugged in the radio and reported back to McLaren. The significance of this was that Berger was still leading in his McLaren and, since I had dropped out, Schumacher was now catching him in the other Benetton. Senna was able to tell them that my tyres were perfect and the same probably applied to Schumacher. Senna's brain was so switched on. All I wanted to do was jump in the middle of the track and put myself out of my misery by being run over.

Ayrton and I then shot the breeze for a while. Finally, a motorbike came and picked him up, leaving just me and an abandoned pair of racing cars. I thought I'd return the compliment and climbed into Ayrton's car. I began poking around, checking the way he had his belts, the location of the padding, noting all the switches and various things on the steering wheel. Little did I realise that two years later, I would be driving the latest version of that car.

When I reached the airport that evening, I poured one of the biggest whiskies I have ever had. I knew that race had been a defining moment but, at the time, I didn't know why or if it was good or bad. If I had won that race, if it had been Michael's car that failed instead of mine, the victory would have elevated me to a completely different level of GP driver. But it had been good because I had blown Schumacher away and demonstrated that I could win a Grand Prix. I downed that huge whisky, just to get the disappointment out of my system. Of course, because racing drivers drink very little and I was dehydrated in any case, I was several sheets to the wind when I got on the plane.

That race remains a major part of Montréal's bitter-sweet memories. I have had some good results and some near-misses. I remember sharing a Jaguar sportscar with Jan Lammers in 1990 and we were leading. When I handed over to Jan – who was a great sportscar driver – I warned him not to go into a dip at the exit of the hairpin. Because sportscars are so heavy, the transmissions take quite a pounding. Two laps later, Jan dropped a wheel into this nasty dip – and bang went a driveshaft. We were out of the race. In no time at all, I was out of my overalls, into a hire car and heading for downtown Montréal with a couple of guys from the team. We were going to a bar for a beer; anything to get away from the racetrack and thoughts of what might have been. When we came across a 'No Right Turn' sign, I, very arrogantly, said those signs were for other people. The guy who was driving took me at my word, turned right – and got hauled off by the police for his trouble. We didn't see him again for the rest of the evening. You learn not to mess with the Canadian police; they're serious people.

Montréal is arguably one of the liveliest cities we visit on the F1 trail, and the pubs, clubs and restaurants cater for every taste. That is just as well because we sometimes need the relief after a difficult day at the track. And I'm not just talking about drivers losing a race. It is a misery working for television there because the commentary box, located on the opposite side of the track, is a half-mile walk from the paddock, while the TV compound is even further.

I have found the best bet is to travel to the compound using the two ITV golf carts either side of the pedestrian bridge and then hitch a ride on a boat which travels along a little waterway that runs round a massive casino in the middle of the island and leads to the commentary positions. It is either that or walk to a footbridge and then fight your way through the fans filing towards the grandstands beyond the commentary boxes.

All of this presents a problem when I am doing the grid walk for ITV moments before the start of the race. If I relied on either the golf cart or boat or going on foot, then the first pit stops would have taken place by the time I joined James Allen on the microphone. The trick is to complete the grid walk and then bolt down the track, the goal being a hole in the fence, just below the commentary boxes. Logistically, therefore, Montréal is a nightmare. Socially, it is tremendous fun, both in the cosmopolitan city and in a paddock that borders the rowing lake.

Given the competitive nature of the teams, it should be no surprise that someone one year decided to build a makeshift raft and challenge other teams to a race on the lake. This quickly caught on and every team entered the spirit of an impromptu competition, the one rule being that you could only use material found in the paddock. Some of the inventions sank within seconds but others became more and more impressive. Of course, it soon became super-competitive and some of the carbon fibre creations were quite brilliant. The race, which was held on the day before practice began, was sadly scrapped for reasons that were never made clear.

There is another aspect of the Canadian Grand Prix that has become a victim of F1 taking itself too seriously. We used to travel to Montréal a few days early because the organisers would lay on all sorts of entertainment. There would be white water rafting, horse riding and organised tours of Québec province. These were wonderful jollies and everyone – team members, media, trade representatives alike – would make the most of a rare chance to relax together. That doesn't happen any more. It simply faded away. Now we turn up, go racing and go home.

Talking of which, a number of drivers were given a not-so-fond farewell one year when dashing to the airport. A policeman was lying in wait with a radar gun and he managed to nab about one third of the field. He famously said to one driver: 'You're fifth on the grid at the moment; you were doing 87 mph. Pole position is the guy on 96 mph.'

The hire car companies must hate it when the Grand Prix comes to town. Apart from having to scrape the ultra-sticky official passes from inside the windscreens, the rental people find their cars have been returned looking as if they have taken part in a motor rally. This is because the route in and out of the circuit involves travelling down a rough gravel road that runs alongside the ship canal.

Detroit

Staging a Grand Prix in Detroit highlighted a curious anomaly about the United States and its relationship with Formula 1. Here is a country boasting the 'World Series' for a number of sports, none of which are actually played outside North America. And yet, when a true world championship came to town, they had no idea what it was about. Absolutely none.

It is true that a hard core of incredibly knowledgeable American F1 fans would come from far and wide. But you could have Niki Lauda, a triple champion, walk into a bar or restaurant in downtown Detroit and they would not have a clue who he was, never mind know how to spell his name. But the great thing was that a lack of knowledge did not prevent the local people – or, most of them, anyway – from eventually accepting the event with typically loud enthusiasm.

As with the introduction of any noisy street race that effectively cuts through the commercial life of a busy city, there were heavy initial objections. It was the same in 1976 when Long Beach in California hosted the first street race for F1. The organisers laid on a fleet of coaches to take the disinterested inhabitants out of town. When they returned, the excitement of those who had

Length: 4.192 km

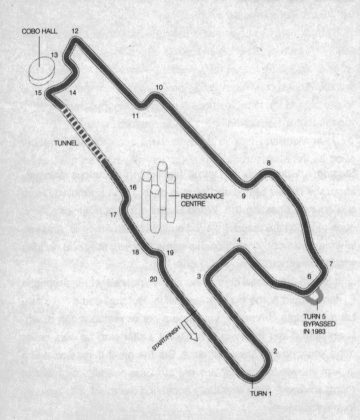

COBO HALL

12

13

15   14

11

10

TUNNEL

16

RENAISSANCE
CENTRE

17

8

9

18   19

4

3

7

20

6

5

START/FINISH

TURN 5
BYPASSED
IN 1983

2

TURN 1

DETROIT
(UNITED STATES)

stayed to witness the spectacle was such that half the coaches became redundant. By the following year, they barely filled one with dispassionate locals.

Detroit took longer because the organisation in the first year, 1982, left quite a bit to be desired as secretaries, trying to get to work, snagged their tights on concrete walls lining the track. This was enthusiastically reported by local newspapers that were slow to get behind the race. You could understand why when examining the motor racing tradition in North America.

Journalists and fans in the area were accustomed to places such as the Michigan Speedway, a two-mile banked oval, which allowed a lap average in excess of 220 mph. Formula 1 cars turned right as well as left but that did not impress the average American because a race through the streets was never going to reach half the speeds to which they had become accustomed. But, believe me, the quick bits were really fast. And incredibly bumpy. It was a terrific combination. I revelled in the challenge from the word go.

The track was defined by temporary concrete walls, and the American street system of blocks meant most corners were either a 90-degree left or right with part of the road ahead left as an escape route. But that was usually the only concession to helping a driver out of trouble if he made a mistake. Otherwise, it was going to be a hard landing. But it was the same for everyone and put the emphasis on precision. You either loathed that or loved it.

Attempting to be neat and tidy was made tricky by the manhole covers, gutters and all of the imperfections that add to the complexity of street racing. And the difficulties experienced were not confined to the drivers. Because of the venue's temporary nature, there was no room for a proper paddock behind the pits. The cars were kept in Cobo Hall, a rather tatty arena used for the Detroit

Motor Show and other major exhibitions. The plus side was that the mechanics could work under cover and in relative comfort. The downside was that Cobo Hall was at one end of the elongated track and the pits were at the other.

I use the word 'pits' advisedly. They were, in fact, a piece of the main straight along the waterfront that was portioned off by concrete blocks. There were absolutely no facilities, and the teams had to tow the cars and bring their equipment by truck, then lay out tools on the pit lane itself and set up shop in the open. It would be impossible today, given the masses of telemetry and electronic equipment needed just to start an F1 car, never mind run it through practice and a race. But on my first visit in 1984, no one complained too much.

Besides, there were advantages, such as staying in the Renaissance Centre, a skyscraper hotel towering over the track and located alongside the pits. There was a revolving restaurant on the top floor of one block, served by a glass-sided lift running up the outside for more than 70 floors. Since I am not comfortable with heights, I would spend the journey studying the back wall of the lift rather than admiring the stunning view of the city and the Detroit River with the shores of Canada on the far side.

The biggest advantage of all for a racing driver was the convenience. You could be staying on, say, the fifty-second floor, order breakfast through room service and get dressed for work. Carrying your crash helmet and wearing flameproof overalls, you would look slightly out of place when stepping into a lift to join hotel guests and business people on their way to the shops, offices and restaurants on the lower levels.

The trick then was to find the correct exit leading to the track because the base of each of the four towers looked exactly the same. Get it right and the revolving doors would spit you onto the short walk to the pits, where your car and team would be waiting. Getting into a racetrack on a Grand Prix weekend has never been easier.

It worked just as well in reverse, of course. When it came to refreshment between practice sessions, F1 did not have the magnificent catering it has now. And Tyrrell, my financially strapped team at the time, had absolutely nothing. No matter, because restaurants were close at hand. I remember in 1984, my first season of F1, sitting in a cafeteria with Paul Newman, Carl Haas (the actor's partner in a racing team) and Keke Rosberg, the 1982 World Champion, hardly able to believe this was happening as we had coffee together while waiting for the next practice session. And, to be honest, I could hardly wait to get back in the car.

Like all street circuits, Detroit was difficult to drive because the car was never settled at any point. It was leaping, bouncing and sliding, while you tried to ignore 90 per cent of the signals and sensations coming at you. The trick in these instances is to quickly identify the 10 per cent that is important. If you try to address everything, you will be either off the road or very slow. A driver receives feedback on four points: feet, backside, hands and eyes.

The brake pedal sends most of the information to the sole of the right foot through a slipper-thin driving boot. Everything on a racing car is solid – there are no rubber bushes to absorb the shock, for instance – and the various sensations come right through the car.

Your backside is like a personal gyroscope that gives a great feel for what the car is doing or about to do. The fact is that you can't react after the movement has started. It has to be totally instinctive. That is one of the reasons why a driver must have the seat and cockpit as snug a fit as possible; it is essential if he is to feel the slightest lateral force which is about to affect the handling.

WORKING THE WHEEL

Hands on the steering wheel are perhaps an obvious source of feel although it has to be said that the messages coming through are stronger than drivers perhaps realise. When you twist something, you create torque. When the steering is turned, the front wheels become loaded and the resulting torque in the steering column tells you a great deal about what the car is doing. As I point out to young drivers, this can be the first sign that a car is going to let go.

As soon as the back of the car loses grip, it slides and that eases the torque through the steering wheel. It is the same on a road car to a certain extent but the difference is that the feeling is filtered out by high sidewalls on the tyres, rubber bushes and the effect of power steering. In a racing car, you get this feedback through the wheel as the torque releases. It means the back has stepped out or maybe the car has begun to understeer: either way, you get a different feel through the steering wheel.

Then, of course, your eyes provide information, although, in this case, they are slightly behind the game, such is the need to be dealing with the car's wayward reaction from the split second it starts. When a car is cornering, it has to slide; something has to give. Normally, the back end will slide through between three and five degrees. If it reaches nine or ten degrees, then you are into a big slide. The back of the car is some distance behind the cockpit, which means that by the time your eyes have registered the slide, it is heading towards 10 degrees and it is too late. In the high-speed world of motor racing, eyes are a secondary source of information, albeit the primary source of direction.

People ask: 'How can you be doing 200 mph, be inch-perfect into a corner and correct a slide at 150 mph?' It is because you have got these signals coming at you. On a street circuit, you are being bombarded with information. The messages are not

The early stages of my crash at Turn 3 in Melbourne, 1996.
This is the 'don't let me go in the trees' moment.

The atmospheric setting at Rio as the pack rush to the first corner. The
fanatical fans can be seen in the unsheltered grandstands on the back straight.

1973 and the great Ronnie Peterson in his Lotus 72 demonstrates
the tortuous switchback nature of the Interlagos infield.

The mad dash down to Imola's Tosa hairpin.
Ayrton Senna snatches the lead from Alain Prost in 1989.

On my ear! Tabac Corner, Monaco 1984. Moments later I was strapped into the spare car and ready to go until I asked: 'Which circuit am I at?'

A classic landscape view of the arid Paul Ricard track.

The unique location of Circuit Gilles Villeneuve, Montreal, with Turns 1 and 2 in the foreground and the Olympic rowing lake and ship canal to the right.

The Renaissance
Centre – the ultimate
'paddock hotel' –
dominates the
Detroit GP circuit.

Working the wheel
hard in the glorious
Bentley Le Mans
car, 2001.

From '95, yet another of my flying Ligier laps
at the super-smooth Magny-Cours.

Happy days on the victory rostrum with Senna: Silverstone 1983.

Heading towards the stadium at Hockenheim.

Through the twists and turns of the Hungaroring watched by the vast crowd on the natural but dusty grandstand.

Eddie Irvine hustles his Jaguar through the supposedly
deterrent bollards and kerbs at Spa's famous 'Bus Stop'.

The Monza podium 1992. The legendary Senna won.
I beat team-mate Schumacher but you wouldn't know from our faces.

Jack Brabham on his way to victory at the first GP I ever witnessed; Clearways, Brands Hatch 1966.

My Ligier-Honda in the final chicane at Suzuka in 1995. F1 cars, fans, fairground… fun.

The infamous wet Australian Grand Prix of 1989. It would get much scarier yet.

necessarily arriving any faster, but there are so many more of them because the car is sliding, ducking and diving and the driver has to filter and discard irrelevant details.

For instance, you can be bouncing towards a kerb but you know the car is going to stick before you get there. So, you drive through it. On the other hand, there can be a really nasty bump and you think: 'Right, I've got to sort that out. If I don't get the car to work at that point, I'm going to hit the barrier.'

That's why there are a lot of crashes on street circuits. Sometimes a bump can catch you unawares, the car will skip or bounce and there isn't enough space to sort it out. Bang! You're into the barrier before you know it, just as Ayrton Senna did at Monaco in 1988. It happens so quickly if your concentration slips just when your tyres are getting old, or driver fatigue is creeping in. It does not take much to provoke a tiny error that will have enormous consequences. That's the thing about street circuits: the reward is immense and the driver can really make a difference. But the penalties are high.

The streets of Detroit were no different. The first corner was a long left, a good corner which you could attack. It didn't seem to matter where you finished on the road at the exit; you could simply floor the throttle and drive from there into the short straight that followed.

The 90-degree right at the end brings back memories of meeting a breakdown truck, just as I did in Montréal. This is an alarming habit employed by marshals in America when they go to the aid of a stricken car – and almost cause another accident in the process. There was a repeat here as I rounded the right-hander to find a recovery vehicle on the track.

Each corner is blind thanks to the presence of the concrete walls, and it is the same for the next right into Woodbridge Street at the top of a small hill. The following section was changed and made faster after the first race in 1982 but, whatever the layout, I found I could attack every corner when racing the little Tyrrell-Ford in 1984 and 1985. That car was like a pocket rocket, particularly through a sweeping chicane that led to a heavy braking zone for the first of two 90-degree corners.

The track went left around a hotel and then right into Larned Street, which, in fact, was the back straight and led to a decent overtaking spot into another left-right. At 2.5 miles, Detroit was not particularly long, a fact that became obvious as Cobo Hall marked the opposite end of the track and a quick downhill run, through the Atwater Tunnel that ran beneath a shopping plaza. A right and left flick brought you back onto the waterfront for a quick blast towards the final chicane positioned just before the pits.

Detroit was very rewarding to attack if your car was working well. One of the reasons I enjoyed Detroit and circuits like it was that it was possible to find more time. Drivers like to talk about the excitement of high-speed corners and whether or not they can be taken without lifting from the throttle. But the fact is that you don't actually spend much time in that type of corner. You can perhaps make a few hundredths of a second if you are brave to the point of being stupid. But time spent in the apex of a first-gear hairpin or a tight second-gear corner is, of course, much greater. If you change your car or your driving style, you can make two-tenths of a second. If you have nine or ten slow corners in a lap then it really makes a difference and can give you a second or more in your top pocket. That is simply not possible on the predominantly quick parts of Silverstone or Spa.

It is necessary to increase the car's ride height even though that will compromise the aerodynamics; the exact reverse of what is required at places such as Magny-Cours. The car needs to be quite soft in set-up because, if you hit a bad bump with your right-front wheel and you have a really stiff chassis and roll bar, then the load simply gets transferred into the left-hand wheel and makes the entire car skip. You want some compliance in the car, not wallowing like a Cadillac but able to absorb some of the imperfections in the racetrack.

The other important requirement for a street circuit is the ability of the car to turn into the corner crisply and accurately, which brings another compromise. You can be comfortable going round a slow hairpin with some understeer as the front slides. That feels reasonable. But it is slow because you are not on the throttle pedal early enough.

The car must be what we call 'on the nose'. In other words, the back is skittish and the car feels slightly uncomfortable. You think you're bound to spin it somewhere. But, by making the nose of the car turn in immediately, even if it means the back is gently stepping out of line, you can pick up the throttle earlier and be powering out of the corner. Then comes the need for good traction. Street circuits are all about being 'on the nose' on the way into the corner and excellent traction on the way out.

Tracks such as Detroit come to you in terms of finding the right compromise with the set-up of the car. The circuit will offer more grip as the cars clean off the diesel, dirt and all the rubbish accumulated over the previous 360 days of the year. There is no point in making drastic changes to the car if it is unbalanced. You have to build up as the weekend goes on and move your settings gently towards the track because the track itself is coming towards you at quite a rate of knots as it improves. If you meet in the sweet spot towards the end of the second day, you have a good set-up.

The gear ratios tend to be very short because of the need for massive acceleration on the short straights. Sixth gear in Detroit will be fourth at somewhere like Monza, which is all about long straights and maximum speed. You end up with a catapult that hammers your neck muscles thanks to the constant violence of the acceleration and braking. You have to shift gear without damaging a dog ring in the gearbox while the car skips through the corners, a problem drivers do not encounter these days thanks to semi-automatic gearboxes, which do the delicate work. These are a driver's dream because he can keep his hands on the wheel. A tiny microswitch is operated by a paddle behind the steering wheel, the usual arrangement being that the right-hand paddle is for the upshift while the one on the left takes care of downshifting. A third lever operates the clutch and that can be a bit tricky because, as you turn the wheel, the paddles disappear from your hands, especially when getting in and out of the pits.

The steering wheel is barely a turn and a half from lock to lock. When tackling corners on the circuit, the driver can't miss a shift. A click of the microswitch can have the hydraulics and electronics punching out one gear and putting it straight into the next in 20 milliseconds. The biggest benefit comes when braking because the semi-automatic box takes away the clumsiness of having one hand off the wheel while dipping the clutch and selecting the correct gear as the car bounces around.

When going up through the gears, the ability to keep your right foot flat to the floor while the electronics weave their magic dramatically reduces the work rate and the opportunity to make errors. The cars may be more reliable as a result but, for me, this has removed a fundamental part of the racing driver's role in the cockpit. The core skill of a footballer is to strike the ball with his head and foot. The core skill of a racing driver is to turn the wheel, open the throttle, shift the gears and press the brakes. That is no longer the delicate balance of coordination and feel it once was and racing is the poorer for it.

Whatever the system of gear-changing, driving on a street circuit means there is never a feeling of being fully settled and in control. At first, you are constantly dealing with a car and a circuit that appear to be combining in their efforts to pitch you into the wall. But once you have found that sweet spot, it suddenly becomes easy. People will say: 'He's not even going within a metre of the walls, yet the stopwatch says he is going quickly. How's he doing it?' Conversely, if you are constantly grazing the barrier and frightening yourself silly, you are probably going two seconds a lap slower than the man who has taken pole with about half your work rate.

Once you have the car sorted, you simply go faster and faster and faster as the track improves and, if everything has worked out as planned, you reach a crescendo during qualifying. That was the way it fell into place on my first visit in 1984 as I qualified eleventh in a normally aspirated Tyrrell-Ford that was extremely underpowered compared with the turbo Ferraris, Brabhams, Lotus and Renaults ahead on the grid.

I was a couple of places in front of my team-mate Stefan Bellof but, for some reason, Ken Tyrrell had convinced himself that Bellof was quicker than me around Detroit – and this despite Stefan having already written off one car against the wall during practice. On race morning, Ken devised a system, the gist of which was that if we were running in tandem and the driver behind felt he was being held up, then he would raise a hand while passing the pits.

As usual, the Tyrrells were much faster in the race compared with qualifying when the turbos had been running at maximum boost. It wasn't long before I was at the back of a queue of turbos, with Bellof latching onto my tail. It was pretty obvious that we were not going to get much further for a while – at which point Bellof stuck his hand up and Ken called me into the pits because, allegedly, I wouldn't let Stefan past. Two laps after that, Bellof smashed the car into the wall at the last chicane and three-wheeled to a halt directly under Ken's nose.

One by one, the cars in front either ran into the wall or into mechanical trouble. Suddenly I was third and rapidly catching Elio de Angelis. With seven laps to go, I pulled a move on his Lotus at the final chicane and set after the leading Brabham-BMW of Nelson Piquet. I was on a charge, the car really working well as I closed in.

I was ready to have a go as we came out of the chicane for the last time and headed towards the flag – only to find the track half-blocked by celebrating Brabham mechanics as they welcomed Piquet's second win in seven days, Nelson having broken his 1984 duck the week before in Canada.

It seems ridiculous now to think of mechanics standing on the racing line as cars charge towards it, but that's the way it was. The habit was banned shortly afterwards but it seems ironic when my good friend Charlie Whiting, then the Brabham chief mechanic but now the man in charge of F1 safety in his role as FIA Race Director, led the on-track celebration. Even if Nelson had run out of fuel, there was no way I could have passed him without mowing down most of his team.

Either way, my first F1 podium was a moment to savour, even though the ceremony now seems from an altogether more amateur age. Today, the podium is sponsored and must be a certain size with a certain colour of carpet and backdrop. The routine is carefully organised and must be strictly observed as only the first three finishers and designated officials are allowed on the rostrum.

In 1984, as with other races of the era, it was a free-for-all. At Detroit, because of the temporary nature of the facilities, the podium was actually a low-loader that trundled onto the track. Anyone who was standing around seemed to jump on board. My wife Liz was with me, as were a number of mechanics from Tyrrell, Brabham and Lotus, with Nelson, Elio and I lost in the middle. It was hilarious.

Not so funny was the fact that our second place would eventually be taken away because of political manoeuvring over the ballast pumped into the Tyrrell during the race, as happened in Rio de Janeiro. It angers me to this day. That said, I still have the cup, which sits in pride of place at home. I bought and paid for it on 24 June 1984 and woe betide anyone who tries to take it from me.

Naturally, I felt pretty pleased with myself afterwards, a mood that was to be punctured without ceremony by Ken who said: 'The way you overtook de Angelis was stupid – and Jackie [Stewart] thinks so too.'

Taken aback, I said: 'I'm sorry, Ken, but I don't think so. I was following de Angelis and he was missing second gear. He was really slow out of the little left leading towards the final chicane. I had followed him for two or three laps, worked out he had a problem, nailed him on the short straight leading to the final chicane, blocked his line on the way in and then cleared off after Piquet.' I said I thought it was a brilliant move – and I still do. But Ken could see that I was getting over-confident.

Sure enough, I went to the next race in Dallas – another wacky street circuit – and was super-quick on the morning of the first day. I was going to be on pole; no question about it in my mind. On my first lap of qualifying in the afternoon, I had a puncture when going through a chicane. I hit the wall three times, the first two impacts destroying the front of the car, leaving my feet to take the brunt of the third. I broke my left ankle and right foot and was out for the rest of the season. Ken could see that coming. I couldn't.

WORKING THE WHEEL

I was back in action in 1985 and looking forward to a return to Detroit. This would represent the last hurrah for the normally aspirated engine, the Tyrrells now being the only cars on the grid without the benefit of a turbo. It was satisfying to find we were every bit as competitive without our so called illegal advantage for which we were banned the previous year. I qualified ahead of Bellof again in the back quarter of the grid but again we knew we had an advantage in the race because, with less power, the Tyrrells were the only cars that could use the softer tyres and the extra grip they brought to the street surface.

As the field began to thin out, Stefan dropped back (he had damaged the nose of his car against the back of mine) while I went on the attack, passing Alain Prost in the McLaren and Michele Alboreto's Ferrari. That put me into fourth place.

But it soon became fifth when I backed off too much for a yellow flag and Alboreto got a run at me and retook the place. The Tyrrell was incredibly nimble and I was right on Michele's tail when we came to lap Philippe Alliot in a RAM, a car which was desperately slow at the best of times but, on this occasion, was fifteen seconds off the pace because of some problem or other.

On seeing the blue flag, Alliot dutifully moved out of the way and let Alboreto through – without realising that a little blue Tyrrell was tucked behind the Ferrari. Alliot pulled into the Ferrari's slipstream and took me clean out of the race. There was absolutely nothing I could do. My incredible momentum came to a sudden halt in a tyre barrier. I was absolutely gutted. It could have been a major result for Tyrrell.

The Grand Prix would only last for another two years in Detroit (I retired with mechanical trouble both times) before it was considered uneconomic by the city to meet the demands of the teams in terms of upgrading the track. I was sorry to see it go, even though you had to be careful in certain parts of downtown. We were warned not to go beyond a certain street and, if you doubted the danger, then a ride in a yellow cab would confirm the stories. The cabbie would speak to you through a tiny grill in a sheet of bullet-proof glass that ran all the way down the back of his seat. But there was another side to Detroit, and I also remember wonderful sailing regattas. We would be taken no more than 10 miles out of town and into the most beautiful suburbs on the edge of Lake Michigan. It was part of the contradiction of F1 coming to Detroit.

As I said earlier, when Grand Prix racing first arrived in 1982, the local sports writers could not get their heads around the concept of motor racing on a stop-go circuit with the resulting low average speed. There is a quote in the *Autocourse* annual from the *Detroit Free Press* in which a sports journalist, George Puscas, more accustomed to baseball and ice hockey, gently mocked Alain Prost's 82 mph average to take pole position that first year with his tongue wedged in his cheek, Puscas wrote:

'This is a fast town, no matter what anyone says. We've got guys here who hit 82 on the streets of downtown Detroit almost any night. They do it about a quarter to two, trying to make last calls in their favourite bar. And they're not our best either.

You want to see real speed, check a high school parking lot. I make it 8 to 1 you'll find some kid in a TransAm hitting 82 mph. In reverse. If not our jails, our courtrooms are filled almost any Monday morning with guys who have made a serious run at 82, which is not fast at all, or maybe 100, which is getting there.'

And on it went. Gradually, though, both sides got to know and respect each other. Detroit was a great place to be and a great track on which to race. An average of 82 mph may not have sounded much but, believe me, it really was a brilliant feeling when the car was working well.

Length: 13.880 km

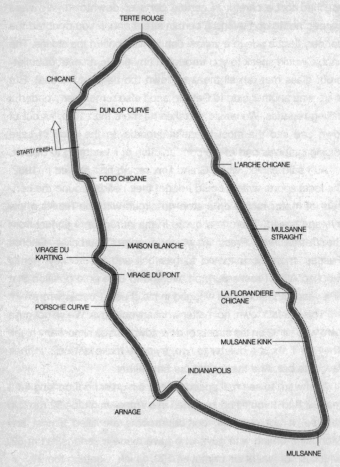

TERTE ROUGE

CHICANE

DUNLOP CURVE

START/ FINISH

FORD CHICANE

L'ARCHE CHICANE

MULSANNE
STRAIGHT

VIRAGE DU
KARTING

MAISON BLANCHE

VIRAGE DU PONT

LA FLORANDIERE
CHICANE

PORSCHE CURVE

MULSANNE KINK

INDIANAPOLIS

ARNAGE

MULSANNE

LE MANS
(FRANCE)

Le Mans

Racing at Le Mans is the equivalent of cramming an entire Grand Prix season into twenty-four hours. A Grand Prix lasts for about 190 miles and a Le Mans car will cover sixteen times that distance at an average of 130 mph. But the big difference is that, at Le Mans, there is no servicing. Whereas a Formula 1 car will be lovingly taken apart and rebuilt between each race, at Le Mans the fuel is added, the tyres are changed, the windscreen is cleaned and off you go with speeds reaching 230 mph. Talk about a different world.

I have a love/hate relationship with twenty-four-hour races; they seem to take all day. (Nobody ever laughs at this but it's my way of saying they go on forever. And then some.) But that is part of the attraction because, at the end of it, particularly if you have won, the sense of achievement is on a par with winning the Monaco Grand Prix or the Indianapolis 500.

I was lucky enough to be in the winning Jaguar at Le Mans in 1990. They say that 50,000 British supporters make the trip each year and the place was awash with partisan Brits at the end, so much so that it seemed to me that Britain had rented this part of France for the weekend. It was an incredible atmosphere.

Each time I raced at Le Mans, I was more or less the lead driver for a works team – Jaguar, Nissan, Toyota and, more recently, Bentley – and I tended to carry much of the workload. That is one of the many reasons why I like sportscar racing: you play a much greater part in the team. Being a businessman by profession, it suits me to work at a management level and help steer the project through development, chassis set-up, tyre choice and so on. I feel really comfortable doing this even though it means making a commitment to do some of the less attractive aspects of preparing for Le Mans, such as a thirty-six-hour test at Magny-Cours. Pounding round and round this deserted track in the dark, in the rain, is one of the hardest things you will ever do as a racing driver.

Experience has taught the Le Mans organisers how to illuminate the kerbs so that they show up well, even when drivers are dealing with the incredible high-speed braking zones. Magny-Cours, on the other hand, was not built with twenty-four-hour racing in mind. As a result, you can't see a thing at night. You find yourself squinting while trying to pick out the actual track and yet, at the same time, pushing on as hard as you can. If you don't take the car to the limit, there is no point in putting yourself through this excruciating test.

The ultimate irony is that there is absolutely no substitute for racing at Le Mans. You can test as much as you like, wherever you like, but on the Le Mans track you quickly discover that this place is totally unique. It could hardly be otherwise on a circuit where we used to reach 240 mph before chicanes were inserted on the Mulsanne Straight in 1990. Even now, the speeds remain extremely high and, the point is, the full throttle running goes on for a long time.

Because the track is so different to anywhere else – and, at

8.484 miles, exceptionally long – one of the greatest difficulties arises straight away. Despite the variety of problems that lie ahead, there is only one day set aside in May for testing. During that time, the car has to be set up, the tyres tested, the fuel economy established and, hopefully, all drivers fully up to speed.

So a five-car works team will have fifteen drivers, all from different backgrounds with different driving styles and different requirements. Some of them have never been to Le Mans before; others are old, wise heads. You have got to somehow make this lot work as a unit and it becomes very difficult, starting with qualifying on Wednesday and Thursday evenings.

Because the Mulsanne Straight is a Route Nationale during the day, it can only be closed off for qualifying at around 6 p.m. Once that's done, you only have two sessions lasting two hours each. It is then immediately apparent that the length of the lap is going to cause problems.

Say you want to do a single timed flying lap. It is necessary to have an 'out' lap from the pits and another to come back in again after the quick lap. That one simple exercise will take about twelve minutes. Then more time is spent while the car is adjusted in the pits, a time-consuming operation because of the fully enclosed bodywork and heavy-duty parts necessary on a Le Mans car. By the time all of that has been completed, twenty minutes have passed and all you have to show for it is a single flying lap. And there is a massive amount to get done in preparation for a race that is going to last twenty-four hours. This is a huge factor because all three drivers have to get through qualifying – both in daylight and darkness – not to mention the set-up and tyre choice. It is extremely difficult to achieve all of that in the time allotted. It's the same for everyone and, like it or not, that is but one of the many distinctive challenges of racing at Le Mans.

In the middle of all of this, the faster driver of the three will be itching to have a run on a set of qualifying tyres in order to post a decent grid time for the car. Getting the best out of qualifiers at Le Mans is another exceptionally difficult challenge. In order not to work the sticky rubber too hard early on, it is necessary to coast through the out lap. While you are doing that, someone in the middle of a flying lap in a quick car will come at you from nowhere. You complete your out lap and nail the throttle. It's now or never. During the course of the qualifying lap, it is common to pass at least ten cars because of the massive variation in speed between an out-and-out sports racing car such as a works Jaguar, and a GT car such as a Porsche 911.

Appearing on a dual carriageway near you, a Porsche 911 would blow anyone's mind. In a top-flight sportscar race, it looks like a snail when caught by an all-singing, all-dancing Le Mans car. We would just dismiss the Porsche; swat it off like a fly on your nose. The Porsche drivers are on their personal ragged edge and we're blasting past them with our lights full on. And the performance difference is not limited to the straights. The downforce on a Le Mans car means our stopping zones are a little over half those required by a GT car even though we may arrive at a higher speed. It takes your breath away the first time it happens and emphasises the need for everyone to be extra careful.

One of the curiosities of Le Mans is the number of different classes. Try as I might, I have never been able to get my head round the various categories and what they actually mean. It is an alphabet soup of championships and classes – GT2, GT3, ALMS, GTS, Group C1, Group C2, LMP1 and LMP2, to name but a few – and you can't help wondering if this is a deliberate ploy to destabilise sportscar racing.

Although the race starts at 4 p.m. on Saturday, the official pro-
ceedings get under way on the previous Monday. And they take
place with all the quirkiness of a sporting classic that has been
running since 1923.

Scrutineering is held in Place des Jacobins in the centre of Le
Mans. The intention is to build up the pre-race atmosphere by
allowing the public to see the cars at close quarters. This may
have been easy in the days when you drove your Bentley touring
car to Le Mans, raced it for twenty-four hours, and then drove
home again. A quick trip to scrutineering would have been nothing more than a few more miles on the clock, with a stop for
afternoon tea or a glass of champagne on the way back. Indeed,
for the first six years, in the days of the Bentley Boys and victory
for British Racing Green, the track actually ran to a hairpin in
the town.

Now, it is a right palaver. The cars have to be loaded onto a
truck at the circuit for the journey through a traffic jam and into the
city. This has to be a vehicle brought specially to the circuit for the
purpose because, by this stage, it would be impossible to winkle
the team's transporters out of the cramped paddock, where they
have been set up and locked together like a Rubiks Cube for the
weekend.

The drivers have to sign on and receive a plastic tag that has to
be worn all weekend. It feels like something you would be given
as a pass at a cheap disco and I hated having to wear it on my
wrist and to fumble inside my gloves and overall sleeves to show
it when asked. It seemed absurd, when I was standing there with
'Martin Brundle' on my crash helmet and 'Martin Brundle' on my
overalls, to sign a piece of paper to say I really was Martin
Brundle. It is necessary, however, because the identification tag
informs the officials which driver is in the car at any given time;

there are rules concerning the amount of time each driver can spend at the wheel and, of course, they need to know each driver's best lap time for qualifying criteria.

There is more downtown action on Friday night when the fans converge again to see the drivers being driven around the city centre. The purpose of the exercise is to generate spending in the local establishments, which is fair enough. The trouble is, this becomes a zoo because fans don't often get access to drivers in this way. And, in the background, police are turning a blind eye to burn-outs, drag races and wheelies – by the fans, not the race drivers!

The adults stay behind railings – but not the children. There are hundreds of them, each with pen and paper, and they come right up to the vintage cars carrying the drivers. I seemed to spend most of the time warning them to keep their tiny feet away from the wheels. Inevitably, in the background, are a few guys who've had a bit too much to drink, but the atmosphere is good-humoured. On one occasion, I was handed a pint of beer. It probably was not good for the image but it tasted great at the time and added to the pleasure of being among the fans, having a chat and sharing the build-up to the race. This is why racing drivers do what they do. If nobody watched us, would we still do it? If the answer is yes, then we should go racing on Wednesday afternoons and have the weekends off.

For the drivers, the action in the city centre is another facet of Le Mans and the preparation begun months in advance. When it comes to eating, the teams bring their own catering and the drivers will have already begun to pre-load on pasta. I can remember one particular race in the late 1980s when we took so many carbohydrates on board, we all felt fat and sluggish. But it was very good for performance through the race. It is much more sophisticated now, in line with improved fitness among the top drivers.

At Le Mans, however, you come across all sorts of drivers. It could hardly be otherwise with fifty-five cars entered for the race. There simply aren't 165 world-class drivers ready to do the job. That can make the drivers' briefing an interesting experience. During much of my time at Le Mans, I was also a Grand Prix driver and therefore accustomed to short, sharp drivers' briefings. I would have been sitting next to Gerhard Berger and Michael Schumacher, Ayrton Senna and Keke Rosberg; drivers who knew exactly what they were about.

At Le Mans the 165 drivers, of all shapes and sizes, are cor-ralled into a briefing that is conducted half in French and half in English. A percentage of those present are professional racing dri-vers. But there are also some weekend warriors and other drivers who perhaps race in national events or do a bit of sportscar rac-ing but, above all else, simply want to say they have raced at Le Mans. I wouldn't decry them in any way – we all came through that phase – but you will see one or two answering their mobile phones and generally not paying attention. On one occasion, I stood behind a guy who had his baby daughter in his arms at a driver's briefing, she kept asking if they could go home and I was thinking 'I don't believe this'. Maybe that's the charm of Le Mans. On the other hand, you can find yourself having raced in a Grand Prix the week before, only to sit in the drivers' briefing at Le Mans, hoping that the person next to you pays more attention at 3 a.m. in the mist on Sunday morning. It's a completely different ballgame.

The period before the start of the race is also very different when compared with the orderly and familiar routine at a Grand Prix. Yet the pressure is just as great. The programme, the budget and the expectation generated by Le Mans spawn similar demands. F1 drivers are protected during the Grands Prix, staying out of sight in the motorhomes and generally not being expected to stand around and chat as the start of the race approaches. At Le Mans the paddock is more haphazard and the drivers tend to be more in the public view. Anyone can lean over the fence or march into the team enclosure and say: 'Hi, I'm from Timbuktu Television. What's your feeling about today's race?' As a result, when you finally climb into the car, it's serenity itself, a wonderful escape from the mounting excitement.

In any case, you need to start thinking about the start because the first lap is ridiculous. This may be a twenty-four-hour race but everyone goes like crazy on the first lap. They know that the TV coverage is usually live for the first couple of hours. So you have to deal with heroes who are not going to be anywhere come four o'clock the next day but, boy, are they are going to make the most of their fifteen minutes of fame. For the rest, there is a long night ahead. And most of the day after that.

Unlike twenty-four-hour races at circuits like Daytona in Florida, the beauty of Le Mans is that there are actually only about six hours of darkness. Nonetheless, you must keep eating and drinking beforehand, but there is a point where you have to be using reserves. I remember seeing a Japanese driver at Daytona have fluid added intravenously to his system. People will try all sorts of things in order to stay awake at night.

I've always had a lot of stamina, so I didn't have a problem with long-distance races. But I've seen super-fit guys simply crash out in the physical sense. I had a team-mate who was finished by midnight. It is hard, no question. If you do a triple stint – one stint between refuelling lasts for about forty minutes – you are in the car for close to two hours. And that is just three of ten stints you might be called on to do during the race.

The year I won Le Mans, I drove for almost thirteen hours as team leader in two cars. I was sent out as the hare in one car to break the Porsches and reserved a seat in another, which won. That was the deliberate strategy, and it worked very well. But, physically, that's tough. Mentally, it is supremely hard just to keep your concentration and stay on top of all that is going on around you.

This, after all, is one of the world's most famous motor races. When people talk about the great racetracks of the world, they mention Spa, Monte Carlo, perhaps the old Nürburgring. I always find it strange that Le Mans is never included. It is a magnificent circuit. You can tell that by the reaction of top drivers – be it Mario Andretti, who has raced on every conceivable type of venue from dirt tracks to 250 mph ovals, or Colin McRae, more accustomed to the demands of world class rallying. They absolutely love it.

I can't think of anything more thrilling than driving a pukka Le Mans car on a circuit for which it has been specifically designed. I think Le Mans cars are the most beautiful racing cars ever built. They are always super-sleek, elongated and elegant, thanks to the need for high top speed. And it doesn't take long to begin stretching the car's legs once the first few corners are dealt with.

The Dunlop curve follows immediately after the pits and this long, sweeping right-hander can be tricky, particularly for the faster cars that carry a lot of speed into the chicane that follows. The GT cars can't do that and it is possible to find a closing speed of 100 mph on a slower competitor and a few dramatic moments as you rush into the chicane that follows. Michael Schumacher famously spun a Mercedes there and got away with it – as he always does.

After a downhill section, the next chicane starts with an almost 90-degree right, followed quickly by a second or third gear left, which then deposits you straight into the original Esses. It is as bumpy as hell in there and often has spilled oil just to add to the excitement. In its original form, there was nowhere to go if you got it wrong or had a problem when arriving at high speed over the crest of the hill. Go off there and you were going to hit something so hard you felt sure the entire car – particularly when it was getting tired towards the end of the twenty-four hours – was going to be vaporised in an instant.

The line of the original track continues its bumpy way to Terte Rouge, a right-hander which doesn't look much but is actually a great corner. In 1999, I asked the organisers to install some extra tyres and move others back. The following year, Eric van de Poele arrived at Terte Rouge with a stuck throttle and went straight into the wall. It was a massive accident because a Le Mans car is twice the weight of an F1 car. The inertia when you crash is simply horrendous.

To make matters worse, the driver's seating position is not as secure as in an F1 car where the seat is tailored like a Savile Row suit around the driver. That's not possible in a sportscar because the cockpit is being shared by as many as three drivers. There is a common setting for the pedals but that presented a problem for me because I have not been able to articulate my feet very well after my Dallas accident in 1984 and required an unusual pedal set-up. Otherwise, everything else in the cockpit, from the position and size of the seat to the location of the steering wheel, has to be a compromise.

It is not uncommon during a pit stop to see a driver – the tiny

Jan Lammers, for example – about to climb in holding a piece of two-part foam, covered in tank tape and with Velcro on the back, to be used as a packer. At the other extreme, I have shared many winning cars with John Nielsen, who is about twice my size and can drive for ever. The situation is aggravated further because the seat belts have to fit any number of different size drivers. We used to have two different buckles – a practice that has since been banned – to cater for Nielsen, who would have a long buckle, while I would use a shorter version that had been stitched onto the webbing. The end result is that the drivers do not have the lateral support they enjoy in a single-seater and it's a miracle that we have not seen a greater number of fatal injuries in sportscars. Van de Poele's shunt was a good example of a driver escaping a massive impact.

Lots of drivers get it wrong at Terte Rouge. It has a wicked kerb on the inside. Because a Le Mans car is low, wide and stiff, if you punch energy into the right-front wheel, it transfers through the car. By exciting the front suspension, you pay the price through the effect created in the rear of the car. Terte Rouge is bumpy on the way in and yet you are carrying a massive amount of speed through the corner. And then there is this old-style, razor-edge kerb waiting on the inside. It can flick the car towards the outside of the corner and, the more you drift out, the bumpier it becomes – all of which is the last thing a Le Mans car needs, particularly at a critical corner such as this because Terte Rouge throws the car onto the start of the Mulsanne Straight.

Before the advent of the two chicanes, we would be flat-chat all the way, day or night, wet or dry, with just a kink to keep your attention about two-thirds of the way down. We reached between 235 and 240 mph in the Jaguar and yet the driver would be doing absolutely nothing, apart from just sitting there and trying not to think about anything going wrong.

WORKING THE WHEEL

Because this is a public road, it is crowned in the middle and has distinct grooves either side where the trucks haul up and down between Alençon and Tours. It means you have to be properly organised when preparing to overtake a slower competitor. It is necessary to coax your car out of the groove, ease it over the crown and catch it on the other side. Depending on the stability of the car and the design of the tyre, you need almost to push the car to make it move and then, when it does go, it happens suddenly and you have to collect it back together again. You travel down the Mulsanne Straight on one side or the other without wandering too much while gently making your way through the traffic as if on a motorway. It's the only option when speeds are so high.

Even when they added the deviations, we continued to see up to 215 mph on Mulsanne and the combination of the two chicanes played into the hands of experienced drivers when braking on the way in. It is similar to braking in an F1 car in that the driver needs confidence to carry a lot of speed. It's very bumpy and, as the race goes on, each chicane progressively becomes like Brighton beach as drivers consistently get it wrong, particularly at night, and shoot straight across the run-off area, spraying gravel all over the racetrack. Frequently you will see a red and yellow warning flag that usually means oil but, in this case, 'slippery track', which is covered with gravel, bits of carbon fibre and whatever else might have come adrift from racing cars. The debris builds up to the point where there is a narrow groove fringed by gravel and that's the only line through the chicanes.

Drivers of the faster cars hate it when they catch traffic at a chicane because you feel you've put on the handbrake and almost come to a standstill. Once through the right-left-right of the first chicane, the pace picks up very quickly. A Le Mans car effortlessly builds speed because there is so little drag and the engines tend to have a very lazy feel. If an F1 car revs to 19,000 rpm, a Le Mans engine will not exert itself beyond 8,000 rpm. But the torque is incredible, so much so that you could pull away from standstill in fifth gear with the 7-litre V12 Jaguar. The car just accelerates on and on, without fuss.

The second chicane is a left-right-left with a very quick exit that leads towards the right-hand kink. Whereas this used to really hold your attention when approaching at 240 mph, it is now a simple matter of continuing to accelerate through on the way to Mulsanne Corner.

But, first, there is a steep hill which had the crest eased following a car becoming airborne there. This is the problem when a Le Mans car leaves the ground. Because there is a huge floor plan area, it will begin to act like a sail, even if the car becomes only slightly airborne. Get the nose up and the driver is guaranteed to be looking at the sky. We saw that all too graphically in 2000 when three Mercedes got air beneath them and flipped backwards. One went into the trees and the driver, Peter Dumbreck, was doubly lucky because the car landed the right way up and the trees had been felled at that point.

Having arrived at Mulsanne Corner still in one piece, you have to deal with a very fast sweep into a really tight little right-hander. I once took a look at what was down the escape road and rather wished I hadn't. There is a roundabout at the end, which means, if you have a major brake or suspension failure, you would hit the roundabout and maybe a barn and a couple of trees and lamp posts. So, best to ignore that when braking and changing down from sixth to second because it is possible to make up more time at Mulsanne Corner than anywhere else on the racetrack.

WORKING THE WHEEL

A lot of drivers brake and then turn into the curve, and then brake again. In actual fact, you can stay on the power through the curve even though it's very bumpy and the car's touching the ground. Saying that, if I've been round Mulsanne Corner 2,000 times, I've only got it right for about half that number. The temptation is to go in too fast and the big heavy car, bouncing around on the bumps, doesn't want to be hauled into the tight right at the end.

The problem is that the weight transfers onto the left-front corner of the car because you are still turning and braking. You then ask the car to do a 90-degree right but, as you come off the brake pedal, some of the load is released from the front-left and the car seems as though it is falling over at the back. You need to be smooth with the release of the brakes, but that's difficult because your feet are bouncing all over the place, even though the rest of your body is held tight against the seat. The overall effect is that the car feels as if it has come to a stop instead of sweeping through the corner. Very often you spin into the gravel because you can't quite stop these forces fighting each other instead of helping you head towards the next corner.

The tree-lined run to Indianapolis is quite narrow with two distinct right-hand kinks. These are tricky because of the need to take a racing line and cut the corner at each of them. They would not be a problem if you had the road to yourself but, nine times out of ten, there will be a slower car ahead. And if there is more than one, you will be in trouble if you don't get past them before reaching either of the two kinks. It is guaranteed that the first car will cut across and the rest will follow, completely unaware of your presence because you have just homed in on them out of the blue. When that happens, you have to come off the power and then accelerate again. For that reason, I always made sure I had flasher lights. Over the years, that developed into a button that I simply had to touch in order to trigger a predetermined number of flashes, usually five, just to be absolutely sure they knew I was coming – which, usually, they did not.

Indianapolis itself is another two-part corner with a very fast entry. All things being equal, you should be able to go into the first part at around 150 mph before dealing with the 90-degree left that follows. This is another area where the driver really does not want to admire the surroundings. There are a couple of houses, some more barns and one or two front gardens waiting to trap the unwary. It's a great corner, but best not to look too closely. Then comes Arnage, which is a different proposition; slower, bumpy and slippery. Many drivers have gone straight on at this clumsy, horrible little corner, which I never really enjoyed.

No time to dwell on that, however, because you are immediately heading back towards 200 mph and the pits. Now you can really get going because this is a newer part of the track. It is wider and a bit smoother as you head into the first right of the Porsche Curves, which are absolutely brilliant. Fast, sweeping, a little bumpy but with loads of grip thanks to a good surface. This is a piece of proper racetrack instead of a public road borrowed for the weekend. You have hung on to the car for the best part of seven miles and all of a sudden it is like coming off a B-road onto a motorway. Your machine suddenly acts like a racing car.

The next left-hander, Virage du Pont, is taken at around 150 mph as it sweeps downhill between two concrete walls. This is another one of those 'if I crash here, I'm going to get vaporised' areas which require intense concentration, particularly in traffic.

Following immediately is Virage du Karting, a fast and rewarding right-hander where you must hug the inside line as if it's your favourite granny. The sting in the tail is the final left, Maison

Blanche, a horrible off-camber corner, which is the worst thing in the world for a sportscar to deal with. It is not what you need because, by now, you are carrying too much speed and, as likely as not, you will come across a couple of slower cars. In fact, when exiting Arnage fifteen seconds earlier, you will have seen them quite some way in the distance. They're already in the Porsche Curves but you can be sure they will get in your way before the tricky exit. That's how fast a pukka Le Mans car is in the Porsche Curves.

There is one more delight in the shape of an easy chicane, the name of which I have never known despite my thousands of laps and which, on an empty track, is merely an acceleration zone. However, in traffic, after having catapulted out of the Porsche Curves, it is easy to find a slower car using both sides of the road and hanging you out to dry with two wheels on the grass.

This can be critical as your entry to the pit lane is effectively blocked if you don't take immediate action. The last thing you want is the awful sinking feeling that comes with the realisation that you should be going into the pits. Apart from traffic getting in the way, it is also possible to miss your pit signal on the previous lap. The team will always radio through and you will confirm. There was a time when the pit signal crew was stationed at Mulsanne Corner, operating by radio contact with the team, miles away in the pit lane. But now it is another full and eventful lap and three and a half minutes before you swing into the pit lane. During that time, drivers have become engrossed in a battle or been carried away coming through the Porsche Curves and simply forgotten to head for the pits.

It's one of the biggest fears. If you miss the pit lane, you will run out of fuel. There is no amount of pussy-footing that will get you around another 8.5 miles because, if everyone has done their calculations correctly, the car will be close to running out when it is due to stop. It is essential to wring the tank nearly dry because, otherwise, you will have to make two more stops and you will not win. That's how close it can be.

Finally, there are the two Ford chicanes. The first is a fast left-right, which needs to be attacked for a hot lap with wheels on the grass coming in and going out. This feeds immediately into the final complex. The organisers have tried everything to stop drivers cheating when coming through the tight left-right: bollards, big kerbs, all sorts of devices that never really work as they are intended.

The competitiveness of the entry over the years has come in waves. But if it is a strong year with several major manufacturers such as Jaguar, Porsche, Mercedes-Benz and Toyota slogging it out, then I always say that if you ever lift the bonnet on a Le Mans car, you're not going to win. Le Mans is no longer simply about endurance; it is about out-and-out speed as well.

Pit stops are everything. The drivers make twenty-eight scheduled visits during the race, so it is absolutely crucial to plan them properly. The rules say that, for safety reasons, refuelling and tyre-changing cannot be done at the same time. That's why it is important to find a set-up on the car that is going to be kind to the tyres and give as many as three or four stints before a change is necessary. Calculations are complicated further by track temperatures during the day being much higher than they are at night, which means a different tyre compound. And, because the circuit covers such a large area, there is every chance of rain at one end but not the other.

The greatest fear, however, is a puncture. The driver does not necessarily know he has a problem when travelling at high speed because the centrifugal force keeps the tyre walls upright. But when the tyre finally blows at over 200 mph, the effect can be devastating.

I'll never forget going down the old Mulsanne Straight in the middle of the night during the race in 1987. I was flat out as usual when I began to see bits of bodywork on the track. There were no warning flags so I figured that, whatever this was, it must have just happened. I slowed as more and more debris appeared to the point where the track began to resemble the scene of a plane crash. As I was dodging various bits and pieces, I noticed out of the corner of my eye some purple bodywork, the same colour as my Silk Cut Jaguar. One of my team-mates had clearly had a massive accident. Eventually I came across what looked like just the chassis lying on its side. In fact, the gearbox and entire rear suspension were missing, as were the doors and windscreen. But I couldn't see the driver.

I radioed back to the pits: 'Has one of us had an accident?' I was still doubting what I had just seen. There was no reply. 'I think one of our cars has had an accident on Mulsanne,' I said. Then a voice came on, asking me to repeat what I had just said. Clearly, the team did not know but they quickly worked out that it was Win Percy, who had just joined the race for the first time as reserve driver in a car shared by Lammers and John Watson.

It turned out to be the ultimate nightmare of Le Mans: a puncture. When a tyre finally goes at these speeds – say, for example the right rear – then it takes the rear wing, rear bodywork, and right-rear brake. The whole lot sails away and now you are in a car that has three wheels, no brakes and is about to take off. By some miracle, Win's car landed on the barrier and came back down on the track side rather than going into the trees. It skidded and bounced and slithered for about a kilometre, spraying parts and debris as it went.

He had not had the chance to spot the signs, which are difficult to see during the build-up of heat that eventually leads to the blow-out. Because the tyre starts to grow, the engine will not pull quite the same number of revs, plus the tyre itself is creating a bit of additional drag. I would watch the revs like a hawk. If, say, the engine ought to be pulling between 6,700 and 6,800 rpm but was, in fact, only showing 6,500 rpm, I would become concerned and start to ask questions. Did I come out of Terte Rouge too slowly? Did I get balked in traffic? Why is it doing this?

Because of the length of the circuit at Le Mans, there is a Safety Car at each end. One picked us up and off we went at a crawl while the wreckage was cleared. And now you get cold. Very cold. It's three o'clock in the morning, you have been working hard and become sweaty. All of a sudden you are doing a mere 60 mph. The cockpit is peppered with vents, designed to keep the driver cool. Now they are directing chilly air, so much so that you start shaking. To make matters worse, because you are running at severely reduced pace, fuel is being saved at an exceptional rate. That means you will have to run even longer than planned before the next stop. The tank of fuel seems bottomless; you're not coming in the pits; you're not going to change drivers; you're not going to do anything apart from trying to stay out of the accident debris because you know your chances of picking up a puncture have just gone up one hundredfold thanks to the shards of carbon fibre and other bits and pieces. By now your teeth are chattering and you are so, so cold.

The radio that night was too quiet for my liking and we trailed behind the Safety Car for just under two hours because so much of the crash barrier needed replacing. During that time, they found Win. He was sitting on the other side of the fence, some way from the scene, getting his breath back. He'd had the shunt of all time and he was OK. A truly remarkable escape, one that reminds you of the race's unfortunate past.

Motor racing in Europe almost came to a halt in 1955 when a car flew off the road at Le Mans and killed more than eighty spectators directly in front of the pits. The twenty-four-hour race has a reputation similar to the Isle of Man motorcycle TT in that many competitors from all walks of life have lost their lives. Grand Prix driver Jo Bonnier was killed when his Lola went into the trees on Mulsanne in 1972 and, fourteen years later, the young Austrian driver, Jo Gartner, suffered a similar fate.

You can't get away from the fact that this race is distinctive, not only from the point of view of driving but also the completely different challenge and the element of risk. The organisers do their very best to reduce the danger, which is why you are prepared to put up with Safety Car periods, even if they do sometimes last for hours.

Once the Safety Car disappears, the feeling of being cold soon goes because there is so much to think about, especially at night. Traffic is such an important factor. You have got to have a car that is good when working through back markers, which means the set-up has to be benign. You don't want a car that is moving around too much at speed. This is not an F1 car in a race lasting for an hour and a half. At Le Mans, you cannot fight a car for twenty-four hours. Above all, the car needs to be capable of changing direction quickly and easily in case a slower car pulls across in front of you. It must work on all parts of the track and not just the racing line.

One of the problems is that the faster cars sit lower on the ground. I can clearly recall looking up at the back bumpers of Mustangs and Camaros and finding myself beneath the whale tail of a Porsche 911. I have got to assume – and I also use this principle on the public road – that everyone is going to run into me until they prove otherwise or I know they've seen me.

All of this is compounded at night because every car carries a massive set of lights. It is necessary to tweak your mirrors so that they are offset and you need to move your head to check what's coming. You don't dip your lights at Le Mans, a full set on whatever car you have just overtaken will dazzle your mirrors. So the problem for the back markers is that something can be approaching with lights stronger than anything on a road car. The slower drivers cannot judge how fast that car is approaching simply because they can't look closely in the mirror without being blinded. You might be lapping half a minute faster than many in the field and perhaps a minute faster than a few of them, a performance differential that is even bigger when it rains. And that's another problem.

I much prefer an enclosed car at Le Mans, if only from the safety point of view, but the difficulty is that it has a large, heavily curved windscreen like a jet fighter. Apart from becoming covered in flies and oil, it is shot-blasted by the grit and bits of gravel straying onto the track. There is some help in the form of plastic rip-offs – much as single-seater drivers use on their helmet visors – which are removed from the windscreen and the lights during pit stops. Because the screen is such an unusual bubble shape, very often you get a distorted vision. During preparation for the race, I would search for a screen that was not rippled in any way in the main area of vision – if it's bad, it can be like looking through a poor pair of glasses – and quietly ask my chief mechanic to put it to one side for my race car.

One problem the technicians seem unable to overcome is finding a wiper that can deal with the curved surface. Clearing it at 220 mph is impossible because the wiper simply lifts off the surface although, fortunately, the water streams off the screen and over the car. The trouble starts when you reach a slow corner, or, worse still, coming into the pits at night with a wet windscreen and lights shining from above and all around. You just can't see where you are going and the wiper is the most pathetic, feeble little thing, rather like the wiper on an old Morris Minor.

So, you are coping with that during a wet race while perhaps coming across the same rather slow car every six or seven laps. The overwhelming picture I have in my mind is coming through Terte Rouge, looking down Mulsanne and seeing a dozen cars heading towards the first chicane. Rather than become frustrated, you have to get on with the job. It's rather like a video game; overtake cars as and when they come. One after the other.

As the race wears on, the pendulum swings the other way when more and more competitors drop out. I have turned onto Mulsanne on occasions on a Sunday morning and not seen a single car on the road ahead. You are sitting very low in this racer with its phenomenal speed. You've been with it for sixteen or seventeen hours now. It's comfy and hot, all snug and cosy in the cockpit as you build up speed. As this lovely, lazy old friend pushes you towards 200 mph, the scenery is rushing to meet you and all of a sudden, for the first time, the pair of you are all alone on Mulsanne. It is just such an incredible experience, this feeling of being completely at one with your racing car as it gives you all it's got with such incredible ease.

Then you hear a strange noise. What was that? What *was* that? Could be anything. Check the gauges; everything is OK. Dab the brake pedal; yes, brakes still there. Don't know what that noise was but we're fine. How much longer to go? Yep, that's OK. We're leading. Everything is looking good.

It is the most wonderful feeling.

You have got through the very spooky period just before dawn, the stint that no driver wants to do. If it is not raining, it is almost always misty. You can be hurtling down Mulsanne and, suddenly, there is mist. Before you have time to react, the road is clear again. But there has been a brief period when you have been travelling at 200 mph completely unsighted. This mist seems to float about the place and you don't know when it will appear.

In the evening, the aroma of barbecues makes its way into the cockpit as you rush past the many campsites. The enormous crowd at the start on Saturday gradually drifts away for dinner, returns in the evening to watch a bit more racing or wander through the village at the back of the paddock, where there is a fairground and all sorts of weird and wonderful sights. That's another of the many bizarre things about Le Mans; you could spend twenty-four hours there, rarely see a racing car and yet have a memorable time.

As the race moves into the final stage, the spectators start coming back and the grandstands fill up. The finish at Le Mans is so much better than the end of a Grand Prix. The sense of achievement is shared by the crowd because there is a feeling of having been in this together and seen it through to the end. The camaraderie within the team, between teams and with the public is quite brilliant, unlike anything else in motor sport. And, of course, when I was part of the winning team with Jaguar, the scenes at the finish were incredibly emotional, very different and far beyond the scenes on most Grands Prix podiums – with the exception, perhaps, of the special feeling I experienced on the rostrum at Silverstone. Monza has a podium that stretches across the pit lane and out towards the edge of the track, allowing the drivers and the crowd to share the pleasure of the moment.

The day after the race, there is a curious emptiness. Everyone

Magny-Cours

No one would argue that Grand Prix racing isn't glamorous. It seems strange, therefore, that I should spend a large proportion of my time as an F1 driver in Nevers, a modest town in the middle of France. In racing terms, the only attraction of Nevers was that it was close to Magny-Cours. And the only attraction of Magny-Cours was that it hosted the French Grand Prix and provided the base for Ligier, the team for whom I drove in 1993 and 1995.

Of course, with a racetrack – a Grand Prix track, no less – on their doorstep, it was only natural that Ligier should use it for testing. I spent day after day pounding round and round Magny-Cours. Even more bizarre, and definitely less glamorous, was the fact that much of the work was largely a waste of time. It's true that Ligier would be very quick at every French Grand Prix but it did little to establish a competitive pace anywhere else.

I am in a minority among drivers in that I quite like the track. The racing line is not that obvious. There may be corners that require the traditional angle of attack and textbook driving, but there are others where you take an unusual route. It is a technical circuit in that you need to really know your way round. Given my role with Ligier, that was not a problem; I got to know Magny-Cours

Length: 4.411 km

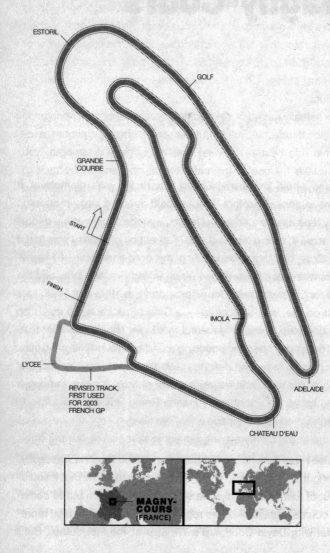

ESTORIL

GOLF

GRANDE
COURBE

START

FINISH

IMOLA

LYCEE

REVISED TRACK,
FIRST USED
FOR 2003
FRENCH GP

ADELAIDE

CHATEAU D'EAU

MAGNY-
COURS
(FRANCE)

inside-out and gained a good working knowledge of how to set up the car, although that set-up remained unique to Magny-Cours as there isn't a bump on the circuit worthy of the name. I don't know whether that has something to do with the foundation or a stunning quality of construction but, more than any circuit in the world, Magny-Cours remains billiard-table smooth, year in, year out.

We actually got rid of the traditional rear suspension springs on the Ligier. It meant we could put the car on virtually optimum aerodynamic ride height. Knowing that the surface is smooth, you could make full use of the car's height and angle of attack to create downforce. Normally, you present the car to the track and that angle will change as the car accelerates and brakes, and the springs and shock absorbers cope with the uneven surface and allow the car to move. Because of the absence of bumps at Magny-Cours, you could more or less lock the car in its optimum position and drive it like that. It was a fantastic experience from a driver's point of view. There was some suspension movement, but not a lot. The majority of the compliance came from the squash of the tyre.

In 1993, I was third fastest in qualifying with my team-mate, Mark Blundell, fourth. It was a fantastic feeling to roll onto the grid directly behind the all-conquering Williams-Renaults of Damon Hill and Alain Prost. I came home fifth that day and fourth two years later. I remember the team patriarch, Guy Ligier, didn't want me to come in for my scheduled pit stop during that 1995 race because I was running third in his home Grand Prix. He was really enjoying the moment and simply didn't want to know that I would run out of fuel if I didn't make a stop. I had no option but to come in, of course, but I could have regained third had I been a bit more forceful with David Coulthard's Williams at the last corner. But, when you are with Ligier, you don't carelessly throw away fourth at the French GP. Guy Ligier applauded me when I came in; goodness knows what he would have been like if I had finished third.

I now manage David, of course, but I quite often regret not actually taking a flying run and bouncing off the side of his Williams. I don't suppose he would have appreciated it, but a very welcome place on the podium would almost certainly have been mine because of the close proximity of the final corner to the finishing line.

That was one of the more curious things about Magny-Cours at the time. The timing beam was on top of the exit of the final, very tight right-hander. You could afford to give up the traditional line on the last lap and, even if you were missing a couple of wheels as the result of contact while pushing past the guy in front, you would still cross the line and register the completion of the final lap. I wish I had done that in 1995. As ever, Ayrton Senna was the first to spot the significance of the finishing line position. He used it during qualifying. His attitude was along the lines of: 'I'm going to banzai the last corner, carry way too much speed, grab the advantage and then I'll spin or I'll crash – but who cares? I'll have done the time.'

That's no longer possible thanks to a revised final corner brought into play in 2003, but the character of the track remains the same. You can give Magny-Cours all the spit and polish you like, but it will always be, at best, an average racetrack. Having said that, the first sequence of curves, a fast left and a long, long right through Estoril, is one of the better corners in motor racing. That combination leads onto the back straight and provides the main opportunity to overtake while braking for the Adelaide Hairpin.

A couple of very fast chicanes follow. The second of these is quite tricky and there have been some big accidents as drivers get the line wrong and bounce across the run-off area. If the track is super-smooth then the gravel traps are always super-bumpy and a car will go flying through the air with no trouble at all.

I've had my moments at Magny-Cours, but only because I have spent so much time there. That said, I had one of the nastiest accidents of my career while testing a Ligier in 1993. As I rushed towards Adelaide Hairpin at about 180 mph, I braked in the usual place, about 85 metres before the corner. The deceleration is incredible at that point. And that was when my right-front suspension collapsed and departed, complete with the wheel and the right-front brake, just when I needed them most. Losing a brake line like that effectively means you've got no brakes at all.

This may seem a very basic failure, but it happens quite frequently. It is caused by a significant load transmitting through the suspension in a reverse direction. The suspension should be able to cope and, clearly, this incident was due to a design fault. It broke like an egg. Off went the wheel and suspension, and ended up in a grandstand off to my right. Luckily, this was a test session and the circuit was closed to the public.

I was helpless, as the car, which had collapsed on one side and become a toboggan, hit the beginning of the run-off area. The gravel should have been level, or slightly lower than the track surface. It was actually sitting three or four inches proud and that sent me and the Ligier into the air. I hit the tyre barrier 100 metres away and the tyres crashed into the cockpit. I woke to see my mechanic leaning over me. I remember thinking that was unusual because the pits were a long way away and yet, suddenly, he was by my side. In fact, the fire marshals should have been first on the scene. I knew that because, during thousands of laps around Magny-Cours, I couldn't help but notice two *pompiers* always sitting in the middle of the circuit. I often thought how boring it must have been for them to sit there, doing nothing, day in, day out. Then I had a massive accident before their very eyes. Their big moment had arrived. But they were clearly convinced I was either dead or badly injured, and were too frightened to move. There was blood everywhere because the tyres had hit the chin bar of my crash helmet, which had then hit me on the nose. I had to go to hospital but I had no injuries other than a bloody beak.

There have been some spectacular incidents at Magny-Cours over the years, most noticeably in 1997 when Jacques Villeneuve did his usual trick of trying the impossible, this time going through the Estoril Curve faster than was sensible. His Williams ran over the outside edge of the corner and into a huge shunt from which, typically, he eventually emerged, dusted himself down and said it was good fun, one of his better accidents.

Any incident on the track would have been the subject of discussion over dinner simply because there wasn't much else to do or talk about in Magny-Cours. I used to stay in the Renaissance, a hotel in the village, and it became a home from home. Because I tested at the track so often I knew the code on the hotel's front door. The food was terrific: all the more reason to get hacked off when I couldn't actually get a room in the Renaissance for the Grand Prix because F1's mega VIPs had claimed them. That was very frustrating because staying outside the village meant dealing with race traffic that is always seriously congested at Magny-Cours.

In fact, just getting from the UK to this part of France is a nightmare. The answer is to fly in by private plane to the small airport at Nevers. Otherwise, you face the misery of flying to Charles de Gaulle, driving round Paris and then two and a half hours spent motoring south. On paper, Magny-Cours looks reasonably close and convenient. In reality, it requires an epic journey, which was a good enough reason to treat myself to the hire of a private jet more often than not.

It was also good to be able to get away quickly at the end of a test session because, likely as not, you would wonder if all the effort had been worth it. The most frustrating thing about Magny-Cours is that it can best be described as a 'Happy Hour' track. The surface may be extremely smooth, but it is very temperature dependent. It gives up grip, almost at the click of a finger. The minute the temperature rises, the car starts sliding or the tyres give up. Maybe this is a French characteristic because Magny-Cours is similar to Paul Ricard. The performance of the tyres can decline very quickly, unlike Monza where you can actually go slightly faster after ten laps. At Magny-Cours, you have to set your best time in the first lap because, after that, you could be two seconds slower. Again, similar to Paul Ricard, this is not helped by a succession of corners that are either long or lead directly from one to the other.

The difference between perfect conditions and anything else is marked. You can go out at 9 a.m. and set the most stunning time and not get near it until it is cool again at around 5 p.m. I remember I did 1 minute 13 seconds with no trouble at all and yet pole position the previous year had been 1 minute 16 seconds. You never see that in F1 because, usually, you are always looking for hundredths and tenths of a second. Yet, early in the day at Magny-Cours, a driver can demolish the official benchmark time because that qualifying lap had been established at a Grand Prix just after midday.

It would be an amazing experience to feel the car working so well; a great way to begin the morning. Then you would start working on the car to improve it further. But, no matter what you did, the car would just go slower and slower. At about 4 p.m. the lap times would start to improve. All of a sudden, by 5 p.m., you were flying again! And you had learned absolutely nothing.

Ligier would pay the price when the season moved to a bumpy track. We had no idea how to set up the car because Magny-Cours was too smooth. It was, and still is, hopeless for tyre testing and that is a complete disaster because, more than anything else in motor racing, tyres dictate your performance. You can spend all day working on areas such as suspension settings, differentials and roll bars and have nothing to show for it. But try a different compound or construction of tyre and suddenly you find a second. Each tyre can take eight man-hours to make and yet, during qualifying, you can write off a set of those in five miles. A really good set might last for half a Grand Prix. In motor racing terms that is extreme, a massive 100 miles!

Tyre technology is very clever but some of it remains a mystery. That chemical relationship between the rubber and the Tarmac, plus variables such as car set-up, humidity, temperature and dirt on the track, do not shake down to a simple formula. The way the various companies make racing tyres is superb but, when it comes to the basic business of how that tyre reacts to a race-track, then there is almost an element of voodoo and educated guesswork. I have lost count of the number of times a driver, in the post-race press conference, will say: 'The car felt really good on the first and third sets of tyres but I don't know what happened with the second set. They were fine when I ran them briefly earlier in the weekend.' There is no doubt that tyres which ought to be identical can vary. And no one really knows why.

A more easily measured and understood factor is tyre degradation, in other words, the drop in performance as the laps go by. You have to take into account the car becoming lighter and faster as the level of fuel goes down and offset that against tyre degradation. Let's say you are going to do twenty-five laps on a set of tyres. There is a relatively predictable downward slope because, on a brand new set, you might do a lap in 1 minute 10 seconds. Twenty-five laps later, it would not be unreasonable to expect that set of tyres to do 1 minute 12.5 seconds, meaning the degradation is 0.1 seconds per lap.

The degradation may be as little as 0.2 seconds in total over a long run on a circuit such as Monza, which is not hard on tyres. At Magny-Cours, however, it could be 3 seconds – which is mighty frustrating for a driver with new tyres. As you leave after a pit stop, the tyre is shiny and you've got much more grip. You think you have time in your pocket, a lovely feeling. But that is when you need to stop yourself from getting too carried away. If you push the tyre immediately, it will give you a reward. But the downside is that the performance will drop off much faster in the following laps.

The choice is simple: you can be careful, treat a new set of tyres with respect and have less degradation over the laps that follow; or you can have the glory laps at the beginning and then pay a massive price in performance from laps ten to twenty-five. Magny-Cours is one of the most extreme examples I know. A driver cannot simply try harder and make up the difference. If you have not got the grip from the tyre, you cannot do the lap time. End of story. A driver needs to minimise that effect by carefully choosing the set-up for his car and driving sensibly.

A typical test day at Magny-Cours would require the use of a control or base-line set of tyres, which the team will refer back to throughout the day. You would make a run, change the car and then return to the control tyres to make a true comparison. At, say, 2 p.m. it would be necessary to bolt on an old set-up and fit the control tyres just to see if you really were any faster with the new piece that had been tried on the car. And, as you reached late afternoon, the track would become faster all on its own, so you wouldn't know where you were. It is a frustrating process.

All of this would be going on mid-week in a pretty desolate area. Having said that, Magny-Cours gets dressed up quite nicely for the Grand Prix. The organisers go to a great deal of trouble, so much so that I reckon they have the best grass-painting anywhere in the world.

I usually do a circuit guide for ITV on the Thursday evening before the race. Naturally, you need background silence when doing a piece to camera and racetracks are comparatively quiet at that time. But not Magny-Cours. It is amazing how many people can get onto a racetrack in the early evening. If they are not cutting grass, or painting it, there is an army of sweepers and they seem to scrub that circuit to death. The result, however, is a circuit that looks extremely smart in the July sunshine.

Apart from the track surface, Magny-Cours has several curious aspects. Elsewhere, the commentary boxes are opposite the pits and require a hike before and after the race. In Magny-Cours, they are directly above the pits, which is very handy, particularly when I'm scuttling back to position after my grid walk.

The paddock, on the other hand, seems divorced from the pits thanks to a location a few hundred metres' walk from the back of the garages. The motorhomes are arranged like a circle of wagons in a Western movie and the unusual family atmosphere is exaggerated by that fact that there are very few corporate guests. The paddock is therefore one of the quietest of the season – and arguably the better for it. Because there is no glamour or razzmatazz in Nevers itself, everyone stays in the paddock to eat. Magny-Cours is a good place for media dinners or simply the chance for rival team personnel to take the rare opportunity to socialise over a beer. It is almost like an F1 Club where everyone gets together during the warm evenings. A nice place to be.

When I was driving for Ligier and perhaps staying on for yet another test, I could see for myself how quickly the track would revert to its usual feeling of cold, grey concrete in the middle of nowhere. If you think of the glamorous image of France, Nevers does not spring to mind. Quite the contrary. I remember once wandering around the town trying to find a pizzeria on a wet mid-week night. It was hardly the stuff of romance.

Length: 5.141 km

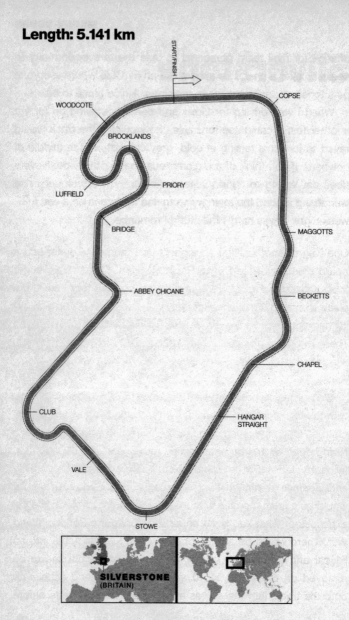

COPSE

WOODCOTE

BROOKLANDS

PRIORY

LUFFIELD

BRIDGE

MAGGOTTS

BECKETTS

ABBEY CHICANE

CHAPEL

CLUB

HANGAR
STRAIGHT

VALE

STOWE

START/FINISH

SILVERSTONE
(BRITAIN)

Silverstone

One way or another, first as a spectator, then as a driver and a board member of the British Racing Drivers' Club, I have spent thousands of hours at Silverstone. You can tell how much the place means to me by the fact that this almost excessive familiarity has not blunted the circuit's appeal for me in the slightest. There is a very special feeling each time I arrive at the place, which is affectionately known as 'The Home of British Motor Racing'.

One of my favourite images of Silverstone has nothing to do with the excitement of a race day or spraying champagne on the rostrum. Quite the reverse, in fact. My vision of a perfect day as a racing driver would be breakfasting at home in Norfolk and then flying my JetRanger helicopter for the 29-minute flight – visibility and weather permitting – to Silverstone for a mid-week test. It would be a crisp morning with the sun beginning to warm the flat expanses of what had been an airfield during the Second World War. There would be a team briefing, then I would settle into an F1 car and wait for the barrier at the end of the pit lane to be removed on the stroke of 10 a.m. Engage first and accelerate onto the track, into the curves at Maggotts and Becketts before powering through the left-hander at Chapel to face what remains, for me, one of the great sights of motor racing.

I'm not talking about a fast, sweeping corner nor a breathtaking piece of scenery. I'm referring to Hangar Straight, a wide stretch of Tarmac that says everything about the character of Silverstone. There is something so inviting, so enticing about Hangar Straight, which dips slightly and then rises gently towards the vast expanse of Stowe Corner, a fast right that seems to dare you to have a go.

I never believed I would have been in a position to say that when I made my first visit here with my Uncle Keith to watch Jim Clark winning the 1967 British Grand Prix. Silverstone has always had a great atmosphere and tradition. It was the scene of the very first round of the F1 world championship in 1950 and British drivers always seemed to do well at home. I also remember seeing Jackie Stewart win here in 1969 and 1971. And then there was an emotional win for James Hunt in 1977 and for John Watson four years later.

But the race in 1973 provokes the strongest memory for me as a spectator, which is not surprising because Jody Scheckter caused a massive accident right before my eyes. My uncle and I used to stand at Copse, the corner at the end of the pit straight. On this occasion, however, I ran down to the outside of Woodcote, which, at the time, was a very fast right-hand curve leading onto the pit straight. It was an amazing place because you could see the cars bucking and moving around on the bumps at about 170 mph.

Jackie Stewart led the field through there at the end of the first lap in 1973. Scheckter was the Young Gun of the day, the South African driving in only his fourth Grand Prix. He was running near the front but slid a touch too wide at the exit of Woodcote, put the left-rear wheel of his McLaren on the dirt – and away she went.

At first it looked as though he would get away with it, as the

McLaren went across the track without contact and then nudged nose-first into the pit wall. But, as soon as it started to roll back in front of the pack powering through Woodcote, you knew there was going to be trouble. It was heart-in-the-mouth time. I stood there and watched as all hell broke loose; wings, wheels, bodywork and dust flew everywhere.

I ran towards the scene of the chaos and climbed the grass bank. And there was Andrea de Adamich, trapped in a Surtees that had careered straight into a barrier attached to the wooden sleepers beneath where I was standing. The race had been stopped. Nine cars were either written off or badly damaged. Considering the carnage, it was amazing that de Adamich was the only driver to be injured – and he was lucky to get away with just a badly broken right ankle and fractures to the left ankle. It was an unforgettable incident and I'm reminded of it each time I see de Adamich in and around the commentary boxes doing work for Italian television.

These days, a spectator would not get near the edge of the track, never mind the scene of an accident. Things were much more relaxed thirty years ago, particularly in the paddock where you could wander at will. Silverstone was particularly good because there was so much room. Part of the internal runways would be used as a paddock for the support races and I remember drifting among the touring cars and spying a red and gold Lotus Cortina. When my uncle said: 'D'you wanna have a sit in it, boy?' I didn't need to be asked twice.

Uncle Keith opened the door and I climbed inside. I was sitting at the wheel, happy as Larry, when someone spotted me and shouted: 'Oi! What d'you think you're doing?'

My uncle said: 'Don't be like that. He's only a youngster. They're the drivers of the future.'

It didn't wash. Martin Brundle, F1 driver and British GP podium finisher of the future, was unceremoniously thrown out of the Lotus Cortina.

I first raced at Silverstone in 1977 when driving a Toyota Celica in the British Touring Car Championship. We would use a little caravan; and my future wife, Liz, and her sister would sleep in the front of the truck. It makes me smile twenty-five years on when I go karting with my son and people come up to me and say: 'Now you know what it's like at the other end of the scale, mate!' Well, I've been there. I've scraped ice off the inside of a caravan window at Silverstone.

We raced on a horrible little triangular club circuit that amounted to no more than three straights and three right-hand corners. That said, there were some good races on that wide track since cars were able to run three, four and five abreast. The various layouts have changed a lot over the years. I was involved with some of them at the design stage when working with the BRDC, which actually owns the entire site. But, whichever way you do it, it will take tens, if not hundreds of millions of pounds to make Silverstone truly glamorous.

Initially, the circuit more or less followed the perimeter road, which meant it was very fast. The Scheckter incident in 1973 spelled the end of Woodcote as a quick corner, the installation of a chicane bringing one of the few places where a Formula 3 driver would need to come off the throttle when using the Grand Prix circuit. Otherwise, it was super-fast through Copse, quick through the left-hander at Maggotts and into Becketts, which, in those days, was a single-right and one of the slowest parts of the circuit at a 'mere' 100 mph. Then it was flat-out down Hangar Straight, flat through Stowe, same again through Club Corner and the fast left at Abbey Curve before taking a slight breather off the throttle on the approach to the Woodcote chicane. Then hard on the power all the way through and away on another lap.

As I said, there have been many variations since then but I must admit I like the circuit in use today. This was the result of fairly major changes for 1991 when Maggotts and Becketts were replaced by the wonderful sequence of curves. The slight infield diversion between Stowe and Club was added at the same time, as was the infield complex running from Bridge round to Woodcote. A final alteration in 1994 saw the introduction of the chicane at Abbey, which was necessary even though it meant Abbey was no longer flat and capable of allowing you to approach Bridge at terrifying speed. Even now, however, Bridge remains one of the best corners among many at Silverstone.

You start the lap by being hurled straight into the fast action at Copse. I like to take people to the inside of Copse because it is the ideal place to appreciate and be stunned by the out-and-out cornering performance of an F1 car. Even those who watch F1 on television and think they know about the speed and forces involved simply cannot believe the energy being generated by an F1 car on the absolute limit through Copse. Here, you see the cars, you hear them, feel them and smell them as they appear to defy the laws of physics at 180 mph. This corner encapsulates that image for the spectator and it is no less awesome when sitting in the car.

You are blasting down the pit straight, often with a westerly wind on your tail to help push the car towards 195 mph, making the approach to Copse one of the fastest parts of the circuit. Then it is a quick lift off the throttle, drop down a gear – so easy with the paddle shift on the steering wheel – and hard on the power while turning into the initially blind right-hander.

Copse has a tiny flat kerb on the exit. It used to separate the track from grass but, in the interest of safety, there is now a Tarmac run-off area. Even so, pointing a car into Copse at those speeds is like threading the eye of a needle. There is no room for error on the exit. That's why you see a lot of cars coming out of Copse and spinning to the inside, where the pit lane exit is.

With Copse dealt with, now you are really on the move and heading towards the supremely challenging Becketts complex. There is a quick left on the way in at Maggotts, which means a weight transfer and the car rolling slightly as you then immediately flick right for the first part of Becketts – with the throttle wide open all the way.

If you haven't actually done it, you wouldn't believe it possible. Indeed, those of us fortunate enough to have tackled Silverstone in an F1 car can't quite believe it either. When I walk the circuit and do a track guide for ITV, I stand at the entry to Becketts and think: 'Now, let me get this straight. They come through here flat out. They definitely do that because I've been flat out through here in an F1 car. But that cannot be possible. Absolutely no way.'

You are aiming for a little serrated kerb: tricky to pick out even in the sunshine; very difficult on a grey day. On top of that, you are often turning across the wind, which means the car moves around a little more than you would like at those speeds.

The downforce curve and the drag curve increase dramatically between 100 and 200 mph. There is an old saying that an F1 car will drive upside down across a ceiling at 150 mph because the downforce exceeds its weight. That curve rises steeply to the square of the speed. If you then put that car into a 20 mph headwind, you have even more downforce. It really pushes the car down and is a wonderful feeling, which seems to increase a driver's confidence in direct proportion to the extra grip. The important thing is not to touch the kerbs because they can really unsettle the car and get you into trouble. The various forces in the aerodynamics and suspension will begin to fight each other and the car will start to move around. Meanwhile, you are focused on the next part of Becketts, a fast left that can be frustrating because the car always seems to slide and leave you in suspended animation.

Throughout all of this, you are working with the fact that even a racing car doesn't like a change of direction when it's already working hard. Having dealt with the left, the second part of Becketts follows in the shape of another right-hander that creates more hard work. No matter what type of car I have driven through there, be it a touring car, F3, sportscar or F1, they have all tended to drift wide and you run out of space on the exit of Becketts. It couldn't happen in a worse place because you are immediately faced with a very fast left through Chapel and onto the all-important Hangar Straight. It goes without saying that a poor exit from Chapel will penalise you all the way to Stowe.

With the engine singing, the car is allowed to gradually drift from right to left, as you diagonal the straight and aim to be on the correct side of the track about 200 metres before the right-hander at Stowe. You don't want to be in the process of crossing the track when you get to the braking zone. You have to be perfectly positioned because Stowe has a very fast entry and this is where you see plenty of overtaking, as a rival, having got a better run though Chapel, uses the momentum to get alongside on the approach to Stowe. I have been overtaken, not only going into Stowe but also, on one startling occasion, round the outside. It could only have been Ayrton Senna.

This was during a F3 meeting in 1983, the first wet race we had encountered at Silverstone. Senna was on pole and I was second fastest. I beat him on the run into Copse and continued to lead as we powered down a very wet Hangar Straight. When we reached Stowe, I took the normal line and began to four-wheel drift towards the apex of the right-hander. When Senna flashed past my left-hand side, off the racing line and apparently without braking, I thought: 'Ha! That'll be the end of him. He'll fly off the road.' But, to my complete surprise, he simply drove round me and into the lead. This was Senna's karting experience coming into play. He knew that the rubbish and bits of rubber lying off the racing line actually offered more grip than the slick, slippery surface I was delicately trying to negotiate. I was attempting to work out what had happened when the race was stopped because there had been a big crash.

When the wreckage was cleared away and the field set off on the parade lap, I thought: 'Right, I'll have a go on that outside line at Stowe.' In doing so I hit a puddle of water and just stopped the car from spinning off at 120 mph. Now I was really confused. We started the race and Senna beat me off the line. We reached Stowe and I decided against any further experiments. Senna carried on in the lead and won the race.

When we got to the podium, I said to Ayrton: 'Your line round the outside of Stowe didn't work in the second part of the race.' And he said: 'I don't know about that. I didn't try it again because there had been too much rain.' How did he know that? He had this sixth sense. It was absolutely maddening. But I learned a lot that day.

Mind you, I got my own back at Silverstone a few months later when there was another round of the British F3 championship that was also part of the European F3 series. That meant the local drivers could race on the faster and softer tyres used by the Europeans but, if they did, any points earned would not count towards the British championship. By this stage, Senna was thirty-four points ahead and he could afford to run the European tyres and try to win the race outright. I stuck with the harder tyres specified for the British series and, while I was the fastest of the local runners by quite some distance, I was only twelfth on the grid. With about twenty minutes of practice remaining, my entrant, Eddie Jordan, and I decided we were doing the wrong thing and opted to make the switch of tyres and forget about the home title race.

The additional grip from these tyres was absolutely incredible. During my one quick lap, I don't think I lifted my foot from the throttle all the way to the Woodcote chicane. I was on pole. Senna was third fastest. He had beaten me nine times in a row and this was the first time I had put one over on him. I legged it off pole. Senna quickly passed Johnny Dumfries, who had been second on the grid, and gave chase. And then he spun twice while trying to catch me.

For the next six races, he either crashed, or we collided, or I beat him fair and square. Suddenly, I was taking massive bites out of his championship lead. Ayrton simply could not compute this. A guy in the same car on the same day was beating him. And the harder he tried to put things right, the more mistakes he seemed to make.

When we went to Snetterton, another former wartime airfield in Norfolk, I gave him half a car's width on the track, leaving the option to pass on the wrong side of the road on the back straight. I thought: 'If you're going to pass me, mate, you're going to have to go the long way round.' He elected to take the half-car option, went on the grass – and we touched. The next thing I saw were the rivets in the undertray of his car in my mirror. As he crash-landed, he floored the throttle in an attempt to hit me amidships with what remained of his car as I turned into the next left-hander.

He missed me and hit a breakdown truck. A few weeks later, they had to remove his car from my shoulder after we had tangled at Oulton Park. It made for an incredible climax to the championship and all of that started at Silverstone.

At the time, the track ran straight from Stowe to Club but now it tightens and runs through Vale before swinging left and then right, making Club much slower than before. Stowe remains a good corner because it still has a wide entry that continues to allow overtaking. But the narrower exit means you've got to be precise. It's very high speed with enough grip to allow you to attack the corner. Then comes a really tricky bit, which catches drivers out because you pop over a blind crest in Vale and reach the braking area for the first part of Club. There is plenty of grip, which explains why there is a lot of overtaking as drivers can afford to leave their braking very late; often too late.

Once into Club, it feels as though you should be going flat out all the way through the right-hander but, in fact, you've got to make a choice. You can either take the inside route, which is shorter but puts more lateral load in the car, or you can travel a greater distance but allow the car its head by going on the outside line. Club looks simple but it requires you to give a bit on the way in, otherwise you will pay the price on the way out.

This is the most westerly part of the circuit and it's from here that you begin to appreciate its sheer size. Set in more than 800 acres, Silverstone has arguably more space inside than any track other than Le Mans. Brands Hatch, in its entirety, could be dropped into the space between Hangar Straight and Abbey. But a drawback of such a wide-open space is the almost continual presence of crosswinds.

Silverstone is 505 feet above sea level and there is more undulation than you would think. The most noticeable part is the rise from Club to the new Abbey chicane. I'm not a great lover of chicanes but this one works quite well. You brake while going up the hill and you have got to take the speed right into the first part, a left-hander. It is essential to be neat and tidy because Abbey has three different levels of serrated kerbs that could rip your car to pieces.

The chicane was introduced because of an accident in 1994, an ill-fated year following Senna's fatal accident at Imola. The rear wing flew off a Lotus driven by Pedro Lamy as the Portuguese driver came through Abbey Curve. The car barrel-rolled, cleared a spectator fence – fortunately, it was a test day, so no fans were present – and landed, in flames, in a pedestrian tunnel passing beneath the bridge. Frightening – and quite incredible. I don't know how many times a stunt man would have to try that to make it work. A chance in a million, I would have thought. How Lamy got in there was matched by the mystery of how he survived. So that was the reason for the installation of the chicane at Abbey.

There is tremendous grip on the exit of the right-hander that hurls the car out of the chicane and into the dip leading to Bridge, so-called because this very fast right-hander is just beyond the vehicle bridge leading to the infield. Bridge, frighteningly quick before the introduction of the chicane, remains a challenge because it is seemingly impossible to take it flat.

When driving for Benetton in 1992, I remember seeing the telemetry readout measuring the progress of myself and Michael Schumacher through Bridge, and, similarly, the comparison between Michael and Johnny Herbert a few years later. Schumacher is simply immense through there. He has a technique that somehow allows him to go 10 mph faster and a way of dealing with Bridge without letting his car scrub off too much speed.

Into the final complex now, rushing out of Bridge towards the left at Priory. It's an 'arrive-and-drive' corner: arrive, knock off a bit of speed and sweep through. The next left is the really tight Brooklands, a corner that has never really worked. It is actually better suited to the national circuit that joins at this point. You cheat across the kerb, which is too low, and the corner nips on the exit. There is very little satisfaction and yet this is an important corner because it sets you up for Luffield, which used to be two corners and was much better. Now it is effectively one corner, difficult to get right and not particularly satisfying in terms of driver feel but rewarding in lap time because it catapults you into Woodcote. This is no longer what it was; more a sweeping curve which is an extension of the pit straight.

Before the introduction of the final complex, we would have what was popularly known as the 'Silverstone Finish' because the old Woodcote corner, and later the chicane, always seemed to be the place for the final move on the last lap. I remember a BMW County Championship race in 1980 where I was fighting Nigel Mansell for the lead. We were flat out and side-by-side through Abbey, rushing towards the chicane. The tricky bit was getting your braking just right: if you were too late, you never made the chicane and would be penalised.

Nigel and I were door-mirror to door-mirror and I decided I wasn't going to brake until he did. I was on the inside so I was going to lean on him if push literally came to shove. Sure enough, he spun off and I went on to win the race, which was pretty helpful at a time when I was trying to make my way into the world of international motor sport. That chicane was the business and I was really sorry when it went.

The start line has been moved further towards Copse because the back of the grid found themselves on the Woodcote curve and unable to see the lights. When the chicane was in operation, it was necessary to avoid it and the last few rows of the grid would form in the escape road, which tended to be very grubby and an unsatisfactory place from which to start.

My most vivid memory of starting a race at Silverstone was when I appeared to be attempting to barbecue half the grid. That was in 1994 when driving the McLaren with the famous Peugeot that caused so much grief at Interlagos and elsewhere by trying to consume itself at awkward moments.

This was a very important race for me. I was in McLaren number eight – Senna's old number – at the British Grand Prix. You can't imagine how excited I was. Even though it was a difficult year, I was enjoying Silverstone because of the fantastic partisan support and the fact that I have always gone well at home. I had been on the podium two years before and, despite starting the McLaren from ninth on the grid, I was full of hope and very much looking forward to the race.

As I took off on the formation lap, the engine was sounding sick – not for the first time that year – and I noticed some blue smoke. I was not too worried because it was necessary for the mechanics to fill the tank to maximum, which caused a bit of oil to find its way into a cylinder and emerge in a blue haze. It was soon clear that my problem was more serious than that as the engine sounded worse and worse. I thought about going into the pits, but there seemed little point, so I took up my place on the grid with the intention of giving the engine a rev in the hope of clearing the trouble.

As the start lights came on, I held the engine revs as usual at 11,000 rpm. I looked in my mirrors and saw a massive sheet of flame erupting from the rear of the car. The oil breather on the Peugeot engine fed into the air box so that surplus oil vapour could be sucked back into the engine and burned. Unfortunately, the entire system had become pressurised and the engine had actually started to consume its own lubricant. Oil was being pumped into the air box and it was no surprise that such copious amounts should emerge from the engine in a sheet of flame. The entire thing erupted.

Immediately after the start, I abandoned the car, walked straight into the pits and disappeared. I shut myself in a cubby-hole in the McLaren truck and cried my eyes out. No one could find me. I was broken-hearted, absolutely distraught. This was the British Grand Prix, my home event, and the telemetry later showed that I had driven no more than 322 yards in a 190-mile race in which I had hoped to do well.

But the trouble didn't end there. Jean-Pierre Jabouille, a former F1 driver who had become the head of Peugeot Sport, was keen to cover his company's backside. He was also desperate to get his mate Philippe Alliot – our test driver – in the car for a race. Jabouille was looking for any excuse. After the race, they got the McLaren back to the pits, added some oil and it fired up. The engine was fine. Peugeot then issued a press release to the effect that I should have carried on. They conveniently forgot to mention that the fire had melted the car's rear suspension, undertray and rear wing, that the engine had used eight of its fourteen litres of oil and was never going to last.

I was then blamed for using the wrong revs on the start line even though the problem was evident on the warm-up lap. It turned out that I was holding the revs in a zone in which the harmonics made the piston rings leak, which ultimately allowed the pressure to go from the cylinders into the sump and send the oil on its way to create the pyrotechnics. It later transpired that Peugeot, in order to reduce internal friction, had gone from three piston rings to two. No one had told me about that or the crucial rev band. Worse still, McLaren, because of internal politics, chose to remain silent about Peugeot's one-eyed account. If I was bitterly disappointed before, I was absolutely livid now.

This race had come off the back of two very eventful British Grands Prix in succession. The previous year I had been heading for a possible third place when the gearbox on my Ligier gave up six laps from the end. That would have made it two podium finishes in a row after a memorable race in 1992.

That year I fought with Senna's McLaren for almost the whole race. I had made a great start, getting ahead of my Benetton team-mate, Michael Schumacher, by jumping from sixth to third at the first corner. Michael tried to pass me going into Becketts but locked his brakes and flew off the road. Senna was right behind me and we began this tremendous battle. It was the first time I had been in a really competitive car since becoming an F1 driver eight years before and, appropriately enough, this was the first time I had been able to fight with Senna since our epic F3 races in 1983, many of them right here at Silverstone.

It was a fascinating contest because the Benetton was really good through Stowe, Club and Woodcote, whereas the McLaren was strong through Copse and Becketts. It was nip and tuck until lap fifty-two when we came to lap Damon Hill, making his F1 debut in an uncompetitive Brabham. Damon didn't see us coming and I got held up on the way through Copse. It was enough to allow Senna to take a run at me and get by. I was really miffed because he had just taken third place from me, and I knew it would be difficult to get him back because our cars were so similar on overall lap speed.

My frustration did not last long. On that very same lap, Senna broke down at Club and I regained the place. The crowd went berserk because now they had Nigel Mansell leading, Riccardo Patrese second in the other Williams – and me third, again.

It all became too much for the Mansell supporters when we finished in that order seven laps later. Mansell-Mania swept across Silverstone in the form of a track invasion that was quite something to see. As I was going down Hangar Straight, I had to slow to a crawl. I'll never forget the moment when a guy jumped out in front of me with his thumb up. Incredibly, he had a small child in his arms and I had to brake to miss them both. It was pandemonium. You are in an F1 car at the end of a race and yet people want you to stop for autographs. Crazy!

Nigel got as far as Club, where he became surrounded and had to stop. I crept back to *parc ferme*, switched off, climbed out and discovered that the Benetton was hissing like an old kettle. An F1 car needs the cooling provided by air passing through the sidepods at speed. It does not like going slowly and the radiators had boiled dry, so much so that the car was fractionally underweight when measured on the scales. Fortunately, the officials made an allowance for what had been going on during that mad slowing down lap.

The scene on the podium was just incredible, beaten only by the emotion felt when I was in the winning Jaguar at Le Mans. People as far as the eye could see, from Woodcote and along the pit straight. All you could hear was: 'Mansell! Mansell! Mansell!' My sister, Helen, was in the middle of it all and she started a chant: 'Brundle, Brundle, Brundle.' The Mansell supporters were – how do I say this – a different breed and one standing near my sister suddenly said: 'Yeah, she's right! Brundle was third. C'mon, you lot: Brundle! Brundle! Brundle!'

That day demonstrated how Silverstone can bring out the best in a driver if he is really hooked up and in tune with the circuit. We saw it more recently when Rubens Barrichello dominated the race in 2003. He tore through the field, pulling off some brilliant overtaking moves and generally humbling any driver who crossed his path.

This was one of those epic Grands Prix where changing circumstances and the appearance of the safety car allowed the drivers to show their immense talent on a circuit that promotes overtaking. It was wonderful to commentate on because I could relate to what was happening, having pulled off similar strokes and also been on the receiving end of plenty. I knew exactly how difficult it was and could appreciate the level of skill as the leading seven or eight cars battled wheel-to-wheel.

When Barrichello and Kimi Raikkonen went into Bridge side-by-side, for instance, it was a game of dare. Going through Bridge flat out, on your own, is memorable enough in an F1 car; doing it two abreast while trying to keep it all together is almost physically and humanly impossible. But you do it. Or, in this case, one of them did because Raikkonen had to come off the throttle and have a moment on the gravel. And that was just one small part of a race which had everything; another Silverstone classic.

It may be flat and featureless but this track provides the most diverse memories of any venue I have ever raced at. And I am probably not alone in this. With the majority of drivers in F1 having passed through the British F3 championship, they will know all about Silverstone. It is at the core of many racing careers and I'm sure the drivers concerned have similar memories, good and bad.

I can recall, for example, the end of a day's racing in 1977 when I loaded the transporter and set off for home – only to be sitting in a traffic jam at 11.30 p.m. while trying to get out of the middle of the circuit, never mind reaching the main road. Thanks to the absence of decent roads, rail links and trams such as we have in Montréal and Melbourne, it was a miracle that Silverstone managed to stay on the calendar.

And yet, despite that, Silverstone has hosted very famous events such as the Tourist Trophy and the Daily Express International Trophy, a non-championship F1 race that used to be held each spring before the Grand Prix calendar became too crowded. I was driving a touring car in the support race in 1978 and it was so wet that day that I spun five times on the river of water flowing across Abbey Curve. I was in good company. The same corner caught the likes of Mario Andretti – later to become World Champion – during the main event.

I also recall competing in the 1999 Rally of Great Britain when Silverstone provided one of the special stages. I was driving a works Toyota Corolla and I thoroughly enjoyed the 6 (and a bit) miles the organisers somehow managed to find by combining the circuit, infield and car parks. Obviously, I knew my way around the track but the loose surface work was quite a challenge. It was brilliant fun and gave a whole new perspective to a venue I thought I knew like the back of my hand.

These are all great memories of driving at Silverstone but one of the most significant had to be my first test in an F1 car. Marlboro sponsored McLaren and that led to the test drive because of my role in the Marlboro-sponsored F3 series in 1983. My dad kept me company as we drove to Silverstone and I remember being so excited. I hadn't yet got my head round being a professional racing driver. I was still a kid who had been in touring cars, moved on to F3 and found himself racing against this guy called Senna. The next thing, I'm sitting in a McLaren as part of a prize awarded to myself, Senna and Stefan Bellof, who would later become my team-mate when I landed the F1 drive with Tyrrell the following year.

I thought the McLaren – number eight, the number I would race eleven years later – was the business. I remember being strapped into this Grand Prix car and heading out of the pits. I just couldn't believe how good the whole performance package was after what I had been used to. The fastest thing I had driven was a 150 bhp F3 car and suddenly I had 550 bhp under my right foot. And I could compare the performance because I had driven other cars on the same circuit. The car had my name on the side and there was even a mechanic cleaning the flies off my crash helmet, typical McLaren attention to detail and way beyond anything I had ever known before.

It was another of those important occasions for me because it led to a very successful test with Tyrrell back at Silverstone a few weeks later. And it was also one of those beautifully crisp days. The car felt brilliant and the track was dry. I was on my way to being a Formula 1 driver. Hangar Straight never looked so good.

Length: 4.574 km

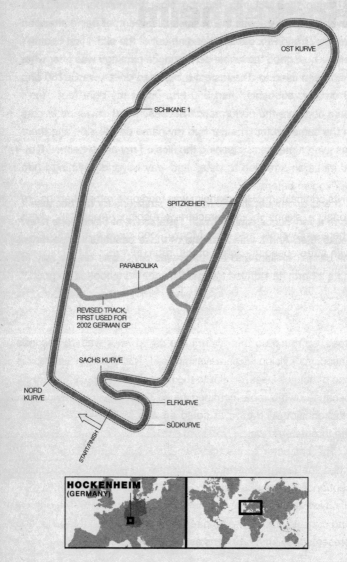

OST KURVE

SCHIKANE 1

SPITZKEHER

PARABOLIKA

REVISED TRACK,
FIRST USED FOR
2002 GERMAN GP

SACHS KURVE

NORD
KURVE

ELFKURVE

SÜDKURVE

START/FINISH

HOCKENHEIM
(GERMANY)

Hockenheim

In its original form, Hockenheim was fearsome rather than inspirational, a skinny 4.2-mile racetrack rushing through the trees. There were similarities with Monza: long periods of full throttle with a top speed in excess of 230 mph, interrupted by chicanes. But Hockenheim was narrow, bumpy and daunting. And that was in the dry. When it rained, which it seemed to do frequently, Hockenheim became terrifying.

The spray would rise off the back of the cars and hang in the trees, so much so that even if the car in front was 10 seconds ahead, your vision was always impaired. The enduring feeling was one of helplessness, similar to the long straights at Le Mans. But, because of the more confined track, it seemed much worse at Hockenheim. All the driver could do was sit with his foot flat on the throttle. And wait.

The character of the track was changed completely in 2002 when the fast back section was replaced by a more traditional sequence of corners and short straights cutting across the middle. Now it is just like any other F1 circuit, albeit with the original and unusual stadium section remaining at the end of the lap, and presents the same problems as any other modern facility.

In the past, the Hockenheim weekend depended on the chassis engineers, aerodynamicists and, above all, the engine builders doing their job, while the driver rushed up and down very long straights linked by chicanes and waited for the more interesting infield section at the end.

The start of each lap was tricky enough back then. Turn 1, the Nord Kurve, was very bumpy, with a little banking and a slight nip on the exit. It was an extremely intimidating corner in the days when the run-off consisted of gravel leading to a barrier. The introduction of asphalt has made the corner similar to Paddock Hill Bend at Brands Hatch in that you could intentionally run wide and actually gain benefit.

Before that was done at Hockenheim, however, there would be a further trap waiting just when you thought you had got through the corner. Because of the little rear wings needed for the long straights, the absence of downforce would suddenly announce itself as the car stepped out of line on the bumpy exit and flicked into a spin. This usually ended against the barrier on the inside of the track, apparently defying the laws of physics, which would favour the outside wall.

Not long after leaving Turn 1 and preparing for the first long run through the trees, a hoarding across the track would provide a suitable reference point for checking to see how many revs the engine was pulling and compare it with readings on previous laps. Racing cars do not have speedometers; in fact, the actual speed reading is irrelevant, which seems a strange thing to say when ultimate speed in the form of lap time dominates motor racing. But the driver needs to know about temperatures, pressures and, most importantly, engine revs and lap time. Speed is dictated by how many revs you are pulling and the gear ratios you are running. A miles-per-hour reading is only necessary in the pit lane where there is a speed limit and, even then, an electronic limiter controls the speed. But, elsewhere, revs are the key and the hoarding across the track at Hockenheim would provide a useful reference as you set off for the first period of maximum revs on the way to the Jim Clark chicane or Schikane 1.

Before this right-left-right sequence was introduced, the track continued its long, lazy curve to the right. During a Formula 2 race in 1968, Jim Clark is believed to have suffered a disastrous puncture. It is hard to credit now but, in those days, there was no barrier, no protection whatsoever between the track and the woods lining the circuit. Clark was killed instantly when his Lotus spun off and slammed sideways into a tree.

This happened in an era when fatal accidents were a regular occurrence on racetracks. It is a measure of Clark's standing, therefore, that his death caused deep shock throughout the motor racing community. Like Ayrton Senna, Clark was so naturally gifted, so in control of his car that he seemed indestructible. That's why 7 April 1968 is remembered vividly within motor sport in the same way that people can recall exactly what they were doing when they heard Princess Diana had died.

I was eight at the time, helping out as part of a support team for my dad on a rally, and I remember sitting on a grass bank near Spalding in Lincolnshire when the news came through on the radio. I had seen Clark win the British Grand Prix at Silverstone the previous summer – his last victory in Britain, as it turned out – and even though, at that age, I wasn't fully aware of his importance, I could sense the gravity of the news through the reaction of the men around me. Here was a twice World Champion who, at the time, had won more Grands Prix than anyone else, a Scottish farmer who had earned the affection of many through his modesty despite being one of the greatest drivers of his era. And suddenly he was dead, killed in a relatively unimportant Formula 2 race on a track very few had heard of. You could understand why people were stunned at the time and yet, looking back now, you wonder why this sort of thing did not happen more often.

Apart from racing with the absence of crash barriers, the drivers did not wear seat belts. Seat harnesses were just beginning to be accepted in 1968, but they were not mandatory. It is difficult to imagine that now. It was a throwback to the front-engined racing cars of the fifties when it was preferable to be flung from the cockpit if the car crashed. That was considered to be a better option than having the car land on your head if it went upside down; or being trapped in the cockpit if the car caught fire – which they did with frightening regularity.

But it is inconceivable to lie in a rear-engined car such as Clark's Lotus without a seat harness. I can't go on the road minus a seat belt, let alone think about doing 200 mph at Hockenheim without one. But in 1968 this was part and parcel of what racing drivers did. Clark's death helped to improve safety, both in and out of the car. And, appropriately, a leader of the crusade was Jackie Stewart, a close friend and fellow Scot.

A memorial to Clark was placed just beyond the chicane that was added not long after his death. This zigzag was made tricky on arrival, as the car tended to jump on the bumps. It never ceased to amaze me how late you could leave your braking when doing close to 230 mph. You told yourself that it was possible to wait until just before the marker board set 100 metres before the corner, but at those speeds it felt that you were much too late and there was absolutely no way you could stop. But, somehow, the speed decayed rapidly and you made it through the corner while, in the days of manual gearboxes, fumbling through the gears and keeping the car in check on the horrible bumps. It was possible to try overtaking but it was so easy to lock a brake and lose vital retardation. Fortunately, the original piece of racetrack acted as an escape road – a well-used escape road, I might add.

When dealing with the chicane itself, it felt necessary to hustle the car across the bumps. You seemed to be fighting the car, pushing like crazy and emerging with the thought that no man on earth could get through there faster than you had just managed. But the trick was to have the car set up so that hustling was the last thing necessary. If you were battling with the wheel, you were probably doing 50 per cent more work than would have been necessary had the car been set up correctly.

Ironically, the small stone cross in memory of Clark had become hidden behind a substantial crash barrier. Not that a driver would have had time to notice thanks to the tremendous acceleration that came with running skinny wings creating very little drag. Because of the long gear ratios, it felt like driving a Le Mans car because of the ease with which speed built up. The Hockenheim gear ratios were spread apart as they had to deal with slow corners and several maximum speed areas. If you had a six-speed box, one of them had to cope with a 50 mph hairpin or a tight chicane while, at the opposite end of the scale, a ratio was needed to help the car exceed 230 mph. It gave a lazy feeling when going up these spread-out gears, unlike Monaco where the driver is changing gear so frequently that, at times, he is selecting the gear he has just left a few seconds before and his feet are constantly dancing on the pedals.

At Hockenheim, your right foot was pressing the throttle onto the stop as hard as physically possible. I don't know why we did that because the car was not going to go any faster as a result. It must have been a preoccupation with returning to maximum speed as quickly as possible while rushing towards the Ost Kurve chicane at the top of the track.

Before the Ost Kurve chicane was installed, this was a very quick right-hander but, once again, it took a fatality to bring the realisation that speeds had out-stripped the corner's practicality. When Patrick Depailler was killed during testing in 1980 due to a failure on his car, it was not long before plans were laid to have the chicane installed.

The approach was almost a carbon copy of the previous one; a bumpy, narrow straight surrounded by trees. The chicane changed over the years. It used to sweep round to the right before a scrappy and undulating left and right, the profile altering from time to time even though the effect was much the same. My main memory of the Ost Kurve chicane is going in backwards in 1993. Mark Blundell and I were really quick in the Ligiers and I was lying third on the first lap. The brakes and tyres were still a bit cold, so I braked earlier than usual. That was my downfall because I hit one of the violent bumps in a manner I had not experienced before and it spun the Ligier through 180 degrees. I went down the escape road backwards, flicked the car towards the correct direction and rejoined the track, still in third place. This was much to the chagrin of my mate Blundell, who thought he had waved goodbye to his team-mate and yet, here I was, rejoining the track in front of him. Mark had the last laugh, however, as I was given a 'Stop-Go' penalty for bypassing the chicane. It was not as if I had used the escape road to steal an advantage. I had been absolutely terrified – as you would be when going in backwards at 200 mph. If I had hit anything, it would have been a wall of aged tyres, which is like smashing into concrete.

The final version of the Ost Kurve chicane did away with jinking left and right, leaving us to go straight ahead, which I always thought was more dangerous, particularly if there was a problem with brakes. A car often fails under braking because there is a lot of loading, similar to the type I experienced in my major smash at Magny-Cours. That's the problem with a sudden failure of this sort. One minute, everything is under control. The next, you hit the brakes and serious loads go through the suspension, causing a failure. With the revised layout of the Ost Kurve chicane, you were aiming at race fans sitting directly ahead in the grandstand. This chicane was always a favourite spot for the slow-motion replays on television. That's when you would appreciate just how little contact the tyres actually had with the track thanks to the kerbs, surface changes and some wicked bumps.

Once through the actual chicane, you were back on the original Ost Kurve, doing a mini Wall of Death while trying to get the car into a straight line as quickly as possible. I refer to it when commentating as 'the line of least resistance'. Whenever you can feel load through the steering, it must be because you are actually slowing the car down. So, the exit from the Ost Kurve needed to be as smooth as possible by allowing the car to run up to the edge of the track and just skim the grass. Jackie Stewart refers to it as 'giving the car its head'. Whichever way you describe it, you loosen your grip on the steering and let the palm of your hand guide the wheel while allowing the car to go where it wants – within reason. At the Ost Kurve, it was important to make the exit as clean as possible because yet another massive straight was waiting.

However much horsepower you have in a racing car, there never seems to be enough and that was particularly evident on the old circuit at Hockenheim. You were only halfway through the lap and all you seemed to be doing was waiting for the engine to build up speed on the way to yet another chicane, this one named after Ayrton Senna. (To my mind, racetrack owners the world over are doing Senna a disservice by naming silly curves and chicanes after the great man.) This combination had a really fast sweep to the left on arrival, then a pathetic little right followed by a bumpy exit on to yet another straight.

Another day, another chicane; whatever they've put before you, hit the brakes, turn the wheel and just drive round the obstacle as fast as you can. There's no point getting upset about it, no point trying to work out what you think they should have done. What you've got is what you've got. It is the same for everyone, so you simply bounce round it to your best ability.

This chicane was particularly terrifying in the wet. Derek Warwick ended upside down because he arrived sooner than he realised and found another car in the braking zone. It was like driving in fog. There have been instances in the rain at Hockenheim when I couldn't even see my own steering wheel. This can be a defining moment for a racing driver. You are in the pouring rain, you can't see where you're going – but you press the throttle a little bit harder, relying on peripheral vision, hearing and blind faith. People ask when Michael Schumacher is going to retire and I reply that Michael will know long before we do because there'll be a pivotal moment when, instead of pushing his foot hard against the throttle, he will lift off – and it will bother him. Only he will know that it happened; it will be imperceptible to the world at large.

The chicanes were mechanisms to stop Hockenheim being a flat-out blast from the moment you left the stadium to rejoining again. Regardless of how this loop to the Ost Kurve and back was configured, it was largely irrelevant, and I can understand why the circuit was changed. The way it was, you could make a tenth of a second on the straight by trimming the wings but then lose it when braking on the bumps. Yet you could make at least a second by setting up the car just right for the stadium section at the end of the lap.

It was a lonely business pounding between the trees and it seemed particularly strange during the pre-race driver parade as we stood on the back of a flat-bed truck and chatted to each other for the want of something better to do. There was a little grandstand at the Clark chicane and another at the Ost Kurve. Otherwise, there was absolutely nothing for about a mile, and nobody out there except marshals.

Almost every driver has a story about breaking down and getting lost while trying to walk back through the woods. There was no perimeter track on the old circuit. The only way the emergency vehicles could move around was on the racetrack itself. So, if you became stranded in the outback, you could either wait to be picked up at the end of the session or try to make your way through the trees.

You would start off in the general direction of the pits but quickly become disorientated because the sound of cars was coming from all around and echoing through the woods. It was possible to end up on the other leg of the track – but no further towards the pits. It was frustrating because, if this was morning practice and there was time left, you knew a spare car was waiting in the pits. But unless you had a GPS navigator in your back pocket, it was better to stay put and accept your fate.

This flat-out drive through the middle of nowhere tended to exaggerate the contrast experienced when arriving in the packed stadium, which is still used today and remains more or less unchanged. There was a danger, however, of making a very embarrassing entrance.

The right-hander leading in was – and remains – a difficult corner because you could never see it. It is deceiving. There seemed to be excess track on the left, but this was too dirty and bumpy to use. Even though you knew the corner was there – it's not as though somebody created it while you were out in the woods – it would catch you by surprise when arriving at such high speed.

In addition, there is a kerb at the exit with a rut just beyond. If you drop off the kerb, your left-rear wheel finds the hole and down you go, into a spin. It was particularly difficult when running cars in the trim needed for the old circuit because the absence of downforce would compound the problem. Then, just when you might have a chance of getting out of trouble at the exit, the kerb stopped and the accompanying hole would ensure you were doomed from that point on. All that foot-to-the-floor stuff, all that hanging on for a couple of miles, would go to waste with the end of the lap in sight.

Whatever version of the track is under discussion, the stadium section provides an entertaining conclusion, starting with the busy entrance and the quick blast to the Sachs Kurve. It is possible to brake quite late – but not too late. The corner is cambered in your favour but, if you arrive too fast and go high on the outer edge, the car will be flicked off the track. It is very easy to get sucked in by following the car in front too closely and, if he goes off, you do the same, almost before you have realised it.

Now you are in the heart of this fantastic stadium with seating all the way round. You can really appreciate the full extent of the noise and the colour during the parade lap to the grid when flares, fireworks and horns go off on all sides – particularly if 'Schumi' is having a good day. It is an incredible experience. Talk about a circuit of two parts. When racing on the old track, it was like taking part in a mid-week test session and then suddenly racing into the middle of a huge event. There is no time to relax and enjoy it, however. Once through the Sachs Kurve, there is a little left-right chicane, which you can take flat with the benefit of grip from new tyres, but not at other times because the car will start to get away from you as the road goes off-camber and into a slight dip leading to the final two corners.

An F1 car never wants to go through the first right-hander. As you come off the little chicane, you are braking, downshifting and the roll in the car is going the wrong way. When this releases, you have horrible oversteer, which was even more pronounced when running so little downforce on the long circuit. This clumsy corner is made even worse because the pit entrance follows on the right, just at the point where you are trying to sort out the car on the opposite side of the track.

The final corner is quick and bumpy as it leads onto the pit straight. With the new version of the track, this is now the second-longest straight; previously, it was a short burst compared to the long hike to and from the Ost Kurve. You can argue both ways about the effect. It is easy to view the track through rose-tinted glasses and claim that Hockenheim is not what it used to be. But, in truth, what they have done is remove a section where the drivers were doing nothing but risking their lives. Nobody was watching and it was boring for TV.

So, instead of heading off into the trees, the track turns sharp right and then curves gently left on a brisk run towards a wide hairpin. This makes sense because it ensures the cars more or less stay together. You need an easy corner followed by a long straight into a wide entry point for heavy braking into a hairpin. There is no doubt about it; this does create overtaking.

The hairpin feeds onto what was the return leg of the old track, just at the point where it left the Senna chicane. But, rather than barrel straight down to the stadium, the track then moves through a flat right and a medium left, neither of which appeared to work until Fernando Alonso and Jenson Button had their epic side-by-side battle in 2004. Then a flat right with acres of space before rejoining the old circuit again and rushing towards the entry, which continues to surprise drivers as they reach the stadium.

A major plus, of course, is that the increased number of laps meant the fans in the stadium can see their beloved Michael sixty-seven times instead of forty-five. On the other hand, when tackling the track in its original format, the cars were really tippy-toe through the stadium. It was a great place to watch and, indeed, it was the only part of the track on which the driver could have fun.

Hockenheim used to be like Spa in that it was very difficult for a driver to keep track of what was going on in the race. The cars would quickly become spread out because performances always seemed so disparate. If you had good power and the car worked on a low-downforce circuit, you were super-quick; if it didn't, you were nowhere and there was nothing a driver could do about it. And, in the interim, you would just lose track of the race.

Commentators would have less difficulty in following what was going on but, very often, it would be a challenge finding something to say as the cars came by with huge intervals between them. Indeed, there were times when just one car could be seen making its lonely way through the stadium.

The commentary boxes are slung beneath the roof of the main grandstand opposite the pits. To get there, you have to brave the German fans, many of whom are unique. Armed with beer and loud horns, they consume one and blow the other with equal enthusiasm.

The same atmosphere prevails as you enter the circuit by a bridge leading across a motorway. This autobahn is one of two that run close to the track and they are, in fact, the reason the stadium was built. Originally, the circuit ran to a hairpin at the edge of town and then speared through the trees, all the way back to the Ost Kurve. Motorway construction effectively truncated the track and the owners wisely put the financial compensation to good use by building this massive stadium at the point where the old circuit was cut short.

If you know the tricks of the trade, you can get into and out of the circuit via the back of a motorway service area. Otherwise, with such a large crowd drawn from the population centres of Mannheim, Frankfurt and Stuttgart, access can be a nightmare. People moan about getting in and out of a Grand Prix once a year, but those who work in F1 have to do it every eight to ten days. It can be quite an issue, but that's part of the job – as much as running the gauntlet of the fans lining the bridge leading to and from the paddock. It is not uncommon to find a big aggressive guy, complete with a stein of beer, who is willing to stand in front of your car until you sign all the autographs. Refusal is not a sensible option. I remember one fan who ran onto the track during the race in 2000. He was a disgruntled ex-Mercedes-Benz employee who wished to make a point in the daftest way possible and was just as likely to kill a driver as well as himself. We thought it could only happen at Hockenheim and then we had exactly the same problem when an Irishman in a kilt took it upon himself to run down Hangar Straight at Silverstone in 2003.

As a driver, the thought of a person on the track really scares you. The terrible proof came at Kyalami in South Africa in 1977 when a well-meaning young marshal carrying a fire extinguisher ran across the track to attend to a car that was on fire. He did it just beyond a crest on the main straight. Tom Pryce came over the rise, running side-by-side with another car, and hit the marshal. Both were killed instantly, Pryce by the fire extinguisher, which hit him on the head.

Racing drivers don't suffer from shock in the same way as ordinary motorists, who might need time off work after an accident at 50 mph. Racing drivers know that, sooner or later, they are going to have an accident. You drive at high speed, week in, week out, testing, practice, qualifying, race. You know that you will make a mistake, or the car is going to break, or someone else is going to make a mistake, or the track conditions are going to become impossible. Whatever the reason, you are going to crash. It's a question of when, not if, and so when it does happen, there is no shock involved, which is why you see drivers jump out of a pile of carbon fibre and run back to the pits, ready to get into the spare car. But he is not ready for a guy in a kilt running at him on Hangar Straight. A driver's office is his cockpit. Like anyone else in their place of work, he gets into a routine; he knows what to do and what not to do. Throw a lunatic on the track and drivers are going to make rash reactions. You never come out of Chapel Curve and wonder if there might be someone on the track in the same way that the drivers accelerated towards maximum speed at Hockenheim in 2000 without expecting to come across a man brandishing a message on a bed sheet.

Hockenheim is easier to keep secure now that they have done away with miles of track in the back of beyond. Despite the radical change to the character of the place, and the July heat, the German Grand Prix remains enjoyable, particularly for the British media, after the hype and fuss generated by the previous race at Silverstone, a return to normality, if you like. There is a lot of tradition attached to the race even though the Grand Prix has only been coming full-time to Hockenheim since 1977. This race seems to mark the start of the so-called 'silly season' as driver moves for the following year are announced. The rumours start earlier each year but something always seems to be happening on that front at Hockenheim. This circuit usually marks a turning point as the championship heads towards the final stage of the season. In 2003, for example, three of the contenders wrote themselves out of the race at the first corner, Michael Schumacher finished seventh and Juan Pablo Montoya shot to contention by leading from start to finish. That's the sort of thing that can happen at Hockenheim even if the drivers are no longer being frightened silly by those long straights to nowhere and back.

Length: 4.381 km

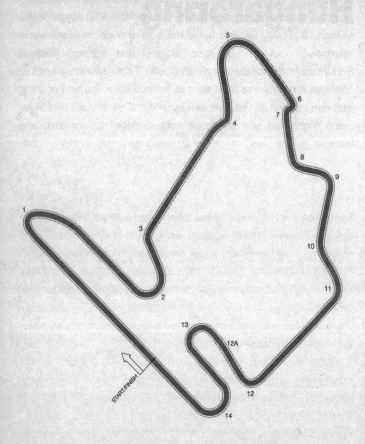

HUNGARORING
(HUNGARY)

Hungaroring

Racing on the Hungaroring has been described as Monaco without the houses. That's a blunt and misleading comparison in some ways and in others absolutely valid. The Hungarian Grand Prix is one of the toughest on the calendar and yet some might argue that the Hungaroring has no place in a book about brilliant racetracks. But every venue has a particular character and, once you get to know it, that circuit assumes a unique identity by offering its own inimitable challenge.

The Hungaroring is a case in point. Here is a track which, through the letterbox slot of a full-face crash helmet, looks much better than it does when beamed into your living room through the lens of a television camera. It may be tight and dusty but I liked the circuit from my first visit in 1986. Nothing has altered my opinion since. If anything, this race, along with the track, has improved with age. As for Hungary itself, the country has changed out of sight since I first went there, over twenty years ago.

Since the fall of the Berlin Wall, Budapest has not been immune from the spread of Western culture; indeed, the impression is that the city welcomed the social and economic change with the same enthusiasm it greeted the first Grand Prix to move behind the Iron Curtain. The arrival of the F1 circus in Hungary provided a culture shock both for the locals, who were in awe of the shining trans- porters and their million-dollar cargos, and the teams, who were dismayed by the quality of the hire cars waiting at the airport – assuming you could get one.

If you booked six months in advance, you got a Lada 1500, a car that was considered a luxury in Hungary, so much so that there was a five-year waiting list to buy one. In Britain, if someone arrived in a showroom hoping to trade in a Lada, the first reaction of the dealer would be to look the other way and pretend he was busy, anything but face the prospect of having to take in a Lada as part exchange. And yet in Hungary, I was annoyed if I couldn't rent one.

The Lada was opulence itself when compared to a Trabant, the car I eventually managed to hire on that first visit, and I counted myself lucky to be at the wheel of this smoking two-stroke. I was not alone. The cream of motor racing society made quite a sight as they chugged around the city, the pungent smell of fumes belching from these tiny little cars with their faded paintwork and cardboard bodywork.

Back then, it seemed that the shop windows were usually empty in Budapest, a city of frayed, somewhat stark elegance, and yet a glitzy Grand Prix was taking place in the middle of this obvious hard- ship. But the feelings I had were nothing like the sadness I felt when arriving for a Grand Prix in Mexico City in 1986 not long after parts of it had been devastated by an earthquake. The city was literally trying to drag itself up from the rubble and there we were, playing extravagant games with racing cars. I didn't feel the same sense of guilt in Hungary but, nevertheless, there was a feeling of discomfort because these people had nothing. There was very little choice when it came to suppertime. Usually, it was goulash soup and a piece of meat. But I have always been struck by the dignity of our hosts, who are polite, determined and justifiably proud of their majestic capital.

The Hungaroring is 12 miles to the east of the city. Even in 1986, there was a motorway, the M3, which was very impressive as far as it went. Which wasn't far. It led towards Miskolc – wherever that is – but in actual fact, for some years, the motorway only went as far as the racetrack. One day, I missed the slip road, drove on for a short distance and, suddenly, it was as though I had dropped off the end of the world. The motorway stopped and, presumably, you had to find your own way to Miskolc on very rural roads.

Whatever your mode of transport or the route chosen, it was worth the effort, even though the circuit and its surroundings had a barren look for the first few years. Set in a large bowl, the pits and main straight are arranged along a high plateau, the track then dropping into the valley, where it runs its tight course before climbing towards the high ground once more. Standing at the back of the paddock, you can see the circuit for much of its length.

In 1986 the Hungarians had done the very best job they could. One of the limiting factors had been the quality of the surface. This was clearly a very low grade of asphalt that had been designed to last for a number of years, the impression being that you could polish it long before it ever wore out. In addition, the track would remain very dirty and slippery off-line. There were twenty-six starters in 1986, every driver going for the same piece of Tarmac. If pushed to the outside, you were immediately at sea, virtually hanging on to the edge of the racetrack while anyone on the inside, on the racing line, would rush past as if you were a beginner.

This was particularly evident at the first corner on the opening lap. Much closer to the pits than it is now, it was downhill from the starting grid and the race became manic immediately as everyone stayed off the brakes as late as possible and went for position. The scramble continued down another slope and into Turn 2, the field opening and then concertinaing into another mad bunch as everyone braked for the long left. Having negotiated Turn 1 safely, Turn 2 would catch you out, a trap that still exists today. Arriving in a pack on the first lap with drivers coping with cold tyres and cold brakes, it is a recipe for crash-bang, and wings and bits of bodywork everywhere.

Even when running on your own, Turn 2 can cause a fair bit of embarrassment. I spun my McLaren during practice in 1994 because the corner is slightly off-camber, downhill and dirty; not what you need when accelerating out of Turn 1. I sat in the middle of the track with my foot on the brake, pretending I couldn't get the car out of gear. Sure enough, they had to stop the session because I was on the edge of the racing line. They recovered my car, took me back to the pits, where it was quickly fired up once more and I was able to rejoin practice and get on with the programme. It was very naughty but I was not the first driver to pull that stroke. Today's regulations outlaw such mischief.

The initial layout of the Hungaroring included a very silly, unnecessary loop that followed immediately. It was created to avoid an underground spring but serious drainage work in later years meant bypassing the loop to a quick right-hander at Turn 3. This used to be a great corner because it was full throttle across a bump in the middle that was nasty enough to cause the car to bottom out. That really got your attention because there was a tricky kerb on the inside. It was a brilliant feeling when you got the corner just right; otherwise it was plain frightening as you hung on and hoped for the best. Then one or two influential drivers complained and had the bump removed, leaving the corner so easy that you can do it with one hand on the wheel – well, almost.

The climb from this point to Turn 4 has seen several memorable moments. In one of the greatest drives among many in his career, Nigel Mansell managed to box in no less a star than Ayrton Senna behind a back marker as Nigel swept through to take the lead in 1989. It was a sensational end to a great performance because Mansell had started from twelfth on the grid – on a circuit where overtaking is supposed to be very difficult.

This is also the place where, in 1997, British hearts sank as Damon Hill lost the lead just as he was about to give the Arrows team what would have been their first victory in twenty years. Damon – the reigning World Champion at the time – qualified in the back half of the grid, his best finish (of just four in ten races) being a distant sixth. But Bridgestone tyres – then in their first year and only supplying the smaller teams – made a huge difference until Damon suffered a technical problem with the throttle. On the last lap, he tried in desperation to ease Jacques Villeneuve off the road on the climb between Turn 3 and Turn 4. But it didn't work. The Williams went on to win with Damon struggling home second.

The last thing on Damon's mind at that point would have been just how great Turn 4 is as a corner. The bumpy left-hander is on a crest and completely blind, with a nasty kerb waiting on the outside of a very narrow exit. The result of getting onto the kerb is like having a pair of giant hands picking up the car and dragging it off the road, or spinning it to the inside and certain contact with the barrier. Go to the outside and you would be in even more trouble, as I discovered in 1996.

The aim, of course, is to stay off the concrete but, when I went over the kerb with the Jordan, I thought I would get away with it and simply drive through the gravel trap on the other side. To my amazement and horror, the run-off area ripped all the wheels off the car. There were some nasty furrows in the gravel and the effect was to shatter the suspension.

The following straight is just long enough to build up speed before pitching the car into Turn 5, a corner that I really liked. This right-hander tightens slightly on the exit, but you can really attack it. There are corners in motor racing where I found myself clench-ing my teeth, particularly during qualifying. Turn 5 at the Hungaroring was one of them. The reason was that the bumps made it incredibly difficult to apply the throttle smoothly. Your right foot would bounce up and down and jiggle the pedal, the problem made worse by modern technology and electronic throttles. Pressing the pedal simply turns a potentiometer that then sends a signal to the engine. There is none of the resistance you would feel if the pedal was connected to a cable running back to the throttle springs and slides on the engine. The oscillation of calf muscles is compounded by the washboard effect of the bumps. The driver finds himself stabbing the potentiometer unnecessarily and causing the power to come in uncontrollable bursts just when he doesn't need it. The only way to sort that out is to simply floor the throttle and have your right foot pushing against something solid. Clenched teeth are required as you hang on and wait for the incredible grip available at the exit of Turn 5. In this corner, adren-alin is the energy source and grip is the reward for getting it right.

That done, a really tricky little chicane is waiting; a right and a left where a driver can make or lose a great deal of time, particu-larly during qualifying. The entry is difficult to see, so much so that the most common mistake is to leave your braking too late. It is easily done when covering 70 metres every second. Get it wrong by a single metre and you will go sailing past, straight into the gravel.

In some ways, it is better to do that than attempt a recovery, which would involve running over a kerb that makes your eyes water just to look at it. The kerb exceeds the ride-height of the car by about three to one and just doesn't bear thinking about, particularly when you are reclined on the floor with your manhood as one of the first points of contact should the bottom of the car take a hammering. So, inevitably, if you brake too late, your instinctive reaction is just to drive off the circuit, go through the gravel trap and rejoin – which every driver has done numerous times.

Yet another chicane follows at the end of a short straight and it was here that I ran into the back of Michael Schumacher during the Grand Prix in 1992. We were racing closely and Michael was tucked up behind Riccardo Patrese in the all-conquering Williams. This was a typical story of our season together at Benetton in that Schumacher had out-qualified me but, in the race, I was faster. Trouble had begun during the first lap when Michael got out of shape and, as I tried to overtake, he simply drove me clean off the road. I've not failed to remind Michael about that during TV interviews because he's done it to other people several times over.

We know he drove Damon Hill off the road when they were fighting for the 1994 championship in Adelaide. He tried the same thing with Jacques Villeneuve at Jerez in 1997 and we have even seen him attempt to nail his brother into the pit wall at the Nurburgring. He is so brilliant you wonder why he feels the need to do it. It is as if he has a mindset that is triggered as soon as a rival attempts to overtake although I have noticed that more recently, particularly in 2004, he has tempered this habit. It is true that drivers can become pretty ruthless once they pull on a crash helmet, but there is a code of conduct, a line that must not be crossed.

WORKING THE WHEEL

You can go right up to that line when racing for position. I have done it, even to Mark Blundell who is almost a blood brother to me. We were racing at Estoril in Portugal and he was making it difficult as I tried to pull off a legitimate pass at 150 mph. I had the line into the corner but Mark was not going to yield. So although I put him in a position where he ran out of road, I would never actually have pushed him off the road. In this case, Mark had a choice. There's a subtle difference between that and simply turning in on a driver as he comes by. After the race, Mark and I shared a hire car and flew home together. It was a little quiet but we got over it: all's fair in love and war – and motor racing, it seems.

Schumacher, however, seems to work to different rules. I was pretty unhappy with him in Hungary in 1992 even before we became trapped behind Patrese. Then, when we reached the back chicane, Michael had to slow more than expected and I tapped the back of his car with the high nose on the Benetton. I didn't think too much of it because contact had been minimal. But it would turn out to be poetic justice. A few laps later, at 170 mph on the main straight, the rear wing suddenly flew from his car and fluttered high in the air like a crisp packet on a windy day. I had actually broken the support for the wing when we touched and now Michael was pirouetting off the track. He didn't find it funny, but I thought it was hilarious.

Turn 9 follows the previous corner very quickly, an in-your-face right-hander that is clumsy, slippery and bumpy. You barely feel under control as the corner tightens on the exit and you appear to have no answer for the track at this point. Nearly every driver will agree that the last thing you want is a corner that seems to tighten on itself. Once you've slowed the car down and done your best through the apex, you want to get on with it. You don't want a corner that makes you have to start all over again.

The fast left kink that follows always seems harmless enough until you suddenly fly off the road for no reason other than catching a bump the wrong way. So far as I was concerned, I didn't want to get that wrong because I was already looking forward to a corner which I always adored.

Turn 11 is very fast: fifth gear but not quite full throttle, with nowhere to go if you get it wrong. And yet the beauty of this corner is that you will be rewarded if you push that little bit harder. All the work is done on the way in and, if you don't get that right, there is nothing you can do: you are going off the road.

When a car slides off and rejoins, it brings a lot of dust and dirt back onto the track. This adds to a persistent problem created by the arid countryside surrounding the Hungaroring. It is common for a driver to finish one practice session with a fair idea of how his car and tyres are working. Yet, when he goes out a few hours later, it is like starting all over again. The movement of thousands of spectators kicks up the dust and this has a much greater effect on the track than you would believe possible. It is much more noticeable at the Hungaroring than anywhere else.

The final part of the track was changed in 2003. It used to run downhill to a right-left chicane that was off-camber and, once again, sent a lot of cars off the road. In 1992, the same year that I had the incident with Michael's rear wing, I remember losing top gear and it really cost me on this final run towards the back of the pits and along the main straight. A piece of metal had got stuck in the selectors and I couldn't get sixth gear. I was running at maximum revs in fifth but everyone was catching me and passing, drivers such as Mika Hakkinen and Gerhard Berger. Then they spun in front of me at this chicane and I performed one of those pathetic 'spin off in sympathy' moves that cost me a place.

That sort of thing can happen with embarrassing frequency.

You can't really see the track because you are glued to the gearbox of the car in front. He has a spin and you do the same. It happens on the public roads but it is not supposed to happen in high-level motor racing. However, going into a blind, very fast chicane, you are instinctively guided by the rear wings and gearboxes of the two cars in front. If they go off the road, you can find yourself sucked into their accident. In this instance, I bounced round the outside but Hakkinen managed to rejoin the track just in front of me and we finished fourth and fifth.

But when it comes to heartbreak at the Hungaroring, the last lap in 1994 was the most painful for me. I was with McLaren, and Hakkinen, who was my team-mate, had been banned for causing a start line accident in Hockenheim. Mika had been the Golden Boy of the team but, in Hungary, I was number one. And, boy, was I enjoying it. Apart from loving the track, I was revelling in the new-found responsibility and the fact that the team were focused on me instead of Hakkinen. I was absolutely flying and the feeling of well-being was increased by seeing my temporary team-mate, Philippe Alliot, really struggle. As I'd discovered at Silverstone in 1994, McLaren's engine partner, Peugeot, had been desperate to get the Frenchman a race drive. This was their chance. And he was absolutely nowhere, qualifying fourteenth, eight places behind me.

I had lapped Alliot on my way to a really solid third place when the team came on the radio and said the battery on my car was starting to go. The engineers in the pits generally know what's wrong with your car long before you do. I backed off and did a number of things to save power. With eleven laps to go, Schumacher, who was leading, came to lap me. That was going to suit me fine because, if he overtook, it would mean, when he completed the race, that I would have one less lap to do. The team reckoned I might just make it, even though the alternator was not working and I was running purely on whatever power was left in the battery. An F1 car is a massive drain on the battery because systems such as the engine and gearbox control units depend on it. These black boxes are power-hungry. But, when they stop, you lose the throttle, the ignition, the ability to shift gears, everything.

I was trying to coax the car home when Michael came up behind me. I moved over and let him through – and that was a crucial mistake. It triggered the thought in Schumacher's mind that I was too helpful. He immediately got on the radio to enquire about the whereabouts of Jos Verstappen, his Benetton team-mate, who was behind me in fourth place. When he heard that Jos was catching me, Michael slowed right down and I had no option but to unlap myself. If I had stayed behind Michael, Verstappen would have caught me and I would have lost my third place. So I had to go back on the same lap as the leader and prepare to do another 2.5 miles.

Michael also let Verstappen unlap himself; another clever move because, as soon as the leader crossed the line, anyone who had been lapped could not complete the last lap. Now Verstappen and I had to finish the seventy-seventh and final lap.

Sure enough, at the top of the hill between Turns 5 and 6, my car ground to a halt. Verstappen passed me. The fact that every-one else had been lapped and therefore could not take fourth from me was absolutely no consolation. When I finally got a lift back to the pits, I looked up at the podium to see Michael, Damon Hill and Verstappen spraying the champagne. The timing could not have been worse. I was two miles short of standing there myself.

By working all that out, Schumacher had shown exactly why he has won so many championships. His mental capacity is one of the things that sets him apart. All the great champions that I've raced against have needed only 70 per cent of their capacity to drive the car while the other 30 per cent is used for reading the track, the race and the politics in and out of the car. If you look at a typical grid, the majority are high-level drivers and there really isn't much more than half a second a lap between them. The difference is their mental capacity. Those who have not had much success in F1 have needed 95 per cent or even 100 per cent of their ability to drive the car, leaving nothing in reserve to sort out everything else that is going on during the course of a race. This incident in Hungary is just one of a number of examples which demonstrate Michael's brilliance in that area. Ayrton Senna, Alain Prost, Niki Lauda and virtually any past champion you care to mention were all the same. That is why they were so good.

Less impressive was the manner in which Berger removed me from what would have been third place in 1993 when going through the penultimate corner, a left-hander at Turn 13. Gerhard had been struggling to get his Ferrari ahead of my Ligier, and I think he must have become bored because, coming into Turn 13, he whacked into the side of me. Cleverly he made sure it was wheel-to-wheel contact in order to lessen the damage to his car.

The impact bent one of the track rods on my car, which meant I needed a quarter turn of the steering wheel in order to keep the car in a straight line. A visit to the pits confirmed there was nothing that could be done. So they gave me a fresh set of tyres and I rejoined. Despite the unorthodox angle of the steering, I was absolutely flying. I actually set my fastest time with the car in that condition, all of which proves that you must be able to drive round any problem and get on with it rather than worry about what's wrong and effectively throw in the towel because the car is less than perfect.

This sets everyone wondering just why so much time is spent measuring and setting up the car to the nth degree when the steering can be knocked completely out of kilter and yet the driver goes faster than at any other point in the race. When the Ligier mechanics later checked the full extent of the damage, they looked at the impressive lap times and threw their hands in the air, the French version of 'Why do we bother?'

Even when your car is working perfectly, one of the trickiest corners on the Hungaroring is the last one. There is a horrendous bump, which has always been there. I didn't mind that because part of the challenge is making your car work on whatever a track surface throws at you. And this one is really difficult. Just as you are getting ready to go through the long right-hander, there is a massive 'boomph!' as this shock passes right through your spine and punches the air from your lungs at the very point when you are trying to hang on to the car and sort it out. You actually spend a lot of time during practice making sure the car can deal with this single bump.

In addition to that, there is never any grip in this corner. You seem to spend ages travelling through the corner, waiting for the moment when you can nail the throttle. It comes at about two-thirds of the way through when the car suddenly hooks up. But it is so frustrating because the main straight beckons and one of the few opportunities to overtake at the end of it. Yet you know if you push too soon, you will be punished.

The first corner has been pushed further down the hill, giving a longer run into a braking area that, as I say, constitutes the main chance to pass someone. But that can be virtually impossible if the driver in front keeps his wits about him – just as Thierry Boutsen did in 1990 when he kept Ayrton Senna at bay for the entire race. Mansell, on the other hand, used part of the pit lane exit emerging from the right to execute a brilliant move on Senna a few years later. It goes to prove that the Hungaroring is not quite as bad as Monaco because it is possible to get by if you bully your way through.

In what seems to be two very brief decades, the Hungaroring has created quite a history, for all its apparent blandness. The first race in 1986, for example, was a very popular event, thanks to the novelty value for the local people and the fact that the admission costs were subsidised to encourage a massive turn-out. Of the 158 F1 starts I made, this was one of the most memorable. I recall standing on the grid and being aware that there was something very different, very strange about the scene. At first, I couldn't work out what it was. Then I realised it was the silence.

There were 120,000 people there that day, the vast majority packed onto the spectator banks rising steeply from the outside of the main straight. I felt like a gladiator in the ring. All these people were looking on in almost complete silence, not knowing what was going to happen next. It's true that a number of fans had come across the borders from Germany, Austria and Italy but, fundamentally, there were a lot of people present who had never seen a Grand Prix live before. The unusual sense of calm was tangible. I felt you could hear the proverbial pin drop.

In the years since, the Hungaroring has often settled the world championship. Nigel Mansell had his golden moment there in 1992 and Michael Schumacher clinched his fourth championship in Hungary in 2001. I'll never forget the latter because, in terms of television politics, this was a particularly low point for F1. Bernie

Ecclestone was trying – unsuccessfully, as it would turn out – to establish his own digital television coverage. He wanted the best pictures and he wanted people to pay to see them. He got the former but failed in the latter, one of the few commercial misjudgements Bernie has ever made. But, at the time, it meant he would not allow terrestrial TV companies such as ITV into the compound to film Michael celebrating his title. We had to resort to filming the new World Champion through a wire-mesh fence. That was a black day for the sport, so far as I was concerned.

But even while all this was going on, everyone was thinking about getting to the airport for the late-evening flight. It remains a drama now because, although the airport is not far away as the crow flies, it is necessary to go into the city and come back out again. But, if it's a performance now, it was a frightening farce during the first few years of the event. Because the traffic was so bad and the road leaving the circuit hopelessly inadequate, the organisers laid on convoys with police escorts. One would leave the paddock every half hour or so and, for some F1 people, this would be the highlight of the year. For many, though, it was plain terrifying.

There might be as many as twenty cars with their hazard lights on, led by a couple of motorcycle policemen who were being paid for the pleasure. The problem was that spectators would join in and, before you knew it, the convoy could be thirty cars and more. To avoid this, one had to drive nose-to-tail and the whole thing became more and more aggressive with every mile. The police would add to the tension by lashing out with their big leather boots in the direction of drivers who were either unwilling or not quick enough to get out of the way.

The journey would become more and more outrageous until, finally, this mob steamed into the airport with half the original number missing. The hire car return area looked like a wrecker's yard, as the cars were given back with panels dented and sides taken out as a result of people losing control and bashing into each other. It was such sheer lunacy that I eventually decided it was safer and probably just as quick to make my own way to the airport.

After the first Hungarian Grand Prix in 1986, we were in no hurry to leave in any case because the next race was just seven days later, across the border in Austria. My wife, Liz, and I liked the idea of travelling down the Danube to Vienna by jetfoil. We thought it would be romantic.

The first hint that this might not be the case came when we edged out of Budapest and noted that the Danube was a serious shade of brown. The trip lost much of its appeal during the remaining five hours, as we saw nothing more than gunboats and trees with the occasional military person on the shore. In addition there was no catering to speak of, just a few curly cheese sandwiches and sickly-sweet orange squash. Unappetising as it was, if you didn't get in quickly, there was nothing to eat. Finally we were deposited somewhere equally unattractive in the back end of Vienna. So much for the romance we had envisaged. Driving a ropey hire car in Hungary had more attraction, which sums up the state of the country at the time.

These days, you have the pick of the bunch when it comes to rental cars. It is a sign of the enormous change that Hungary has experienced since our first visit in 1986. Budapest has become a cosmopolitan city – with prices to match. Whereas a taxi would cost 20p fifteen years ago, the same journey now is £10. You could live like a king on £20 for the weekend; now that will not buy a half-decent bottle of wine.

That does not detract from the experience in any way.

Budapest is a wonderful city and the racetrack remains a huge challenge. Seventy laps of the Hungaroring in the heat of summer puts this race on a par with Monaco. It may not have the grandeur or the billionaires' harbour, but the circuit is no less of a challenge.

Length: 6.973 km

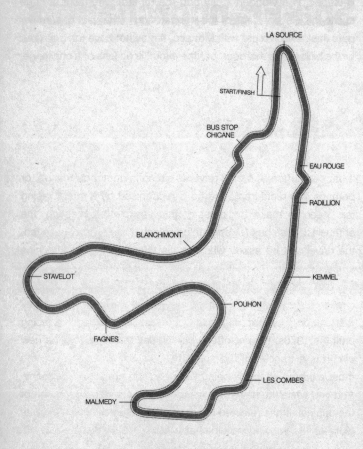

LA SOURCE

START/FINISH

BUS STOP
CHICANE

EAU ROUGE

RADILLION

BLANCHIMONT

KEMMEL

STAVELOT

POUHON

FAGNES

LES COMBES

MALMEDY

SPA
(BELGIUM)

Spa-Francorchamps

It happens often. A racing driver is sitting in an airport lounge, or perhaps in a restaurant, and he is recognised by a motor racing fan. Keen to make the most of this unexpected meeting, the enthusiast searches for something to say. Nine times out of ten, the driver will be asked which is his favourite circuit. And nine times out of ten, the answer will be Spa-Francorchamps.

I can't think of a single driver who would not have the Belgian circuit on his shortlist. But it always means the 'new' Spa rather than the original version, which was in use for international racing until the 1970s. It's not often you can say that. Usually, the new circuit is a truncated and anaesthetised version of the old, the most extreme example being the new Nurburgring in Germany. And yet, while the new track is indeed a shortened adaptation of the original, it has retained the essential character of Spa in all its glory while removing genuine hazards.

It is easy to trace the former circuit, as it makes its way down public roads towards the town of Stavelot and then returns along the opposite side of the valley to the point where the existing track rejoins it. It is simply mind-blowing and no surprise at all that many drivers lost their lives there. It was very fast, extremely dangerous and clearly had to change.

WORKING THE WHEEL

The answer was to use two legs of the old track, where they run to and from the hairpin at La Source, and link them with a new section across the middle. Until recently, that meant the track was of two different types; the new part was purpose built while the old sections remained public roads. Now, much of the original part is no longer in daily use as a public highway but, until a few years ago, drivers faced the usual hazards associated with racing on a main road – white lines, bumps, grit and rubbish. And yet, within three minutes, you would be reaching more than 200 mph several times per lap.

It was very noticeable when driving a sportscar because the grit would make a powerful sound in the wheel arches at those speeds. It was a reminder – not that you needed it – that this was not a superbly maintained and groomed racetrack. It was a public road, albeit it nice and wide but with a crown in the middle and the usual drainage channels at the sides. When practice finished, there would soon be two-way everyday traffic on the same piece of road.

The first leg, starting from La Source, takes you plunging down-hill to the famous Eau Rouge switchback, which then shoots the car uphill and onto the long climb through Radillion to Les Combes, the highest part of the circuit. Now, instead of swinging left and away through the frighteningly fast curves at Burnenville and on towards the town of Stavelot, the track turns right and into the new section.

This link, rushing downhill and then gradually rising towards the far side of the valley, has been designed brilliantly. It includes a left-hander, one of the trickiest corners I have ever encountered, which leads into the downhill charge to Pouhon, a very quick corner that has become the most difficult challenge on the circuit, surpassing the recently modified Eau Rouge. Then on through a fast chicane to a couple of challenging right-handers named Stavelot, because this is where the new rejoins the old.

The effect is to have a new section of pure racetrack leading towards the original, and, appropriately perhaps, the fast right-hander at Stavelot has a nasty bump in the middle. It is most satisfying in any kind of racing car because there is a lot of grip and you are sweeping through with the forests on either side. It is the very essence of Spa and its surroundings in this corner of the Ardennes.

Back on the main road, it is foot hard on the throttle with the immediate prospect of a sweeping right and then left, followed by Blanchimont. This 90-degree left-hander used to be positively horrifying. Recent modifications have reduced it to just plain scary because the introduction of a run-off area on the outside means it is no longer necessary to run between two steel barriers with absolutely no room for manoeuvre. It used to be like a street circuit environment, but taken at 190 mph. You didn't lift from the throttle and, just for good measure, there were a couple of ugly bumps in the middle. The only thing that slowed you down slightly was the scrub of the tyres and the G-force as the car tried to drift sideways. A truly heart-stopping place then, and an enormous challenge even now.

This fantastic, fast-flowing run has to end somewhere and it does so at the Bus Stop, so-called because it is structured like a lay-by. At first sight this appears to be a crude means of slowing cars down as they approach a left-hander leading onto the pit straight but, appropriately for Spa, it is actually an enjoyable challenge. On the approach, you are braking on a curve from very high speed. Suddenly, you have got to be in first gear and swinging left and right between two tiny kerbs. The organisers have tried every way they can – using high kerbs, bollards, tyres – to stop cheating at this point with more elaborate changes introduced in 2004, but a racing driver will always minimise the angle of a corner and the length of the racetrack. That's his job.

There has been plenty of dramatic overtaking at the Bus Stop and I have had a couple of silly spins there. The key to a great corner is that it should just fall short of being flat out, and there used to be a very challenging right-left on the exit of the Bus Stop where a good driver could always make the difference. Unfortunately, it has been smoothed out with very low kerbs and a new piece of asphalt, so much so that it is hardly worth a second thought now. But if the Bus Stop has been made easy, then the sting has been removed completely from Eau Rouge.

The routine on arrival in Belgium was always the same when I was driving. I would fly into Brussels, drive around Liège and reach the village of Francorchamps. With the pits and La Source hairpin just a half a mile away, you would instantly sense the atmosphere, because the road soon became the actual racetrack. And that piece of track would continue downhill from La Source to Eau Rouge, nestling at the bottom of the hill with an even steeper climb waiting on the opposite side.

No matter how many times you had raced at Spa – I have been round it thousands of times thanks to several Grands Prix, loads of sportscar races and twenty-four-hour marathons in touring cars – it was difficult not to look at Eau Rouge as it was and feel a dryness in the mouth. Particularly if you stood in the bottom of the dip with the track coming down from the left and what appeared to be the side of a mountain on the right. It would actually take your breath away for a second or two and I often said aloud: 'I don't remember it being that tight!' The thought of taking Eau Rouge without lifting from the throttle seemed absurd. And yet, by the end of practice, it was definitely on the cards. Of course, you had to have a little confidence lift on a bump or a kerb, and a mental note that it wasn't quite flat. Jacques Villeneuve proved the point when he tried to take it at full throttle in the BAR in 1999 and had a horrendous accident.

I have been through Eau Rouge at full throttle and top gear in a sportscar, but only because that class of car had so much downforce and would appear to be glued to the road, especially on a good set of tyres. I did, however, manage it in an F1 car in 1984. I remember journalists saying that my Tyrrell team-mate, Stefan Bellof, and I were the only drivers on full throttle through Eau Rouge.

It was true. We were coming out of La Source and accelerating in a crazy way down the steep hill. The effect of speed would be heightened by the location of a steel barrier on the driver's right. This marked the edge of the old pit lane that was used for sportscar racing, but not for F1. The track curves gently to the right and drivers would skim the barrier while accelerating hard. If you stood beside the barrier, you could feel it ripple as the approaching car bulldozed the air in front. That in itself is a buzz. Then to watch a driver reach the bottom of the hill, flick left, right and up the hill was just amazing. So you can imagine the effect of watching and listening when a Formula 1 car sweeps in and the engine note does not falter. To watch it happen in the pouring rain defies words.

In fact, the only reason Bellof and I were flat out that day was because the Tyrrell-Fords, the only cars with normally aspirated engines, were comparatively slow. We were actually going into Eau Rouge about 20 mph slower than the guys with turbocharged engines, which were pushing them down the hill at an incredible rate of knots. They had no option but to lift.

WORKING THE WHEEL

In any case, flat out through Eau Rouge is sometimes not all that it seems. I began to work out that it was slightly quicker to briefly lift off the throttle. It is a transient thing because the dynamics of the car change at that point. If you lift slightly in the middle, there is less of the huge compression in the dip that can really unsettle the car and cause the driver to work more at the steering. That would actually make the car slower on the way out of the corner – which was critical because of the very, very long uphill climb to Les Combes.

It's a strange thing. I have never fully understood why this happens but, if you lose speed at the beginning of a long straight, you never fully recover. You would think that the car must eventually catch up again, but it doesn't. So, by keeping the car calm in the dip and powering cleanly out of Eau Rouge, it has the longer-term advantage of maximum speed all the way up the hill.

Of course, such logic did not divert paddock chat about who did or did not take Eau Rouge flat. It was a macho thing, particularly before data acquisition told the story of every twitch of the right foot. These days, your engineer can give you a piece of paper that shows, quite clearly, you were not flat out. But, before the arrival of telemetry, you had to rely on what the driver said.

I can recall the American driver, Eddie Cheever, saying he was flat out in the Jaguar sportscar in the 1,000 km race in 1988. Which he undoubtedly was. But he was also using his left foot to dab the brakes. And, because this was a sportscar, the brake lights would come on. Unfortunately for Cheever, everyone standing in the old pit lane could see the flash of red.

All that, sadly, is in the past. Eau Rouge was resurfaced in 2003 and, whilst it has the same radii and incredible undulation in the racetrack, it is now simply a great risk without being a great challenge because it is absolutely flat out from the word go. Drivers come out of the pits, go though it once on their warm-up lap and, by the time they return two minutes later, it is full throttle. There is no learning process.

It used to be that you built up to Eau Rouge throughout the weekend until your final qualifying lap. You'd start with a bit of a lift from the throttle and a dab of the brakes on the way in, followed by another lift halfway through. Then you would forget the brakes and, eventually, not lift on the way in, leaving just that bit in the middle. Finally, and inevitably, someone such as Villeneuve would go over the top.

But that is no more. Eau Rouge is easy today. Which is why Pouhon has taken its place as the ultimate challenge at Spa. Pouhon also has a fast downhill approach but it is not full throttle on the way in, even though it is on the exit. The driver can make the difference if he stays on the throttle longer and replants it earlier against the stop.

The weather is always a key factor at Spa, regardless of the time of year. It can work both ways. The track was resurfaced in 1985 but, unfortunately, the Tarmac was not cured and traditional overcast conditions were required. Instead, the sun split the trees. It was the hottest I have ever known Spa. It wasn't long before the racing line, which of course gets the heaviest treatment, began to crumble during F1 practice. They ran a F3000 race on the Saturday and that finished it off completely. The Grand Prix was postponed until later in the year.

Thanks to the pine forests that dominate the area, Spa seems to have its own microclimate, particularly at the top of the hill. You can be pretty sure that you will run wet-weather tyres at some point during the weekend. It's a matter of reading the changeable conditions as best you can. Ayrton Senna once refused to come in to change to wet tyres because he was so convinced the rain was going to stop. It didn't and he spent a crucial part of the race on slick tyres. That is part of the challenge at Spa. It does rain hard and consistently but, because the track is such high grip with fast corners, the racing line dries quite quickly, which means there is a critical moment when you can pick up some grip, more so than other racetracks in the wet.

I have had some amazing experiences at Spa. I won sportscar races there and enjoyed good results in F1. But, more than anything else, I'll have to live with the fact that I really should have won my first Grand Prix there. It was in 1992, the year Williams-Renault were dominant. At Spa, it boiled down to Nigel Mansell and Riccardo Patrese, followed closely by Michael Schumacher and me in the Benetton-Fords. It was wet and changeable and the Williams pair were not getting away. I was on Schumacher's gearbox and we had Mansell and Patrese in sight.

As I came out of Les Combes, I felt a new level of grip and I remember thinking: 'I'm fourth. Where am I going to pass Michael? It's going to be difficult because we have identical cars and tyres. I'm going to have to do something different; pull a fast move when it comes to changing tyres.'

The rain had stopped and the track was starting to dry. As we came to the first part of Stavelot, Michael ran wide and I passed him. Until that point, I made my mind up to stop for slick tyres at the end of the lap. The Benetton had a very low front wing. Whenever you went off the track, it was virtually certain that the wing would be ripped off. Michael rejoined behind me. His front wing, surely, had to be broken?

We swept into the Bus Stop with the two Williams just ahead of me and I could see they weren't stopping as they passed the pit entry and started another lap. Also, the track seemed a little wetter at this point. I began to wonder if it was perhaps too soon for slicks. I also noticed that Michael fell away from me as we went through Blanchimont, seemingly a confirmation that he had broken his front wing. I elected to do one more lap.

Michael decided to go into the pits and he received the slicks that were ready for me. If I had gone into the pits, he would have had to wait because he was behind me. I made a critical decision – the wrong one.

Michael rejoined and started to do quick sector times on slicks. I came in at the end of the next lap, the Williams pair doing likewise on successive laps. But, crucially, Michael's pace had been such that he managed to leapfrog all three of us. I ended up side-by-side with Patrese as I came out of the pits and he just beat me through Eau Rouge. I was back in fourth place again.

Michael lucked into what would be the first of many wins, thanks to his mistake at Stavelot. But Michael had noted the state of my rear tyres as he followed me just before the stop. He could see how bad they were and knew he should take the waiting slicks.

Although wet tyres have very clear tread blocks, they become a blur at speed. You can see some discoloration but not the condition of the tyre. Only when you go into a slow corner does the tyre circulate slowly enough for you to see the tread more clearly in your mirrors. But the problem is, if it is a tight corner, you are busy driving the car. You don't go into somewhere like the Bus Stop looking at your rear tyres because you will make a mistake and have a silly spin. You can see the front tyres easily enough. But the following driver has a much better view of your rear tyres. One way or another, Michael was very fortunate at my expense and he has been honest enough to say as much.

That race brought home the fact that it is a long lap at Spa. The race tends to be over quickly in terms of tactical choices because there are a shorter number of laps. (Each Grand Prix must not be less than 305 kms or 189 miles, except in the case of Monaco, which is only 260 kms, or 162 miles, because of the time taken to complete the race thanks to a lower average speed.)

It means pit stop strategy is very critical. If you call it wrong, then there is the best part of five miles to go before you pass the pits again. The race is the same length as usual but it feels different because you might make your first stop after just ten laps, maybe less. And because the track is so long, it is also very difficult to read the race because the cars become spread out. Quite often, a driver can find that he is racing along all by himself with not another car in sight, unlike Hungary, for example. There is no Diamond Vision screen to give you a quick flash of information, no adjoining stretches of track, such as at the new Nurburgring where you can see cars going in the opposite direction and measure your pace. At Spa a driver can feel quite left out and the feeling of isolation is made worse because the car-to-pits radio will only work on certain high parts of the track.

None of this helps in changeable conditions if you are not sure what the ultimate pace should be. Say it is a drying track. You think you are somewhere near the limit, but you don't want to go over it otherwise you'll smash your car to pieces. You don't have small accidents at Spa. I have frequently radioed in to ask for the pace. That's when you discover you are perhaps two seconds a lap faster than anyone else and it confirms your suspicion that you ought to back off slightly. You are effectively running on a narrow track because the road is wet either side of a drying racing line. You are on tramlines that become wider and wider as more and more drivers edge it out. You can go very fast on-line because there is a lot of grip. But if you stray beyond that at Spa, you go straight to the scene of an accident.

It all came good in 1995 when I finished third for Ligier. It was another race of changeable conditions, but this time I called it right by staying out instead of stopping for slicks. The great thing about Spa is that, up at Les Combes and at the following left-hander, the racetrack falls away into a big valley and you have a great view of the sky. The wind tends to be westerly so you can see the weather coming in. I spotted the bad weather making its way across and that helped me decide to stay on wets even though the track was drying rapidly.

The trouble was that every single tread block on all four wet tyres had a blister because of the punishment dealt out by the high-speed corners. Damon Hill was running ahead of me but stopped to take on slicks and then had to change back again. Trying to pass me, he came down the outside going into La Source and he spun – mainly because I didn't know he was coming. He caught me again on the last lap and managed to take second place. There was nothing I could do. My wet tyres were shot and I had to use the wet side of the track simply to keep the tyres cool. Damon passed me as though he had an extra gear, even though I was doing 190 mph. The Ligier-Honda was nothing like as quick as the Williams-Renault in a straight line. It is a classic story of racing at Spa. The race was won, predictably, by Schumacher.

People loved working at Spa as well as driving there. I remember one particular occasion during the European Touring Car Championship. It was pouring with rain and a mechanic was in the old pits on the steep downhill run to Eau Rouge, wrestling with a rear axle. He was lying on his back, and water was gushing down the pit lane, straight into his collar and back out through the bottom of the leggings of his overalls. But he was so busy he didn't notice. That's what working at Spa could be all about.

The twenty-four-hour races brought mixed feelings. The Jaguar XJS touring car, one of my favourite race cars of all time, was beautiful to drive at Spa. It was very fast and seemed to float through the corners. We were nineteen hours into the race in 1984 and, inevitably, someone's engine had blown up and dropped oil all over the track. The marshals put down cement dust to soak up the oil. With just over four hours to go, the Jaguar broke down at Blanchimont. I had been following another car that had kicked up the dust, and the Jaguar, which was very hot to drive, had two scoops sticking out of each side window in order to direct fresh air towards the driver. The fine grit had then been channelled through the fresh air ducts, directly into my face and eyes. I climbed out of the steaming, smoking car and began to walk back to the pits. It was around midday, the sun was shining into my face and a television helicopter was hovering overhead. The cameras captured me trudging along, very unhappily, with my eyes streaming from the dust. I was scowling at the helicopter and my facial expression must have said everything about one of those moments in a twenty-four-hour race when a driver is asking himself: 'Why am I doing this? What's the point?'

Primarily, Spa is about the feeling that comes with driving a really good lap. The pleasure is generated by a combination of the length of the lap, the majestic setting, massive undulation, which you simply do not get anywhere else, and the variety of corners. Hairpins, chicanes, medium-speed and frightening corners: a whole band of challenges behind the wheel of a good racing car on a circuit where the driver can really make his mark. This is a circuit that gives back what you put in. That's why it is so satisfying and why it's the favourite track for nine out of ten drivers.

Length: 5.793 km

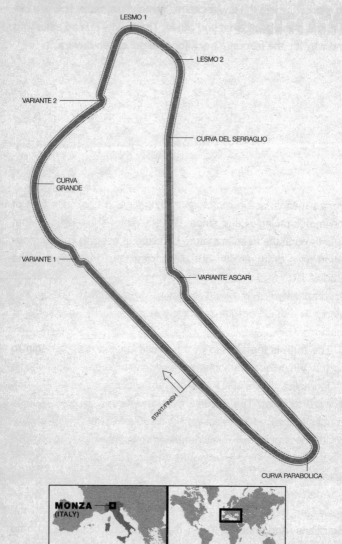

LESMO 1

LESMO 2

VARIANTE 2

CURVA DEL SERRAGLIO

CURVA
GRANDE

VARIANTE 1

VARIANTE ASCARI

START/FINISH

CURVA PARABOLICA

MONZA
(ITALY)

Monza

Monza means fast in motor sport language. It has been part of the motor racing scene since 1922, a pistol-shaped track that cuts through the trees in mature parkland. It used to have a reputation as a dramatic flat-out blast from start to finish but the gradual introduction of chicanes changed all that. Looking at the uncomplicated layout, you would be forgiven for thinking that Monza is a relic from the past and has no place in modern motor racing.

The truth is that a map of the circuit does not even begin to portray the unique atmosphere. I loved racing there and now, as a TV journalist, the Italian Grand Prix remains one of the races I look forward to most. The circuit's past and its frayed surroundings imbues Monza, which is essentially a suburb of Milan, with a wonderful sense of history, inescapable from the moment you arrive in the town, never mind entering the parkland through those ancient gates.

Apart from providing wonderful food and restaurants full of character, the locals have a passion for F1 that is equal to the Brazilians. And let's not forget that this is one of Ferrari's home Grands Prix, Imola being the other. Throw in a warm September afternoon on this classic circuit among the trees and you have a feeling of well-being that is hard to match.

Surprisingly, perhaps, the actual track, for all its apparent simplicity, creates a wonderful theatre for spectators and an extremely tricky test for the drivers. The two Lesmo corners at the top of the circuit used to be very difficult to drive; there were a number of accidents there until officials decided to tighten the pair of right-handers. On such a high-speed circuit (with a lap average in excess of 160 mph) it goes without saying that the car needs to be good in a straight line and stable when braking for the slow chicanes.

These aspects are mutually exclusive. For a good top speed, you need small wings. These create minimum drag but, conversely, they provide comparatively little downforce – required when braking from 230 mph to 70 mph in just over 100 metres. Nonetheless, the need for performance on the straights wins every time, which means the car will always be quite skittish under braking.

You can tell immediately if your team has found a low-downforce package that works. Venture out on the first lap, rush into the Ascari chicane on the back leg of the circuit and hit the brakes. If the car is dancing all over the place and the front wheels lock under braking, and then the rear wheels do the same when changing down through the gears, your heart will sink. And having it right one year does not automatically mean that the same team will achieve the same results in twelve months' time.

Downforce is another one of the mysteries of motor racing. Because it squares with speed, downforce will be colossal at 220 mph and you really feel the effect of it as you hit the brakes. The front of the car will go down immediately as the weight transfers and there is a lot of braking capacity. But in the same way that downforce increases with speed, it comes off just as dramatically as the speed diminishes under braking. All of this is happening in mere tenths of a second. As the downforce comes off, the car actually starts to rise. If you look closely, you can see clear air begin to appear beneath the chassis and this contributes to the mounting problems the driver is experiencing as the car suddenly becomes very lively.

A lot of the downforce comes from the relationship between the underside of the car and its angle and proximity to the road. When the car begins to rise, the effect of this area of downforce reduces and you have to rely on the grip of the tyre and the downforce created by the car's upper surfaces. But because this is Monza and the wings are very small, the tyres are more or less left to do all the work. This is the complete opposite to Monaco, where you carry the largest wings the regulations will permit because you don't need straight-line speed on the narrow streets. Monte Carlo is all about corners, braking zones and traction. The downforce is so great that you can feel the car being pushed into the ground from the moment you get into second gear.

At Monza you really notice the difference, particularly going through the very fast Lesmo corners in their former guise. If you got Lesmo 1 right, then you would be even faster into Lesmo 2 and yet you had to take the 90-degree right-hander flat out. The track is let into the woods and, because the circuit owners are not permitted to cut down a single tree without a major enquiry, there is nowhere to go on the outside of the corner. So, paradoxically, if you got the first of the two corners absolutely right, the second one would be even scarier. And it would be bad enough at the best of times because, of course, the car had very little downforce. If it started to get away from you, an enormous accident was almost certain.

A number of people experienced just that. I recall John Watson crashing there in 1981 and breaking his McLaren in two. He sat in a perfectly intact chassis on the inside of the track, trying to restart the engine. Unfortunately for John, the steaming remains of the Ford V8 were lying on the opposite side of the road, such was the force of the impact.

Lesmo 2 in its former glory was one of those corners where your tongue became dry and you took a bite out of the seat with your backside. The second Lesmo could be a terrifying prospect, particularly if your car wasn't working. And quite a frightening place to be, even if you were not sitting in a racing car.

During test days at Monza, when work was being carried out on my car, I would jump on a moped and take one of the internal roads leading to the inside of the Lesmos. As there were no spectators and perhaps very few cars on the track, it would be so peaceful. All that would suddenly change with the sound of an approaching car through the trees, the high-revving engine giving the impression it was about to disintegrate. You would get goose pimples as the car suddenly burst into view and rocketed through Lesmo 2 without the driver lifting his foot from the throttle. On the approach, you had heard air intake noise, a slightly muffled sound compared to the assault on your hearing as the car disappeared down the straight towards the Ascari chicane. Now your senses would be assaulted by the untrammelled shriek of the exhaust giving maximum decibels.

I could stand there all day, even now, watching F1 cars tackling this top section of Monza. The place oozes tradition. When the track was built, it incorporated massive banking that still stands and loops across the existing circuit. The weathered and over-grown grey concrete is so steep that it is impossible to climb to the top without going on all fours but its presence adds to the feeling of being somewhere special, a place where you can almost hear the ghosts of the past.

The feeling is particularly evident during the mid-week test. You may be watching a single practice lap in a season of many thousands of laps but this driver might go through Lesmo 2 on the very limit. And yet, that lap will quickly become lost in time. You probably couldn't even find a record of it in the archives of the team; that lap on that test day in that year. And yet it remains imprinted on the mind of anyone fortunate enough to have witnessed it. The level of energy generated was no less than it would be in the Grand Prix and it happened in a park, a place you would normally associate with peace and tranquillity on a summer afternoon.

When you fly in by helicopter, it is easy to see how the actual track is almost smothered by acres of trees. It's not a sight I see very often these days since qualifying as a helicopter pilot. Thanks to the restricted space created by the cutting in the woodland, helicopters have been known to fly into each other. You see them reversing out of the wooded glade used for landing and take-off, and it seems pretty chaotic to me. Very Italian; very Monza.

It seems appropriate that Monza should be the place where I actually managed to pull off the stunt of finishing first and second in the same race. This was the 1,000 km race in 1991 in my favourite sportscar, the Jaguar XJR14. There was so much downforce that the Jaguar felt like an extension of the driver; you could almost think it around the racetrack. Teo Fabi was in one car and Derek Warwick in the other; they were both up for the championship. I couldn't do all the races that year because I was primarily driving for Brabham in F1, so I was more or less Jaguar's 'super sub', occasionally driving both cars.

As usual, the plan was to have me start the race in one car and finish it in the other. One of the cars needed an engine change just before the start. They managed to complete the swap, but too late to get the Jaguar onto the grid. It meant I would start this car from the pit lane.

Unlike the standing start used in F1 and most forms of racing, sportscars get under way with a rolling start. These cars are designed for long-haul endurance events and making a standing start with a heavy car (compared to an F1 car) can wreck the transmission before the race is barely up to speed.

There were seventeen cars on the grid and I had to wait until they had all rushed past before getting away from a standing start. Just to add to the difficulties, because Monza is an elongated circuit, one half was still wet and the other dry after an earlier shower. I was on slick tyres for the first time that weekend, but without the benefit of a warm-up lap to discover exactly where the track surface might be slippery. A tricky set of circumstances, to say the least.

I shot out of the pits, passed nine cars and found myself eighth at the end of the first lap. The team, looking for me further down the order, didn't see me go by and thought I must have crashed. Two laps later, I was third. And then came another shower of rain, which mainly affected, of all places, the two Lesmos.

I'll never forget looking in my mirrors and seeing rooster tails of spray. Sportscars with such huge amounts of downforce simply suck the water off the track. It was that wet and yet, despite being on slicks, I couldn't make the wheels spin because of the downforce pushing the car onto the road. So I just pressed on. In four laps, I gained 20 seconds on the Peugeot of Keke Rosberg and took second place by passing the 1982 World Champion going into the Parabolica, the long right-hander at the end of the back straight.

I completed my stint and handed over to Warwick. Then, for the final phase, I took over the sister car from Fabi (who had earlier been delayed for various reasons) and I charged back to finish second behind Derek. When we went up to the podium, I didn't know which step to stand on, so I put one foot on the top and the other on the second level. It was most unusual, to say the least.

Apart from racing for Jaguar, I also tested a lot at Monza for Toyota and found it to be a mighty place in a sportscar. Because of the high-speed straight, a Le Mans car works nicely at Monza, so much so that we got to within seven or eight seconds of an F1 time. In fact, while chasing Derek Warwick during the final stage of that race in 1991, I set a time in the Jaguar that was just 2.9 seconds outside Ayrton Senna's F1 lap record. It would have been good enough for twelfth place on the grid for the previous year's Italian Grand Prix. Anywhere else and you would be 15 to 20 seconds a lap slower. That gives an indication of the nature of Monza; it actually felt better in a Le Mans car than anything I have ever driven in F1. That said, it was still a pretty intimidating place. And very, very fast.

You would be doing close to 230 mph, rushing towards a chicane and hoping the brakes were going to work. I make no bones about it. When testing a Le Mans car, I would have a little dab on the brake pedal while going down the long straights, just to be sure everything was working. The problem with Monza is that a quick lap requires you to fly over the kerbs at the chicanes and that can knock back the brake pads, especially during a long run. The violent action of jumping over the kerb can move the wheel bearing, flex the brake disc and upright, and jiggle the pads. As a result, the next time you go for the brakes, the first part of the pedal travel is actually pushing the brake pads back to the disc. The initial impression is that you have had brake failure. At

230 mph. Le Mans was the only other place where I felt the need to check that the brakes were fully operational, because it would be curtains if they weren't.

In the 1993 Italian Grand Prix, Ayrton Senna's brakes were working adequately but he found the need to use my car to bring his McLaren to a stop, preventing a collision with the barrier. I had made a good start from twelfth on the grid and was holding a comfortable seventh early in the race. Senna, meanwhile, had been having a pretty eventful time. Staring from the second row, he had tangled with Damon Hill's Williams as the pack went through the first chicane bottleneck on the opening lap. The spin dropped him behind me but he wasn't a worry because my Ligier was good at Monza. The Renault engine had plenty of grunt to go with a reasonably low downforce package; quite a tidy little motor, in fact. So, I was minding my own business, having braked from 210 mph and begun to turn into the second chicane, when there was an enormous whack from behind. Senna had hit me hard enough to shoot the Ligier forward into a barrier 100 metres away on the outside of the corner. He had put enough acceleration into my car to throw me right across the gravel and into the metal barrier.

He had missed his braking and it was only on later examination of the on-board footage from Ayrton's McLaren that I realised what he had done. You could see quite clearly that he was adjusting something in the cockpit – probably the balance of the brakes from front to rear because he had been locking a front wheel – and he looked up to find he was into the braking area far sooner than he had imagined. That part of the track through Curva Grande is on a long, right-hand sweep, which runs under a canopy of trees and also beneath a bridge. It's a little dark in there and you need to be paying full attention. Ayrton looked up and he knew immediately he was not going to make the corner and that he was on his way to a big shunt. You could see him start to line up his car to hit the Ligier fair and square in the back in order to save himself from going head-on into the barrier. Unquestionably, he used me.

When we came to a dusty halt, Senna leapt from his car and ran over. He was really agitated. 'Are you sure you're OK?' he kept saying. He was very concerned that he might have injured me but, as soon as he had worked out that I was unhurt, it was as if he had thrown a mental switch and he simply walked away.

Two years later, in 1995, I was heading for what ought to have been another good result at Monza when fate intervened, this time in the form of a puncture. I was really flying, so much so that I did-n't know I had a problem until it was too late. Monza is exactly the same as Le Mans. You pick up a puncture but, because the speeds are so high, the centrifugal force keeps the tyre to shape. In fact, it starts to grow because the rubber begins to get hot, and then it goes bang. As the tread delaminates, it starts flapping and just rips apart. Somehow, you manage to keep the car on the road when trying to slow down. The next priority is to creep around to the pits but the flapping tread begins to mash everything associ-ated with that corner of the car: the suspension, bodywork, rear wing. That's what happened at Monza in 1995 and, to make mat-ters worse, I didn't realise I had a puncture until just after I had passed the pits and was braking for the first chicane. It meant limping along for three miles while the rear corner of the car was being ripped apart.

That first chicane always seems to be the source of controversy and a silly thing happened there in 1996. The kerbs had been re-profiled there and at the second chicane, but the concrete just beyond the kerbs could become dislodged and cause serious damage to a chassis. That, of course, would not stop drivers from taking a risk occasionally. In a bid to stop them from cheating by cutting across this no man's land, the officials placed a pile of tyres on the concrete, just inside the first part of the chicane. What we didn't realise was that the tyres were very firmly fixed to the ground. I discovered that during the warm-up on race morning when I merely clipped the tyres – and broke my front suspension. I couldn't believe it and intended to see the officials about it. But while I was waiting for collection by a recovery vehicle at the end of the warm-up, I started to see the whole thing in another light. I now knew something that the others didn't. So I kept my mouth shut and finished fourth in the race. I was going well regardless of the fact that a number of people – including race leader Damon Hill – hit the tyres and wrecked their suspension. But that did not detract from the fact that you would be ducking and diving under braking while heading close to a pile of tyres that could launch the car into the sky. When talking safety, sometimes a hasty fix is more dangerous than the original problem.

If you stopped on the circuit at Monza, it was important to make sure you stayed with your car, otherwise, by the time the officials arrived with their truck, there wouldn't be much left to retrieve. The fans love memorabilia: steering wheels, mirrors – anything that can be broken off. Before the circuit became as heavily fenced as it is now, this used to be a major problem at the end of the race. The chequered flag would signal not only the finish but also a massive track invasion. The driver's main aim would be to get the car back to *parc ferme*. The team, meanwhile, would pile everything into the garage and bring down the shutter doors immediately. If we failed to do that quickly enough, anything that was not nailed down would disappear. It's not that people are out-and-out thieves; they are simply passionate about F1 and want a small piece of it. The next job that is ahead of you, of course, is to fight your way through the mayhem and crowded roads.

In 1989, I tried to be smart by parking my car inside the grounds, but not within the circuit itself. I walked through a road tunnel and found it was wedged with people coming from each direction. I became stuck in the middle and simply could not move either forwards or backwards, just what I needed after driving a Formula 1 car for an hour and a half. It was far scarier than the actual race. After half an hour I finally emerged and headed towards my car. I got in – and didn't move for two and a half hours. I couldn't even get as far as joining the queue on the park road. Naturally, I missed my plane.

Two years later, I thought I would be even smarter by parking in a street, right outside the circuit boundary. I was with my wife, Liz, and my team-mate, Mark Blundell, and we reckoned we could get away without hiring a helicopter. We had to walk for more than a mile to reach the paddock, but kept telling ourselves it would be worth it because of the quick getaway later on. Some hope.

The return journey on foot seemed twice as long because both Mark and I were knackered. There had been a screw-up during the design stage of the Brabhams we were driving. I'll never forget being at the factory in January when everything went quiet and the designers and engineers went into a worried huddle. The regulations called for the driver's feet to be behind the front axle line of the car and, due to an initial mix-up, they had to move the pedals about three inches closer to the driver in order to conform. That meant Mark and I had to spend a whole season feeling as though our knees were somewhere around our ears. An already cramped cockpit became almost impossible. The Yamaha V12 engine also used to pump heat everywhere and we were always exhausted at the end of a race.

In this state of fatigue, we reached the street – but there was no sign of the car. I had parked in a tow-away zone, which, despite the absence of any warning signs, was being zealously policed.

We eventually discovered that we had to go to the police station, which was 500 yards away. We turned the corner to find a queue of about forty people outside. I was sweaty, tired and hot, so I went to the front and put my nose against the door. The queue went berserk – as only they can in Italy. I pretended not to understand, which appeared to make things worse. The situation was becoming tense when the door opened and I walked straight in.

The policeman explained to me that my car was in a compound, 5 kilometres away. Mark was too exhausted to go any further, so he stayed with Liz and our bags while I set off to retrieve the hire car. With the road chock-a-block thanks to race traffic, there was no option but to jog the 5 kilometres, not easy for me ever since I smashed my ankles in Dallas in 1984. I reached the compound and, sure enough, there was my car – along with a number of cars sporting the same official stickers and obviously driven by F1 people who believed they had the same clever idea. I paid around £80 and returned to pick up Mark and Liz. By the time we staggered onto the plane, Mark and I were destroyed.

It is tempting to stay at Monza until the Monday because the quality of the accommodation, food and social life is second to none. This becomes a very important issue when you are a frequent traveller. The downside of the enormous amount of travelling required by Formula 1 is the queues at airport check-ins, passport control and security checks. Then there is the wait at the baggage carousel at the other end and another queue for a hire car. If you do that every other week for decades, it is easy to understand why F1 people are blasé about globe-trotting.

The upside is staying in great cities such as Montréal, Melbourne, Budapest and Milan. At Monza, effectively a suburb of Milan, the Hotel de Ville provides much of the charm. It is not necessary to book; your room is yours for as long as you want to come to Monza. The management simply assumes you will be there for the next Grand Prix, which is always the case because they treat us so well and the food is superb. The maitre d' has known all the drivers who have passed through over the years. It's like a club, a wonderful experience made even more enjoyable because you are with a group of friends throughout. This doesn't happen at every track. It is unlikely, for instance, that you will go into Northampton for a memorable dinner during the British Grand Prix. Increasingly these days, F1 personnel are scattered in hotels far and wide, the catering handled by team motorhomes at the track. But, when the race comes to a major city, then the tendency is to stay in a large hotel and make the most of the variety of restaurants nearby. You will always have company, which is a major plus, as there is nothing more tragic than having room service by yourself and watching CNN.

A more complicated, not to say expensive, solution is to stay at Villa D'Este, a fabulous place on Lake Como. The trick is to heli-copter in and out, but the worry is always that at least one trip will be affected by mist or fog. The alternative is a nerve-wracking battle with Italian traffic. It is a manic race to get to the circuit on time for practice or, as used to be the case, the warm-up early on race morning. Two or three key drivers would use the Villa D'Este, and some still do. It is a fantastic place. Even so, I stopped staying there because of the stress of wondering whether or not I would get to work on time.

The world of F1 may be moving on to exciting new venues but Monza says everything about the importance of retaining the sport's core values. I wouldn't miss the Italian Grand Prix for the world.

Brands Hatch

I was seven years old when my mum woke me at three o'clock one morning to say that my uncle was going to take me to the British Grand Prix. I'll never forget that moment.

The excitement continued to build as we set off from Norfolk on the long haul to Kent. And it was a lengthy journey in 1966 because there were no motorways or bypasses. We travelled through a seemingly endless number of towns and villages before reaching the Dartford Tunnel. Passing beneath the Thames, we emerged to join the queue of traffic heading along the A20 from London towards Brands Hatch and my first Grand Prix.

The whole experience was just so exciting. I can recall lots of images, from the gates opening, to entering the sloping grass car park, to hearing the public address system, visiting stands selling merchandise and walking along the internal roads where promotions girls were handing out leaflets. My eyes must have been like organ stops. I couldn't take it all in. Here I was, at a Grand Prix, a place where Gods such as Jim Clark, Jack Brabham, Jackie Stewart and Graham Hill would be racing.

We watched from South Bank, the sloping enclosure on one side of the magnificent natural bowl that forms the focal point of

Length: 4.197 km

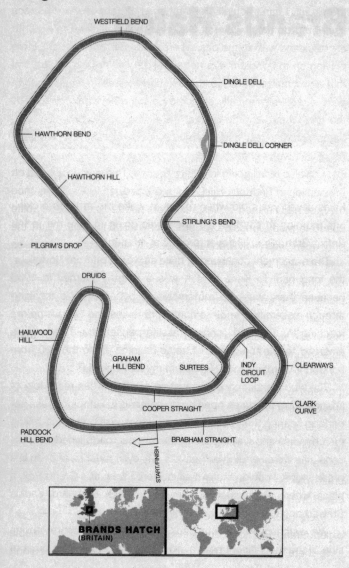

WESTFIELD BEND

DINGLE DELL

HAWTHORN BEND

DINGLE DELL CORNER

HAWTHORN HILL

STIRLING'S BEND

PILGRIM'S DROP

DRUIDS

HAILWOOD HILL

GRAHAM HILL BEND

SURTEES

INDY CIRCUIT LOOP

CLEARWAYS

CLARK CURVE

COOPER STRAIGHT

PADDOCK HILL BEND

BRABHAM STRAIGHT

START/FINISH

BRANDS HATCH
(BRITAIN)

the circuit. I can't actually remember what happened in the race itself but I do recall, when it was over, being allowed to go onto the track and walk to the pits, where Acker Bilk and his band were playing on the podium. I'm not sure jazz was my cup of tea, but that didn't matter because it all seemed so thrilling. I just couldn't believe we were actually standing on the main straight, right by the grid where, shortly before, the Brabhams, BRMs, Coopers, Lotus and the rest had stormed away to start a round of the Formula 1 world championship.

I can also recall going into the paddock. This was positioned on the outside of Paddock Hill Bend and was open to everyone once the race had finished. It was here that I spotted a small and polite queue formed alongside a Ford Zephyr. Sitting inside, with the door open, was Jack Brabham, cheerfully signing autographs – as well he might because he had won the race. But the point was, Brabham was the man of the moment. He was leading the championship and yet the public had ready access, with no trouble at all. Today, assuming the fans could get into the paddock in the first place, a queue for the winner's signature would run three times round the block.

The race day programme in 1966 had carried several supporting events, including a touring car race for thundering Mustangs and Galaxies chased by Lotus Cortinas and a pack of screaming Minis and Anglias. In years to come, I would take the opportunity to watch the support races from the back section of the track where it peeled away from the main amphitheatre, headed over a crest, plunged down a dip and into the woods before looping back towards the central bowl.

There was a little glade that linked the two sides of the so-called Grand Prix loop and I clearly remember seeing a couple lying there, snogging. That really threw me because I couldn't understand why they had bothered paying to come to a Grand Prix if they were not going to watch the racing. My state of puzzlement had nothing to do with being young and impressionable because I can remember thinking exactly the same thing after breaking down in races and coming across similar intimate scenarios while walking back to the pits.

It seemed all the more absurd at Brands Hatch because, wherever you went, the trackside viewing was excellent. And it looked better from the cockpit of a racing car, even though I had my doubts before I actually tackled the track for the first time. That was another occasion I'll never forget.

I had just turned seventeen. I had been grass track and hot rod racing until then but I was thinking of making the step into circuit racing. That idea really took hold towards the end of 1976 when *Autosport* magazine ran an advert offering the works Toyota touring car team for sale. It caught my eye because my family ran a Toyota dealership and, apart from anything else, these were competitive racing cars. There were two Celicas, as driven by Win Percy and Barrie 'Whizzo' Williams, plus a transporter that had been fitted with a highly tuned engine during its original role as transport for the works Ford rallycross team.

Brands Hatch comes into the story because, at the time of the advert, this was to be the scene of the final round of the 1976 British Touring Car Championship and it would give my father and I the ideal chance to take a look at what was on offer. We cruised to Brands Hatch in a big white Toyota Crown and made contact with the team. 'Whizzo' drove me round the paddock in one of the cars and I was just as thrilled when Win Percy spoke to me. He used to autocross against my Dad in the 1960s and was one of my heroes then, and remains so today. It was almost too much to take on board: meeting these stars of the racetrack; riding in this noisy car – albeit at a walking pace around the paddock – and looking over a works team, complete with its impressive truck.

We thought the next best move would be to step outside the paddock and watch the race from Paddock Hill Bend. The track at this point plunges steeply downhill while swinging right before rising just as quickly towards the hairpin at Druids. As we reached the bend, the pack of more than thirty cars came charging over a crest, into the corner and rushed down the slope; I looked at my father and said: 'No way, Dad! No way can I do that.' Ultimately, however, it did not put me off. We bought the cars and equipment and thus began my career in circuit racing, with Brands Hatch included in the programme for 1977.

Once behind the wheel that following year, I was to find that Paddock Hill was not as daunting as I had thought, although it is definitely one of the great corners of the world. That said, the approach, viewed from the cockpit, is arguably even trickier than it seems from the trackside.

The problem is that the corner is completely blind and then, once you pop over the crest, the track falls away quite dramatically. The trick, when flat out on the pit straight, is to aim for a marshals' post, which is positioned on the outside of the corner, just beyond the crest. Initially, you need to convince yourself this is going to work as you head straight towards the barrier. It is total commitment. As you arrive, brake and turn right, the downhill slope suddenly appears and you aim for a nasty kerb on the inside. It is a very tricky approach and just about any car you drive tends to be a handful through Paddock Hill Bend.

There is room on the outside of the corner on the way out. Given the precarious nature of Paddock Hill, this has frequently been a 'Get Out of Jail Free' card. Originally, it was simply grass, then gravel, then, when the angle of the corner was tightened slightly, the original asphalt provided much of the run-off for the revised layout.

The problem was, and still is, that if you were going to use this extra piece of track, you had to commit to it. There is a clearly defined kerb marking the edge of the track proper, but you daren't straddle it otherwise the bottom of the car is likely to suffer. More recently, drivers have been penalised for continually using the additional space. But it can be quite an advantage because you reduce the angle of the corner by coming into Paddock Hill Bend with no intention of staying on the main part of the racetrack, sweeping wide and then cutting back in again. If you do that, however, it is necessary to be ready for an immediate attack from any driver who is following closely.

The track rises steeply towards the right-hander at Druids. As with any uphill braking zone, the laws of physics work for you. As a result, there have always been brilliant overtaking manoeuvres here. No matter what car you are driving, there is a chance to pass the guy in front with a good run through Paddock and then, whichever side he decides to go – and so long as he sticks to it – you can take a look at the other side as the pair of you rush up the hill.

Inevitably, you try to come up the inside into Druids, even though that can force a compromise on the way out of a corner that is tight, fiddly and frustrating. As you charge down the hill again, the difficulty is caused by the next corner, Graham Hill Bend, being a left-hander, which means you are now badly positioned if your rival has remained alongside on the left all the way through Druids.

It's a race to get to the bottom of the hill and the very quick entry to Graham Hill Bend. This corner has been tightened in recent years and you have to be careful because the bit that follows is pinched in the middle. It may be called Cooper Straight, but the track actually curves to the left and it is very easy to run wide. That can be quite daunting because, once on the grass, there is not a lot of space between there and the mud bank at the back of the pits. I have seen drivers get it wrong in Graham Hill Bend and then have enormous accidents, especially if the grass is wet.

If the race is being held on the shorter Indy circuit, then you are already heading towards the final part of the lap. This involves a challenging left and right through Surtees and McLaren. Before you know it, Clearways, the last corner, is upon you, just over the crest of a small hill. The kerbs at Surtees have unsettled the car and now you are desperately trying to slow while downshifting and turning into McLaren and Clearways.

It is important to be smooth through Clearways because it rises then falls, and, just to add to the difficulty, the track is off-camber at the exit. It is no surprise that drivers frequently run out of room after getting it wrong at some point in that swirling complex of corners. All of this adds to the feeling of being on a fast merry-go-round at a fair because Clearways fires you onto the pit straight, into another lap and, in no time at all, you are aiming for the marshals' post at Paddock once more.

If you are intending to visit the pits, it is easy to be concentrating so hard coming into Clearways that you follow the racing line and end up on the outside of the track. That's not where you need to be because the pit lane entrance is on the right. By running wide and then suddenly pulling across to the right, it is easy to write someone off. But, whichever way you should approach the pits, the downhill entrance is very fast. Too fast, in fact, for some people.

When I raced the Toyota Celica for the first time at Brands

Hatch, I was launching myself off Clearways and into the pits with no trouble at all during practice, because, in those days, the pit lane did not have a speed limit. Not long after practice had finished, Ralph Broad came into our garage enquiring after me. This was Mr Broad of Broadspeed, the well-known preparation company that was running the championship-winning Dolomite Sprints at the time. When he asked for me, my hopes soared. 'He's spotted me on the track,' I thought. 'Maybe he's going to offer me a works drive.'

Instead he snapped: 'Will you slow down coming into the pits! You're going to kill us all!' And, with that, he turned on his heel and walked out. So much for my top touring car drive. Not that I necessarily had that as a prime ambition. In fact, I had no aspirations at the time and was purely a hobby racer. Back then I had absolutely no idea that I would race in a Grand Prix at this track.

That moment did not come until October 1985, almost two years after I had started F1 racing. I had missed the 1984 British Grand Prix at Brands Hatch through my Dallas ankle injury and it was Silverstone's turn to provide the venue the following year. Three races from the end of the season, however, Brands Hatch hosted the European Grand Prix. Now, finally, I was going to tackle the full circuit in an F1 car.

I was sixteenth on the grid in my Tyrrell-Renault, not the ideal place to start a race. But, strangely, neither was pole position at Brands Hatch. It is rather like Interlagos where part of the grid dips and another part rises. Pole is not only on the latter, but also where the track slopes from the outside to the inner. The usual job of balancing the throttle and the clutch is made worse by having too much wheelspin send the rear of the car sideways and give no grip at all. It is not uncommon to see the pole position car swamped by the time it reaches the braking area for Paddock Hill

Bend, just at the point where the track narrows slightly as it passes over the tunnel leading from the outer paddock. And just to complicate things even more, the track undulates here because of the effect of settlement at the site of the tunnel.

The hazards of starting at Brands Hatch are the same, no matter which track is in use. The Indy circuit technique remains all the way to Surtees, where the Grand Prix loop begins by going into a long, slightly off-camber left-hander before rising uphill and heading into the country.

The thing that strikes you most is the absence of decent run-off areas. An aerial photograph of Brands Hatch explains why. The boundary of the land and a number of housing estates are nearby; it's as if the circuit has no room to breathe. The lack of suitable run-off is particularly noticeable at Hawthorn Bend, if only because this right-hander is in sight for quite some time as the car really gets going on the outward leg of the loop. Having crested the rise from Surtees, the track remains level before curving right and swooping down to Pilgrim's Drop, which really increases the momentum for the rush uphill towards Hawthorn.

It is one of those 'arrive-and-drive' corners, a quick right-hander that allows you to carry a great deal of speed going in. Which perhaps is a good thing because there is little time to notice there is not a lot of space on the way out. It's a pretty dangerous piece of racetrack that is perhaps engraved on my mind because a driver had a fatal accident there in a powerful Formula 5000 single-seater on the weekend I made my touring car debut. Hawthorn is also remembered as the scene of a fiery accident that killed Jo Siffert when the Swiss driver crashed his BRM during a non-championship F1 race in 1971. Hawthorn Bend is a brilliant corner if you get it right, but not the place to have a mechanical failure.

The fast exit leads onto a short straight and into another quick right at Westfield, after which the roller-coaster ride continues with the drop into Dingle Dell, followed by another fast rise to the blind Dingle Dell Corner. This has been chopped and changed over the years but, when the Grand Prix was held there, it was a fast 90-degree right. If the car was working well, you would glide, almost float, through there. It was as if a piece of rope attached to the inside barrier had been somehow hooked to the car and was pulling you round the corner. Certainly, that was the effect you needed because it was important to get over to the right of the track as quickly as possible in order to be ready for the entrance to Stirling's Bend.

When I think of this left-hander, I instantly have a mental picture of a driver called David da Costa standing on the outside of the corner and shaking his fist at me as I went by in my Celica. A disagreement over the same piece of racetrack had resulted in his Ford Escort going off the road – and he wasn't happy about it.

I had enough to think about without that distraction because Stirling's is a difficult little corner, and quite tricky on the way in. You always think you have carried too much speed into the corner and then, when halfway through, the feeling is that you should actually be going a lot faster. Certainly, it is important to be quick at the exit in preparation for the blast down to the point where the Indy circuit joins from the right on the approach to Clearways. And on you go, the track falling away at the exit as Clearways becomes Clark Curve, followed by a rise and then the charge towards Paddock Hill Bend and the start of another lap of this great circuit.

That Grand Prix in 1985 – my first at Brands Hatch – may not have been a particularly memorable race for me (I retired the Tyrrell with a broken water pipe) but it certainly was for Nigel

Mansell. This was to be his first Grand Prix win after seventy-two attempts, so you can imagine the incredible emotion, not just for Nigel but for his army of supporters. It was that break-through moment for him – like mine ought to have been at Spa and Montréal in 1992 – which turned the whole thing on its head and gave Mansell incredible impetus. He went on to win the very next race in South Africa and would fight for the championship the following year.

Brands Hatch 1985 provided that pivotal moment for Nigel where, instead of thinking you can win a grand prix, you *know* you can. It allows a massive leap of personal confidence and your career, which had seemed stalled, takes off. For years Jenson Button couldn't get onto the podium and all of a sudden he broke his duck with a hat trick early in 2004. That was the way it was for Nigel, and the sport would be the richer for it.

Nigel had a self-belief that was quite incredible. Most sports people are actually quite insecure and what drives them on to do exceptional things is a constant dissatisfaction with what they have achieved. You frequently see sportsmen and women tormenting themselves, driving themselves on with disappointment or discontent. They are never happy and, although they would never admit it, lack confidence.

That had no part in Nigel Mansell's repertoire. He had a supreme, unshakeable self-confidence and an inner strength that matched his physical power, evident from the moment he shook your hand with the apparent intention of breaking a couple of bones. It was the same with the muscular way he drove the car. His overtaking manoeuvres were always dramatic and it remains a mystery to me why he didn't fly off the road more often.

In 1988, Nigel went down with chicken pox and I had to stand in for him at Spa. The thing that struck me immediately was his preferred choice of steering wheel. This little doughnut of a thing was so small that I could barely turn it in order to get the Williams out of the pits. I simply couldn't drive the car. Nigel was an immensely strong guy and it was as if he had to prove it by choosing the smallest steering wheel possible.

Nigel was also a complicated man and wore his heart on his sleeve, but I admired him enormously as a racing driver. He did things in cars that did not appear possible and, of course, the fans loved him for it. Nigel motivated the crowd like few others and the press were with him all the way. There was always a story when Nigel was racing. He would conjure an amazing race result from nowhere or do something that was plainly ridiculous. But you could not ignore him. Nigel delivered that day at Brands Hatch and began his run of thirty-one victories at one of the world's outstanding racetracks.

Every corner at Brands Hatch is a great one, even allowing for the alterations at Westfield and Dingle Dell. The aim of the changes was to pacify both the motor bikers and the car racers, two forms of racing which have different needs. It may be almost impossible to come up with a layout and kerb format that pleases everyone but the basic challenge and thrill of tackling Brands Hatch remains as exciting as it always was.

Before F1 officials limited the circuits we were permitted to test on, the Tyrrell team used Brands Hatch quite often because it was only an hour's drive from their factory at Ockham in Surrey. I have to be honest and admit it was a frightening place to have untried parts fitted to your car. And, if they didn't fail, there was always the chance that the driver might be the one to break at the end of a tough couple of days – as I found to my cost in 1985.

We were about to complete a two-day test and Ken Tyrrell wanted me to run with a set of sticky qualifying tyres on my

Renault turbo. The plan was to crank up the turbo boost and use the tyres to set a time that would create a good impression – probably with a prospective sponsor, although Ken did not say as much.

Brands Hatch is a very physical circuit and the Tyrrell – which did not have power steering – was tough to drive. I was pretty tired after two solid days' work, and made that clear. But they wanted just one more lap, so I agreed. Powering out of Druids, the back tyres lit up as the turbo boost kicked in – and I failed to gather the car together in time to negotiate Graham Hill Bend, where I smashed the Tyrrell into the barrier.

A front wheel sprang back and bent the chassis. I didn't break any bones – but I was trapped in the car. If it had caught fire, I would have been in terrible trouble. A hydraulic ram was needed to force back the chassis and set me free, ensuring that the car was written off. When we got it back to the pits, Ken took one look at the car, one look at me, said nothing and left, in total disgust. As only he could.

I should have said no to that last lap. It is difficult when money is tight and the team wants you to do a time at the end of the day, but I should have taken into account the physical effort necessary to push an F1 car for two days, particularly at Brands Hatch.

Fitness has become vitally important during the last twenty years. It is true that former champions such as James Hunt and Jody Scheckter were in extremely good shape in the 1970s, but they received nothing like the specialist attention drivers enjoy today when it comes to nutrition, fitness, massages and just about anything else you can think of.

When we were racing in Canada one year, I agreed to be wired for a study by the Human Performance Centre at McGill University. I was very fit but, for most of the race, my pulse was very near my maximum. It was partly physical and partly anticipation but, whatever the cause, I could never average 180 bpm for an hour and three quarters on an exercise bike, but that is exactly what happened during the Grand Prix. My pulse spiked at more than 200 bpm when I made an epic overtaking move but, otherwise, it was constantly at 180 bpm. Quite amazing.

I had another surprise during qualifying when there was a problem with my car and I was unable to go out straight away. This was not a drama because the qualifying session lasted for an hour and I could complete my three or four flying laps whenever I wanted. Yet my pulse jumped 30 bpm when a siren sounded to indicate the start of qualifying. I was nowhere near my car – it was still in pieces, in fact – and I was not about to do a lap. I'm not a highly excitable person but just knowing the session had started was enough to set the adrenalin running.

My pulse rate must have gone through the roof at Brands Hatch once – and I wasn't even driving. I took part in many corporate days with Sir Jackie Stewart, which involved a number of fast cars and key clients. The usual plan was that we would drive the guests around the circuit and then they would drive us. I had this terrifying experience with a girl in a Porsche 928. We were using the Indy circuit and I was in the passenger seat as we headed along Cooper Straight with the intention – I thought, quite reasonably – of taking Surtees and McLaren in something approaching an acceptable racing line and then peeling into the pits. As we approached Surtees, I could see my driver had the throttle flat to the floor. We were in top gear and the Porsche 928 is a quick car. It rapidly became apparent that she was not going to be lifting her foot from the accelerator any time soon.

'Lift off,' I said. 'Lift off! Lift off *now*!'

No response.

Her mind was somewhere else. She simply did not hear me. Sometimes people become nervous and either lose their heads or freeze. Whatever the reason, we were into Surtees at a huge rate of knots with the track swinging to the right and grass and all sorts of obstacles I didn't want to contemplate rushing to meet us.

I remember yanking the steering out of her hand and pulling the handbrake. We spun in a plume of blue smoke, backwards onto the GP circuit – and somehow didn't hit a thing. I knocked the car out of gear and switched it off. I wouldn't let her drive me back to the pits, even though it was a matter of a few hundred yards.

That is part of the mixture of memories from Brands Hatch. It is a wonderful racetrack and yet everything is very slightly scruffy. Even when they extended the paddock behind the pits so that we didn't have to use the sloping area outside Paddock Hill Bend, the place was cramped and could just about accommodate the F1 transporters, but not much else.

Before that, the mechanics had to work on a slope so severe that nuts and bolts would roll away if you weren't careful. Then, when it was time for your race or practice session, it was necessary to gather at the appointed hour in a collection area – again, on a steep slope. If you were not there on time, you might miss the chance to get through the single-lane tunnel and fail to make your race as a result. But this, and a cheerful big marshal operating the traffic lights, were part of the charm of Brands Hatch.

I was disappointed when the British Grand Prix was held there for the last time in 1986. It had to happen because it was no longer viable to alternate the Grand Prix between Brands Hatch and Silverstone. Given the investment and infrastructure that was needed, one of them had to go. Silverstone had the space but, at the time, Brands Hatch was the more interesting racetrack.

WORKING THE WHEEL

I was delighted when Jonathan Palmer, a former F1 driver, pur-
chased the circuit in 2003 and secured its future as a racetrack.
With such a prime piece of real estate situated near the motorways just south of London, it was easy to envisage it being used
for something other than motor racing. But it is right that it should
continue a tradition begun in the 1950s because, when all is said
and done, this is London's racetrack. Brands Hatch has the location; it has history. Better than that, it has introduced many
hundreds of people to the thrill of motor racing. Not least, a wide-
eyed kid from Norfolk in 1966.

Suzuka

One of the many unusual things about Suzuka is that it gets dark early and very quickly in October. The air becomes chilly and the atmosphere seems very different. But the patience, enthusiasm and good manners of the Japanese people do not change at all.

I recall walking back to the circuit hotel late one evening after a particularly long post-practice debrief with my team. It was raining and I had a hood pulled over my head as I quickly made my way through the fair ground, which adjoins the circuit. Quite suddenly, a little lady appeared out of the gloom and proffered a pen, saying in her best Japanese-English: 'Mr Blundle, Mr Blundle. Sign, prease. Sign, prease.' I swear my mother would not have recognised me that night. I have absolutely no idea how this woman knew who I was. That's but one fascinating part of the Japanese Grand Prix. It's an extraordinary experience, rather like the circuit itself.

Suzuka was designed by John Hugenholtz, a Dutchman who knew exactly what he was doing when it came to giving a racing driver a supreme challenge. This is the only figure-of-eight circuit in F1, a track that was way ahead of its time when Honda built it

Length: 5.807 km

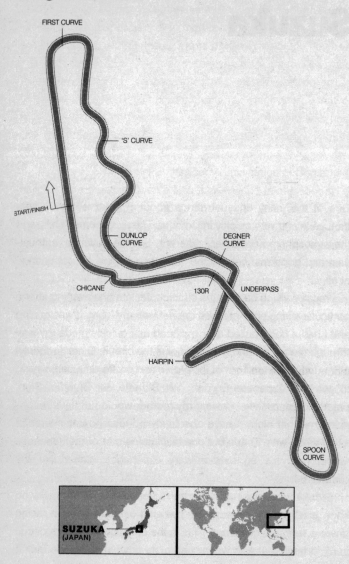

FIRST CURVE

'S' CURVE

START/FINISH

DUNLOP
CURVE

DEGNER
CURVE

CHICANE

130R

UNDERPASS

HAIRPIN

SPOON
CURVE

SUZUKA
(JAPAN)

for testing in 1962. It has got everything: hairpins, blindingly fast corners, undulation, bumps, narrow in places and all the adjectives you could ever wish to apply. Suzuka must rank among the top three racetracks in anyone's book.

The only drawback is that it appears to be in the middle of nowhere rather than, as you might expect, close to a major city such as Tokyo or Osaka. Tucked away among small towns and areas of light industry, Suzuka is difficult to find. When it was first used for a Grand Prix in 1987, I reckoned we all deserved world championship points simply for getting there.

Nobody spoke English and, unlike now, there were no English signs, it was cash only, credit cards were not taken and GSM phones do not work to this day, the Japanese preferring their own unique system. And back in 1987 we had a complicated journey ahead of us once we landed in Japan. I knew a Japanese mechanic who used to work for the helmet manufacturer, Arai, and I asked him to write down the directions in Japanese. I arrived in Tokyo with Liz, who was heavily pregnant with Charlotte, our first child, and the entire journey was a nightmare. I had this long piece of paper covered in Japanese fretwork but I had no idea whereabouts we were on the list of instructions. I kept showing it to people. They would run down the order to see how far we had got, and then struggle to communicate to us how to do the next bit.

This quickly turned into a very tiring process because we had just stepped off a long flight. This was in the days when the journey to Japan involved a stop in Alaska. The express train from Narita airport to the centre of the city did not exist, which meant a long, long taxi ride to Tokyo Central Station and then a number of trains to Nagoya and from there to Shiroko. That part alone took between five and six hours – provided you managed to get on the correct trains.

WORKING THE WHEEL

The only saving grace is that Japanese numerals are the same as Western numbers. That allowed you to work out the time your train left and the number of your seat. Even better, if the doors opened at the arrival time printed on your ticket, then you could get off in the certain knowledge that you had reached your destination. The rail network is that reliable. It is so brilliant that travellers from the UK can't help but think that everyone in charge of the British rail system ought to replaced by a handful of people from Japan Rail to sort out our problems. I never cease to be amazed by the Japanese infrastructure and transport system.

The Bullet Train on the famous Shinkansen line rushes effortlessly at an incredible speed towards Nagoya, the scenery a mix of industry, paddy fields and golf driving ranges, but the suburban line to Shiroko is a slow contrast and the last thing needed at the end of thirty-hour journey. We were absolutely exhausted by the time we reached the Suzuka Circuit Hotel that first year, and every year afterwards. The journey has since become easier thanks to better rail links and contacts such as friends in Tokyo with a helicopter. But the effort is definitely worth it once you catch sight of the circuit. In fact, you begin to marvel before seeing anything of the racetrack.

Suzuka is like a mini-Disneyland because of a fairground bolted on to the side of the track, with the sort of cheery music you associate with rides in an amusement park, and little Japanese children – sweetness personified. It has to be the most unusual route to work. It really is a great feeling as you make your way to the bottom of the fairground, pass under a road and then move up between lively concession stalls to the back of the main grandstand. Emerging eventually at the front of the grandstand, you have your first sight of the track as it descends steeply in front of the pits.

The track has changed very little since its inception, particularly the opening section, which gives drivers an immediate taste of what is to follow. There is something of a theatrical atmosphere about the start/finish line thanks to the pits on the right and large grandstands opposite with a Ferris wheel and roller-coasters in the background. When you stand in the pit lane, there is an aura that is almost tangible, and you get the same feeling on the track.

As you accelerate down the hill, there is the impression of rushing into an arena. Of course, for the start itself, the hill can create problems because you've got to hold your car in position and manage the controls in order to make a clean getaway. The feeling of acceleration is exaggerated by the steep drop and the fact that the track narrows on the approach to the first corner.

This is where Ayrton Senna famously and intentionally nailed Alain Prost as they fought for the championship in 1990. Senna had won pole but the sport's governing body, the FIA, insisted it should be on the right-hand side of the grid, which, unquestionably, was the dirty side of the track. Senna wanted to switch to left, which was on the racing line and had much more grip. Because the officials would not move pole, he was therefore at a disadvantage, particularly with Prost starting from the left. Senna decided he was going to take his rival off the road going into the first corner and win the world championship – which is exactly what he did.

The right-hander at the bottom of the hill is a brilliant corner in its own right and doesn't need the extra dramatics provided by Senna as the McLaren and Prost's Ferrari ploughed spectacularly into the gravel on the outside of the corner. When tackling the corner in a more conventional manner, Turn 1 really needs to be worked in association with the next right, which follows almost immediately. In effect, Turn 1 is the approach and the braking zone for Turn 2, the very place where a wheel parted company from Jacques Villeneuve's Williams and helped Damon Hill win the championship in 1996.

I've seen Michael Schumacher go through the first part without lifting from the throttle. He has come steaming down the hill at 195 mph on fresh tyres and swept through Turn 1 with his right foot hard on the power. It helps to have that big run-off there although a few local drivers have hit the wall and suffered fatal consequences while trying to get through Turn 1 as quickly as possible.

Once Turn 2 has been dealt with, the serious business really begins. The next section – I have always called it The Snake but the official title for the sequence of lefts and rights is the Esses – really shows the power of Hugenholtz's thinking. You could not challenge a racing car or its driver more if you tried. Every discipline is included: braking, downshifting, turning left, short straights, turning right, some cambers in your favour, some against you, with the final piece of braking taking you into the foot of a hill. In addition to all of this, the sequence runs round a small lake, which means concrete walls close at hand and an environment similar to a street circuit. There is just enough grip as the road goes left, right, left, right, left over a crest and into the right at the foot of the hill. It's a 'Yee-hah!' section where you grit your teeth, tense your stomach muscles and really attack as you hook the kerbs all the way through. If you make a mistake, then it simply spits you out, straight into the concrete wall. Nigel Mansell proved that in 1987 when a massive shunt during practice injured his back and took him out of the championship.

I went off in a big way at the same spot five years later. I was hurting before I even went into the wall, thanks to dreadful stomach cramp from a piece of fish I had eaten the night before, an unusual occurrence in Japan because the food is normally of exceptional quality. I was in terrible trouble and I didn't want to go out. In fact, I shouldn't have gone out. I wasn't up to dealing with such a physically demanding circuit, particularly the Esses because you don't have small accidents in there. Luckily, it was wet on the second day, so I didn't need to run because my time (before the crash) on Friday was good enough for thirteenth place on the grid.

On race morning, however, I could barely stand up and just managed to get down some rice, which had the life deliberately boiled out of it by one of the Benetton trainers. I finished third in the race and set the fourth fastest lap. I got through the Esses fifty-three times by running on pure adrenalin, nothing else.

If everything is working well through this sequence and you are hooked up, it feels as though you are winding up an internal motor that is taking you faster and faster. It is rather like a snowball gathering momentum and carrying you with it all the way to the braking point just over the crest of the hill. It is a brilliant feeling. But it is very difficult to get the car right all the way through and some drivers struggle at this point.

When you see the opening left for the first time, it is hard to believe just how fast you can ultimately go through there. It seems to defy all of your knowledge and instinct as to how much a car will stick before it cries 'enough' and flies off the road. If you get any element wrong on the first part, that error is magnified as you go through the rest of the sequence. You will be off-line for the second part. And then you will be even further off-line on the exit of the second part and so it goes on. It is sweet if you get it right but so difficult if you get it wrong.

There is no time to congratulate or chastise yourself because the Dunlop Curve comes next as you tackle the hill. This is a strange corner because, initially, you are looking at the sky, especially in a racing car with your backside scraping on the ground. The corner goes left and left and left, and just when you think you have reached the end, it still keeps going left. Dunlop is constantly turning and there is no run-off on the outside. It is like a James Bond film where they put 007 in a centrifuge test before he becomes a cosmonaut or some such. It is as if you are being slung round this corner and the only thing preventing you from flying off the road is a big metal arm holding the car from the inside. And, just for good measure, the surface is so bumpy, the car keeps hitting the ground. On the other hand, you have a lot of grip because you are going through this never-ending left at high speed. I don't know what it is about the Dunlop Curve, but it is so unusual, so difficult. And I'm not saying that simply because I had a very big accident there during the Grand Prix in 1994.

It frequently rains in Japan but it is not the common or garden heavy thunderstorm on an English summer day. It is of torrential downpour proportions, much as we experienced during the race in 1994. As we came to the end of a lap, I got on the radio to my team and demanded to have the race stopped. The conditions were impossible.

As I followed Heinz-Harald Frentzen down the hill, past the pits, something suddenly flashed past my left-hand side. It was Johnny Herbert, stationary and pointing the wrong way after his Benetton had aquaplaned. It was a total miracle that we did not smash into Johnny and I dread to think what would have happened had two F1 cars met nose-to-nose.

I was back on the radio in seconds, repeating what seemed to me to be obvious. There was no sign of a red flag as we started the next lap, went through the Esses and began the climb through the Dunlop Curve. There was a lot of water running towards the foot of the hill, and large puddles had formed in the divots and bumps. All of a sudden, my car hit a pocket of water and spun through 180 degrees.

It is an eerie feeling. The first thing you notice is that everything goes quiet because you've hit the brakes and stalled the engine straight away. With the road going to the left, you are guaranteed to fly off to the right. Now I was a passenger, spinning towards the outside of the corner and the very spot where Gianni Morbidelli's Minardi had gone off the lap before.

I hadn't seen any yellow flags, mainly because I couldn't see anything while following in the spray of Frentzen's Sauber. As I looked to my right, I could see I was heading absolutely broadside, shoulder on, to a mini caterpillar truck. This was the price for racing on an old circuit that did not have the benefit of an internal road for safety vehicles. In the event of an accident at Suzuka, officials rush onto the track with Honda Accord estates and rescue vehicles such as the caterpillar that was going to the aid of the Minardi. I took one look and thought: 'That's it. I've had it. I'm going to go under this thing.'

My McLaren was undamaged at this point because all I'd done was spin off but now, quite clearly, I was going to have a huge accident. All I could do was stamp my foot on the brakes and that spun the front of the car around. It was something I had learned when heading towards the end of the pit wall in an International Race of Champions event on the Michigan high-speed oval. At Suzuka, I miraculously missed the caterpillar by less than half a metre and spun past the Minardi. But the drama was not over yet.

I smashed into the tyre barrier and I remember seeing a marshal jump in among the tyres at the point where I hit. He was unhurt, but the same could not be said for another marshal who could not get out of the way. I'll never forget this man's face as the front of the car caught him and he was flung through and over my cockpit. The car seemed to skid for ever before finally coming to rest on the inside of Degner, the next corner.

I climbed out and ran back. The marshal was lying on the ground with a bone sticking through the leggings of his overalls. He was in a terrible state.

When I asked to meet him the following year, I could see the lasting effect of his injury. The accident was one of those awful situations where there is very little a driver can do. Even though marshals know the risks, I felt so sorry for the poor man.

Much to my chagrin at the time of the accident, I was officially warned because I had crashed under a yellow flag. It is impossible to explain to anyone who has not been in that situation – fogged-up visor streaming with water being chucked out by the car in front – why you cannot see your hand in front of your face, never mind a piece of coloured rag masquerading as a flag by the side of the track. The officials should have stopped the race and, indeed, they brought out the red flag shortly after I had crashed. It should have happened much sooner and spared the marshal an unnecessary injury.

The walk back to the pits that day did not take too long because the exit of the Dunlop Curve is at the highest point of the track on the loop running behind the paddock. Then a gentle descent begins towards Degner, which is split into two right-handers, both of which are very difficult.

Degner 1 is approached at about 180 mph. It is another 'arrive-and-drive' corner, which means brake, bang down two gears and sweep through. It is a great corner if you stay on-line. But if you catch a bit of kerb, or go in too hard, the price is high, as demonstrated by numerous incidents as cars bounce through the gravel on the outside and arrive at Degner 2, where, at best, the underside is damaged by the kerb and, at worst, they end the journey by hitting the wall.

Either way, the car is going to return with gravel rash along the sides; something the mechanics hate to see because the car has to be stripped down and repainted. They can paint the wings and the bodywork easily but a gravel trap scars the monocoque or chassis onto which the paint is directly applied. This is not a simple respray job. The only way is to strip down the car, return the monocoque to the factory, where it is repainted, baked in the oven and eventually returned. It is an epic task, which is why the team will never feel sorry for a driver who gets carried away and pays a high-speed visit to the gravel at somewhere like Degner. It may look harmless enough but the cost and the effort of repair are beyond belief. Worse still, the chassis becomes a little heavier and weight is 'God' in motor sport.

Assuming you have managed Degner 1 without incident, the second part is waiting. This is even trickier. It is as if, having seen you charge through Degner 1, the corner is saying: 'OK, so you think you're clever, do you? Well, just try this.' Degner 2 always feels tight and it's quite difficult. There is no room for complacency in any sense because the edge of the track narrows as it goes under the bridge forming the figure of eight loop and sweeps into a fast right, which leads directly to a really great hairpin left. It is so easy to lock your brakes and spin off; certainly, this is not a corner to experience brake failure of any kind.

Whatever shape you may be in when arriving at the hairpin, it is essential to make a clean exit because of the long, fast undulating section that follows. The road curves right and it is unnecessarily fast and dangerous. We have seen cars crashing there quite often but there is not a lot the driver can do because there is no skill involved at this point. When the track is dry, it is not a problem. But, in the wet, this right-hand kink needs caution. You are flat out and you feel in control but, at the same time, you are suspicious of this piece of road as you race towards Spoon.

This is a really great corner, which sweeps left into a long semi-circle. The entry is fast and, to a certain extent, the less you brake, the better. It takes a while to realise that because the horizon is coming at you very fast. Having arrived into the first part of Spoon, the car wants to slide to the outside. But a second, tighter apex is waiting and you have got to bring the car in for a second time. Making a racing car do that is quite difficult, particularly when the track also starts to fall downhill. It is so easy to come off the road here.

Now you are heading back towards the pits via a straight which leads to the 130R, a very quick left which is much less of a challenge now than it used to be. The run towards the 130R is long; something I can vouch for from experience, having been forced to walk its length in 1993. I was driving for Ligier then and, for some reason, the French team had terrible trouble making a suitable seat for me. I would sit for hours in the material that formed the perfectly-shaped mould for the carbon fibre seat. But, every time they put the seat in the oven, it folded up. It would shrink in all directions and curl up into a foetal position. It meant I had to make do with a horrible seat made of seven pieces.

When the Ligier broke down, I took out all of the pieces and tucked them under my arm, the idea being that I would return to the pits on foot and put the pieces of my seat in the spare car. With no perimeter track, I had to pick my way through the undergrowth while wearing dainty little driving boots, four layers of flameproof clothing and my crash helmet, which for some reason,

I had chosen to keep on. By the time I reached the end of the straight and 130R, I was ready to quit. So I can guarantee that the straight is even longer than it seems when building towards 200 mph in an F1 car.

The 130R is so-called because of the radius of the left-hander. It is absolutely superb, a legendary corner, and appears to be 90 degrees as you approach, flat out in top gear. The road disappears out of sight and narrows on the exit. There is no run-off at all because the outward leg of the track at Degner is on the other side at this point where the figure of eight crosses. When your car was working well, the 130R could be taken flat out in its original form. Sometimes you had to have a tiny lift-off the throttle but, either way, this corner is thrilling, terrifying and rewarding all at the same time.

As soon as you come out of the 130R, it seems as though you are in a funnel because the surroundings close in. If you make a mistake here, it is a worst-case scenario. Allan McNish had a massive accident here during practice in 2002 when his Toyota spun off and acted like a tin-opener as it sliced through a quadruple-layer barrier on the outside of the corner.

This was also where I first realised just how good Michael Schumacher was going to be. He spun coming out of 130R during practice in 1991 for what would have been only his fifth Grand Prix. Benetton had let him have a go in Nelson Piquet's car and he spun it into the wall and made a right mess. Michael had a confident air about him right from the very beginning and everybody in the paddock was waiting to see how he would be affected by such a massive accident in the car belonging to the three-times World Champion.

The answer came quickly and left no one in any doubt. He stepped into his own car and, on the next lap, went faster than at any other time. Most people would have been circumspect, particularly at that corner. But Michael simply went faster on every sector of the lap. Point made.

By this stage, I knew he was going to be my team-mate for the following year because I'd signed for Benetton in the previous July. I made a mental note that this was someone to watch. The 130R had presented him with no nightmares. Quite the reverse; Schumacher had used it in the most positive way possible.

The corner was changed for the 2003 race. The angle was eased and the surface made smoother. Now the drivers are at full throttle, almost without thinking – which is a great shame. The cars are so good and the track so smooth that the 130R is comfortable rather than a suck-through-your teeth job.

The narrowing zone leading to the final chicane is an area where you can surprise the driver in front and overtake. The right-left chicane is known as the Casio Triangle and it frequently causes chaos because this also marks the entry to the pit lane. On any number of occasions, drivers have taken a run down the inside, only to find the man in front turning into the pit lane.

Because the track curves right on the approach, it is necessary to go from one side to the other in order to take the best line into the chicane. The problem is that, ideally, you need to brake in a straight line. If you are braking while turning, the tyre contact patches with the road are not equal side to side. So if you turn and brake, it is easy to lock a wheel. It is the same in your road car: if you brake and downshift in a straight line you are always going to be better off.

By trying to take a straight run into the chicane, it leaves room on the inside for someone to have a go. So, you've got to feign going down one side and then cut to the outside under braking.

The next problem is that you almost need to come to a standstill because the corner is horrendously tight and the kerbs look as though they are half a metre high. In recent years, they added Astroturf on the run-off to make it look prettier. But that is more slippery than you can imagine, especially when wet.

The left-hand turn follows immediately and it always seems impossible to get the power on soon enough, no matter what car you are driving. You just sit there waiting, spinning the rear wheels or using the traction control. Then, at a certain point, everything seems to come together and away she goes, sweeping into a long right-hander and starting the roller-coaster ride all over again as you rush down the hill past the pits.

At 3.64 miles, it is a long lap, one that means all things to all men all the way round. It is what I call a confidence track. You can't just go out and nail Suzuka. You need to build up and accumulate knowledge and confidence in the same way it used to be when tackling Eau Rouge at Spa. You try this method and that; you go into a corner a little deeper than before; you charge into the Esses a bit harder. Maybe the first time into 130R, you will brake a bit, then you'll simply lift off the throttle, then you'll semi-lift and then finally you'll nail it and hope it sticks. It's that kind of racetrack. You've got to creep up on Suzuka quickly although today's cars seem to inspire confidence much earlier.

It is a terrific circuit on which to sort out the championship. I'll never forget Murray Walker's words when Damon Hill won the title in 1996: 'I've got to stop talking now because I've got a lump in my throat.' Mika Hakkinen won there in 1998 when Michael Schumacher stalled on pole position. Then Michael had an appalling drive in 2003 when he seemed to collide with everything and yet somehow finished eighth, enough to take the title.

For the Japanese enthusiasts, however, the most emotional moment came when Senna clinched the championship at Suzuka, not when he drove Prost off the road in 1990, but when he won it fair and square the following year. The fans are very passionate about their racing and Senna really struck a chord. He was a God in Japan and the popularity of motor racing rose dramatically as a direct result. In the years that followed there would be a constant queue of people waiting for autographs at Suzuka. They would stand quietly with gold-edged autograph cards and the latest in permanent markers. No scrappy bits of paper or half-chewed Biros as in England, and when you had to go, they would politely stand back and nobody would ever argue.

Things changed quite noticeably as the sport's popularity rose still further. The politeness seemed to evaporate. Suddenly, drivers were faced with a crazy, screaming bunch of fans. Every racing driver has thrown away a number of really nice leather jackets and shirts, which have become streaked in permanent black marker pen as a result of the jostling fans. It became so chaotic that it was necessary to bring in security people to keep control.

But generally the Japanese are orderly to a fault. The restaurants close at nine o'clock, not one minute before or after. We discovered that to our cost at the end of our thirty-hour epic first journey to Japan in 1987. We were exhausted and hungry and could not find a restaurant to serve us. We eventually found a taxi and the driver took us to a Japanese version of McDonald's. I pointed to my watch and asked him to return in 45 minutes because, otherwise, I had no idea how we were going to get back to the hotel or, indeed, where it was. I didn't really expect to see him again. It took a while for the food to arrive and I was just starting my hamburger when there was a tap on my shoulder. It was the taxi driver, bang on time, ready to go and expecting me to come immediately.

On the other hand, the procedure when checking out of the hotel is extremely confusing, as the receptionist will produce a tray full of papers and receipts for everything. In a country that has given us all manner of sophisticated electronic devices, it seems bizarre to receive a bunch of hand-written chits. It is one of those curious habits that are part of a fascinating country and a brilliant Grand Prix; just like a little lady appearing from the gloom and asking for your autograph on a wet and miserable night.

Length: 3.780 km

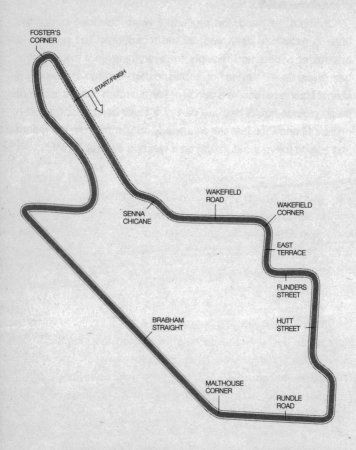

FOSTER'S
CORNER

START/FINISH

WAKEFIELD
ROAD

WAKEFIELD
CORNER

SENNA
CHICANE

EAST
TERRACE

FLINDERS
STREET

BRABHAM
STRAIGHT

HUTT
STREET

MALTHOUSE
CORNER

RUNDLE
ROAD

ADELAIDE
(AUSTRALIA)

Adelaide

There was something absolutely right about Adelaide from the word go. The inaugural Grand Prix through the streets was held there in 1985 and I can clearly remember the conditions as I drove into Adelaide for the first time: blue skies, cool breeze, perfect temperature. But, more than that, there was an immediate feeling of arriving in a city that really wanted to embrace the race and everything associated with it. Believe me, that was not always the case elsewhere.

Whenever we went to street races in some cities in the United States, you had the unmistakable impression that about 30 per cent of the population were really happy to see you, but the other 70 per cent felt you were blocking their streets and making a lot of noise while doing it. Only a small part of the city appeared to be supporting the event and, as ever, the local mood could be gauged by the reaction of the cab driver bringing you from the airport. When he asked why you were in town, his response to your answer would be along the lines of: 'Ah! So that's on this weekend, is it?'

That was not the case in Adelaide. From the moment you landed, the race weekend atmosphere rushed to meet you in the form of promotional bunting, smiling hostesses, motor sport para-phernalia, chequered flags – and this was before you had reached the baggage hall. Added to the mix was the fact that this was the last race of the season so, inevitably, there was always an end-of-term feeling. It would be a case of getting away from the penultimate race in Japan as fast as possible in order to head for Australia. Often you would stop on the Gold Coast or in Sydney for a few days but, in the end, everyone just wanted to get to Adelaide.

I think that confused a lot of people – particularly the Australians themselves – because Adelaide is considered quiet and reserved. It is known as the City of Churches, which perhaps explains the puzzlement over the supposed F1 jet set raving about going to the Australian equivalent of Worthing or Harrogate for the weekend. The important thing was that every man, woman and child seemed to want us in town and we were made incredibly welcome.

I loved the circuit from the very start. The first part through the suburban streets was American in style: turn right, down a block, turn left, down a block, turn right, and so on. Then it opened onto Dequetteville Terrace, renamed Brabham Straight once a year when it became part of the racetrack. The right-hander leading onto the straight was massively quick – and very difficult. It was so easy to get it wrong. There were just two kerbs lying on what would normally be a great big junction full of Tarmac with concrete walls waiting to punish your mistake. Mika Hakkinen had a huge accident there during practice in 1995. Had it not been for the rapid intervention of the medical teams, led as ever by Professor Sid Watkins, Mika would have died.

It wasn't much better at the far end of the straight. I remember my Tyrrell was clocked at 206 mph during qualifying in 1986. But the point was, you were flat out at these ridiculous speeds – and heading for a cul-de-sac. That's all there was at the end of a straight where the track turned right and the escape road was lined with more concrete blocks. It didn't bear thinking about then, and gives me goose bumps even now.

Once we were done with Brabham Straight, the track became what could best be described as parkland in style as it entered the Victoria Park horse-race course. This bit was very quick, sweeping through a left and a right towards the last corner. We all had little trip-ups there. You made your decision before this kink to have a go at overtaking under braking for the final hairpin. But if the guy in front decided to go into the pits, you couldn't slow down because you were already committed.

I ran into the back of Mark Blundell and threw away a much-needed second place in 1995 by doing exactly that. There were numerous incidents at this point: Ayrton Senna hit the back of Keke Rosberg in 1985; Nigel Mansell and Senna had a coming-together there seven years later; David Coulthard managed to hit the inside of the pit wall while leading in 1995. It was a very tricky area.

The truth was that both the pit entry and exit were totally impractical at Adelaide. The first corner was a tight left at the end of the pit straight. You needed to keep the car to the extreme right of the track in order to be in the perfect position and yet the pit exit came from the right – immediately into the entry for Turn 1.

An already dangerous situation was made worse by the technical rules of the day. We were running turbocharged engines in the mid-1980s. For qualifying, you would have extra turbo boost (the engine could only stand a lap or two of this prodigious power), plus special sticky qualifying tyres. So you would practise in the morning with about 850 bhp at your disposal. Come qualifying and you would tiptoe out of the pits, watching your mirrors for fast cars approaching, and gingerly complete the so-called 'out' lap without getting too much heat into your tyres too soon. Then, turn into the pit straight – and floor the throttle. With 1,300 bhp and sticky tyres, it was like warp-drive down the pit straight. The car took off like a rocket.

In 1985, just as I reached the entrance to Turn 1, Nelson Piquet wombled out of the pits without bothering to look. The Brabham suddenly emerged from the concrete on my right. I had to swerve around him, spun off, slammed backwards into the wall and hit my head hard on the back of the cockpit, because the mechanics had forgotten to put the headrest, such as it was, in place. We usually had a little button of foam that was in any case hopelessly inadequate when compared with the cuddly things drivers have around their heads now.

That said, I loved the track although, in the rain, it really was something else. The true horror of racing in the wet at Adelaide was brought home to us in 1989. The warm-up on race morning had been run under threatening skies. By midday, the rain had arrived in earnest and we were given a fifteen-minute familiarisation run, which merely confirmed our worst fears: the track was awash and it was almost impossible to drive. The start was delayed for thirty minutes in the hope that the conditions would improve. If anything, they got worse.

Very few drivers were keen to race. As usual, no one could make a firm decision either way. I had then been in F1 for five years. I wasn't one of the old hands, but neither was I one of the young boys. I was tempted to race even though it was lashing down and the racetrack was waterlogged in places. A few of the more experienced drivers, Alain Prost in particular, said they didn't want to race.

Confusion reigned as we formed on the start line and got out of our cars. Well, most of us did. Ayrton Senna, who was on pole, sat resolutely in the cockpit of his McLaren, helmet in place, ready to start. As usually happened in those days, the matter was resolved quickly and simply by Bernie Ecclestone. He walked down the grid, speaking to the drivers and when he reached me he said: 'Get in your car. The race is about to start.' As I was of a mind to race anyway, I got in my car. And so did everyone else. Prost then elected to stop at the end of the first lap – which, at the time, I thought was weak. Today, I think it was actually very brave.

As expected, the conditions were horrendous. There was not even a breeze and the problem was that the rain tended to hang between the walls and the trees. It simply didn't disperse and we were driving into it at around 150 mph. In fact, Senna was going much faster than that. There had been an incident at the previous race in Japan and Ayrton had lost the race and the championship because of what he perceived to be grossly unfair disqualification for his part in a collision. He was still bristling when he got to Adelaide and, judging by the speed at which he shot into the lead, he continued to be emotionally charged. The McLaren crew were trying to slow him down but he was lapping people after five or six laps. The man was on an absolute mission.

I wasn't going too badly myself, moving from twelfth on the grid to seventh thanks to those who had either fallen off or chosen not to continue racing. Unlike the majority of the field, I was on Pirelli tyres, which were not ideal in the rain. But even the very best wet-weather tyre can only cope with so much surface water. After that, you become a passenger. At 150 mph. Between walls of concrete.

I was flat out in sixth gear on Brabham Straight when, all of a sudden, my car began to aquaplane. Before I knew it, I was spinning like a top in the middle of a ball of spray. I couldn't see a thing and, by some minor miracle, I didn't hit the wall or anything else. The spray died down, I hooked first gear and drove off. I knew there were a number of drivers behind me somewhere.

As I accelerated through the gears, I suddenly had the dreadful thought that I could be going the wrong way. With grey walls towering either side of the car and nothing but mist and spray all around, I had no means of identifying anything. I didn't know how many times I had spun round. Was it two and a half times? Was it three times? Three and a half? I had no idea and neither did I know whether I was heading away from the traffic – or towards it. There was this terrible thought that a car could come hammering out of the gloom and straight into me. Even so, I couldn't slow down or stop in case someone piled into the back of me. Heart in mouth, there was nothing for it but to keep my foot on the throttle. Then I saw the 300 marker board for a corner – and it had the writing on my side. I was going in the right direction. The relief was indescribable.

I was lucky still to be in one piece but I applied a bit more caution, only going as high as fifth gear on Brabham Straight the next time round. The car was continuing to skim across the top of the water but I just about managed to keep it pointing in the right direction. I wasn't flat out but still doing between 140 and 150 mph.

I suddenly felt a huge impact from behind – and Senna sailed past on three wheels. He had driven into me. I had a camera on the back of my car and the picture showed what appeared to be a shark suddenly charging out of the gloom and taking a big bite from the back of the Brabham. Ayrton could not have seen where he was going. Despite continuing pleas from his team to slow down, Senna was in a world of his own and at some point he was going to hit somebody or something. Unfortunately it was his old

F3 sparring partner. The back of my car was not badly damaged but it was enough to put me out of the race as well.

The surprise is that this sort of thing doesn't happen more often. Each car has a red rear light, which must be illuminated in wet conditions. But the truth is you can't even see your own dashboard, never mind the light on the car in front. I always relate it to passing a truck on a streaming wet motorway. There's a moment, as you approach the off-side rear corner of the truck, when your windscreen is completely obliterated. Your wipers can't even cope. For the racing driver, the visor on his helmet is the equivalent of the windscreen on your car. It's a scary moment and there is no alternative but to drive through it. It's exactly the same when running behind another F1 car.

The picture for the viewer at home is slightly false because the TV camera, even in normal circumstances, can see much better than the human eye and it is usually mounted high above the track, beyond the crash barrier. As a result, it is peering over much of the spray and the picture looks much clearer than it is to the driver. Sitting low and directly behind the car in front, the driver is actually looking through 10 metres of spray and much of it drenching the visor on his helmet.

All of your senses become hyper responsive. Usually, vision is restricted to the periphery, which means you are watching out for reference points flashing past: marshals' posts, marker boards, advertising hoardings. But you are also listening intently. You can hear the guy ahead, provided you are consistently running with him. Even though you can't see the car in front, you can hear the driver lift his foot from the throttle on the approach to a corner.

As soon as the speed drops, the spray becomes less; it's as though curtains have been pulled back or someone has turned on the lights. Now you can see the corner and everyone then races into it. You see the car ahead and start entertaining late thoughts about overtaking him going into the corner. You go through it, the speed builds up again, the spray intensifies once more – and you are back where you started.

One way or another, the Brabham Straight played a major part in many of the eleven Grands Prix held at Adelaide. Being monstered by Senna in the rain was the most memorable for me but, for race fans the world over, it was Nigel Mansell's dramatic retirement from the race and the title chase in 1986.

This was arguably one of the most theatrical finales to any championship, largely because it was a three-way fight between Mansell and Piquet (who both drove for Williams-Honda) and Prost in his McLaren-TAG. It was a reporter's dream because, at different stages in the race, all three drivers were in a position to win the championship if they stayed right where they were in the running order. Mansell was the first to fall and, typical Nigel, he did it in spectacular style.

Having a points advantage going into the race, Mansell simply needed to finish third, even if the other two were ahead of him. That's exactly where he was as he started lap sixty-four, with eighteen to go. Coming down Brabham Straight, his left-rear tyre suddenly punctured and Nigel had to fight the car to a standstill in a shower of sparks, rubber and confusion. He actually made it to the escape road without hitting anything, the Williams coming to a halt by the wall.

I was aware of what was going on in the championship battle but, to be honest, I was busy running my own race in the Tyrrell-Renault. I remember seeing Nigel's car parked in the cul-de-sac but I didn't see the incident itself because I wasn't on the same piece of track. In fact, when I think of it now, I see television pictures of the blow-up and hear Murray Walker's voice at maximum revs as he describes the incredible scene. '*Look at that!*' shouts Murray. You can just hear him, can't you?

I had my own problems in that race. If Nigel was disappointed then so was I, even though far less was at stake. I should have finished third but ran out of petrol on the last lap. It was all my fault. The Tyrrell had an 'overtake' button on the dashboard, which gave a sudden burst of turbo boost and power. But at a price. By hitting the button, you were using more fuel for that brief spurt. As there was no refuelling during the races in those days, you were strictly limited to what was in your tank at the start. Everything was carefully calculated to the point where you could only press the overtake button three times. I used mine five times!

I couldn't resist it. Philippe Streiff, my team-mate, had been quick all weekend and he was three rows ahead of me on the grid. I had gradually hauled him in during the race but then he started to get away from me in traffic as we held eighth and ninth places. I was itching to use the button. You're alongside somebody on Brabham Straight and there is this little button on the steering wheel – the Forbidden Fruit – and if you just touch it, you've got another 30 or 40 bhp. No more waiting. Job done. Up behind my team-mate again.

One by one, the leaders were dropping out, Mansell's retirement moving me into the top five. Then Stefan Johansson made a pit stop in his Ferrari. I was fourth. When Streiff stopped with three laps to go, I was third. (Philippe was actually out of fuel, so he must have been using the button even more than me!)

Coming up to the final corner for the last time, my fuel gauge went to zero. To this day I never believe fuel gauges; I always think there is more fuel available than they say. Halfway down the pit straight, the car ran out. I coasted towards the flag on fumes – but the recovering Johansson overtook me on the line. A podium finish disappeared in the dying seconds of a race that had lasted almost two hours. I was gutted. But it was my own fault. For once, the fuel gauge had been absolutely spot on.

The race – and therefore the championship – was won by Prost, the outsider of the three. The irony was that his fuel gauge had been reading 5 litres on the wrong side for most of the race. Prost was the cleverest and most cautious of drivers and, under normal circumstances, he would have backed off, used less fuel and got the readings back on the correct side. But these were not normal circumstances. To win the championship, he had to win the race. Anything less would be no good. So he adopted the attitude of having nothing to lose by pushing hard. If the car ran out of fuel, then so be it. He gradually worked his way through the field and took the lead with seventeen laps to go. But he couldn't relax because Piquet, who had lost the lead with an unscheduled pit stop, was closing rapidly on fresh tyres. Prost's gauge showed a row of zeros during most of the last lap. But it was wrong and he ran out just seconds after crossing the line. Championships have rarely been won by such slim margins.

Adelaide was famous for settling another title in dramatic fashion in 1994, the year Michael Schumacher collided with Damon Hill and sent the Williams-Renault into retirement and second place in the points standings. They had been having a tense battle all year and it continued into the first thirty-six laps of the final race in Adelaide. Michael was leading but Damon was pushing him really hard. The Benetton and the Williams were in a league of their own. Michael got ahead by a second or two but then made a small mistake, ran wide and touched the wall. He was prone to do that under pressure. Unfortunately, when Damon came round the corner a few seconds later, he had missed seeing the impact and just thought Michael had simply run wide. Seizing the moment,

Damon dived down the inside for the next corner. Had he realised Michael was in trouble, Damon would have held back and passed the Benetton with ease on Brabham Straight. But he saw this as his only chance. And Michael drove into him as they turned, side-by-side, into the next right-hander.

Once again, I was on a different part of the circuit. The first I knew of the incident was when I saw Michael standing beside the track. I couldn't work it all out and I assumed Damon must be about to win the world championship. In fact, he was limping to the pits. I remember thinking that Michael's car appeared to have very little damage and I was wondering why he was staring sky-wards, as if talking to God! In fact, he was listening to the PA and the news that Damon's car was too badly damaged to rejoin. Michael, who had a points advantage, won the championship right there. The first clue I had of Damon's plight was my McLaren pit board saying I was up to third place. I joined Nigel Mansell (for his last F1 victory) and Gerhard Berger on the podium. Talk about a bunch of old duffers. Our combined age was 111.

That was actually my joint-best result in Adelaide, since I had also finished third in 1992. The most disappointing moment by far had been the previous year when I failed to pre-qualify, never mind qualify. The entry at the time was so large (thirty-two drivers going for twenty-six places on the grid) that the less successful teams had one hour in which to fight for the right simply to prac-tise. Halfway through 1991, my team, Brabham, had fallen into the pre-qualifying group because of our poor results. It was to be the hardest time of my racing life and this particular pre-qualifying session took place first thing on a Friday morning.

I was usually the king of pre-qualifying because my Pirellis were good on a dirty track – which was always the case as we were the first cars to venture out all weekend. The fastest four would get through; the rest would have to pack up and go home almost before the weekend had started. But, for Brabham, it wasn't a drama. In fact, I'd got through pre-qualifying and gone on to finish fifth at the previous race at Suzuka. I was looking forward to more of the same in Australia on one of my favourite circuits.

On that particular Friday morning, the track was wet, so there wasn't much point in going out straight away. With ten minutes to go, the surface was beginning to dry and everyone prepared for what would be a frantic scramble when the track was at its best during the closing minutes.

I climbed into the car as they were fitting the wheels, put my foot on the brake – and fluid shot straight out of one of the brake calipers. It went everywhere and the pedal went to the floor. The bleed nipple on the caliper was faulty, an unusual occurrence which had perhaps been caused by the nipple receiving a knock. The actual reason was irrelevant at that particular moment. Either way, I was in trouble. When I took my foot off the pedal, air was sucked into the system. So there I was, ten minutes to go, and I had no brakes. They had to change the caliper and bleed the system. We ran out of time. I failed to pre-qualify.

I was a spectator for the rest of the weekend. With my return flight already booked for the following Monday, it was impossible to leave early. It was a case of hanging around and supporting the team, Mark Blundell having qualified in the other Brabham.

I was in the pit lane the following morning, just before the F1 cars went out. There was a practice session for Formula Holden (one of the support races) and this kid came in, jumped out of his car – and he was wearing a set of my Brabham-Yamaha Martin Brundle overalls! This was the last Grand Prix of the season and, because I hadn't qualified, my mechanics had sold the overalls the day before. That's the way it was with the smaller teams; it was the boys' Christmas bonus. I guess the overalls weren't mine to give away but it was a bit of a shock because no one had said anything.

Third was my best result in Adelaide, but I so easily could have finished second in 1995 but for crashing into the back of Mark Blundell's McLaren at that notorious spot just before the final corner. When you consider that I enjoyed second place just three times in my F1 career, the significance of that simple mistake becomes apparent. My team-mate, Olivier Panis, inherited second in a sick car that had been smoking for most of the race. I had broken Olivier's heart by nailing him at just about every race during the season and was half a lap ahead of him in Adelaide when I made that misjudgement at the expense of my mate Blundell.

Making friends in Adelaide seemed easy. It was not unusual to find lots of good-looking girls and children waiting for someone from F1 racing each time we arrived. A few team members even ended up with second families in Adelaide. It was common to see tearful goodbyes at the airport when we left.

Adelaide just had a party atmosphere. Everyone seemed to stay in the Hilton Hotel, which in itself was unusual because teams are generally scattered in various hotels across town. But, in Adelaide, the Hilton was Party Central. It was only two miles from the track and we could swan in to work with ease.

I'll never forget leaving the circuit at the end of the 1993 race. Senna had won (his last victory, in fact) and, not far from the paddock, Tina Turner was belting out her songs in an open-air concert. Ayrton was called onto the stage and Tina was singing 'Simply the Best' to him, with all the fans around. For me, that said everything about Adelaide. It was almost surreal. I was walking across the bridge towards the car park and the fans were going for it. This seemed to sum up the Aussie attitude to sport: in one respect, the Australians are laid back; in another, they can be so passionate about whatever it is they're doing. The Grand Prix in Adelaide embraced all of that and so much more, yet the race in November 1995 would be the last. Just a few months later, we would be packing our bags for Melbourne, thanks to the state of Victoria spending even more dollars to entice F1 on the next adventure in our race around the globe.

As a driver, your mentality is to turn up and drive as hard as you can, no matter where the championship takes you. The calendar is constantly changing, sometimes during the season itself, and the choice of venue is steeped in politics and finance. A driver can play little, if any, part in these decisions and he should not let himself either become involved or acquire favourites when it comes to racetracks.

On a personal level, that is virtually impossible to achieve. With so many positive and negative experiences on and around the circuit, you can only build strong feelings for or against what amounts to little more than a ribbon of asphalt. But every metre of every track poses a different challenge, and each, in its own way, is intensely rewarding. The glamour and pleasure of motor sport is not all it might seem on the surface; it's about how brilliant it feels when working the wheel.